Appointment Northwest

Peter Skrzynecki

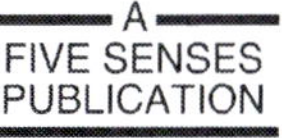

First published by.
Five Senses Education Pty Ltd, 2014.
ABN 16 001 414 437
2/195 Prospect Highway,
Seven Hills NSW 2147

Printed by Five Senses Education Pty Ltd.

Cover image: Peter Skrzynecki

Skrzynecki, Peter
'Appointment Northwest'

ISBN 978-1-74130-997-3

"The mountain wooded to the peak, the lawns
And winding glades high up like ways to heaven,
The slender coco's drooping crown of plumes,
The lightning flash of insect and of bird,
The lustre of the long convolvuluses
That coil'd around the stately stems, and ran
Even to the limit of the land, the glows
And glories of the broad belt of the world –
All these he saw."

Enoch Arden, Tennyson

Acknowledgements: Marie and Dave Williams, Joan Munro, Dawn Mullen, Leonie Farrugia, Fiona Clark, Christine Flynn, Professor John Ryan, Debbie Gwynne, William Oates and Dr Philip Ward of the Heritage Centre, University of New England and Regional Archives, Kevin Coates, Dr Elizabeth Hale, Professor John Scott, Bronwyn Hubbard.

"Memoirs of a Lifetime Spent near Jeogla", George Gray, *Armidale & District Historical Society*, Journal Number 42, April 1999. Armidale & District Historical Society, PO Box 692, Armidale NSW 2350

Scots' Corner: A Local History, B.L. Cameron & J.L. McLennan, 1971

Armidale: A Cathedral city of Education and the Arts, Tony Barker, Cassell Australia, 1980

To the Best of My Knowledge, Marion Diamond, 2010

"Red Trees" and "Jeogla Return" from *Red Trees,* Vagabond Press, Sydney, 2010

I would like to thank University of Queensland Press for permission to use "Moonbi Hills", "Wollomombi Falls", "Wyatts Creek", "Styx River", "Jeogla", "Weeping Rock" from my *Old/New World: New and Selected Poems* (UQP 2007)

For Caroline Lillian Sloggett

ARMIDALE REGION inc. JEOGLA

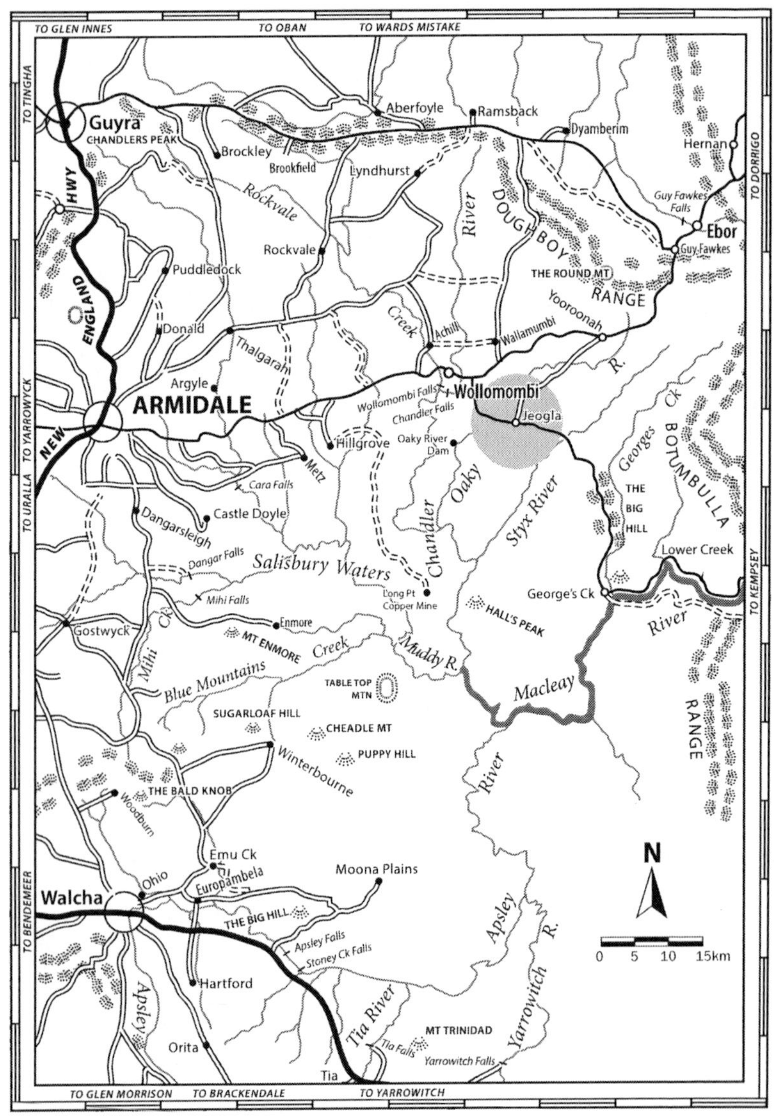

I

Rain

Sunday, January 29 1967

The car door slammed behind me and rain fell as I dashed across the road to the police station. At teachers' college we'd been told, *If you get lost, go to the local police station and ask directions.*

I hadn't brought my umbrella from the car and stood before the duty officer, a big man with grey hair, water dripping off the end of my nose, my shirt soaked, my hair stuck flat to my head.

Excuse me, sir, can you please tell me how to get to Jeogla?

Why do you want to go to Jeogla?

I'm the new school teacher.

The police man put a hand up to his mouth – but it wasn't possible to hide the laugh in his eyes or the creases of his cheeks. He said, Oh, you poor little bastard! He paused, then added, Let's have a look.

Emerging from behind the desk he led me to an enlarged map of Armidale on the wall. Come a long way? he asked.

Sydney.

First appointment?

Yes.

Figured as much. Jeogla will be a test – make you or break you, so to speak. I'm from Harden myself. Love the country. You wouldn't get me to Sydney for quids. We're here. Okay? Go back to the main road, turn left at Central Park – that's Barney Street – and keep heading out of town. That becomes the Grafton Road.

I stepped back, trying to take it all in.

He led me to another map. Now, let's have a gander at the district map. Over here. You'll be turning off at Wollomombi. See, on the right. Just over the Chandler. That's the Kempsey Road and Jeogla's along there. You'll think you've come to the end of the world – but don't worry, you haven't.

I watched as his finger snaked along the map, stopping and starting. The rain fell harder and he raised his voice above it, talking as if I wasn't there.

Road's pretty narrow in parts – he continued – and it winds a bit. So be careful. When you get to Baker's Creek – back down here – it straightens out, then dips and winds again. Remember. Right turn once you're over the Chandler. And that's about it. Good luck, son. It's pretty wild out there.

Thanks. I tried to sound cheerful, but I could still see the smile he tried to hide and hoped I could remember more than just turning left at Barney Street.

The rain eased as I stepped outside. Or maybe I just imagined it had. In any case, a strong gust of wind blew towards Central Park, in the direction I had to go.

It was hard to tell where Barney Street ended and the Grafton Road began, but as I passed through a row of poplars, in the vicinity of the Armidale race course, I guessed that by now I must be on it.

I'd left home a day earlier but only managed to get as far as the outskirts of Tamworth, where I stayed in the first motel I came to. At Singleton, while buying petrol at a garage beside the Hunter, I remarked to the driveway attendant about the rain and the possibility of flooding. He pointed to a row of buildings, and said, *See that brown line running along the tops of those shops. That's the flood of 55.*

If I thought the rain was heavy to Tamworth, nothing prepared me for the downpours that started once I approached the Moonbi Hills. The closer I got to Armidale, the more frequent they became. The temperature dropped. Winds blew stronger and the landscape more bleak. Everything was washed in grey. All I could see were farmhouses, low-lying clouds, mountain ranges, granite outcrops shaped like cannon-balls and spinning-tops, barbed wire fences, cattle and sheep. At times I thought the windscreen wipers would stop working.

The names on signposts after Armidale fascinated me, and I tried to remember them sequentially – Commissioners Waters, Gara River, Metz, Burying Ground Creek, Hillgrove, Cooney Creek and Wollomombi where, for the first time, I saw people.

I'd driven past several houses and what looked like a general store with a petrol pump outside. The sign of the flying red horse stood out distinctively in the rain, as did a red telephone booth beside the entrance to the store. A bakery was next to an open shed with a bus inside. Further along, I could see a small church and a house where four people were stepping out into the rain. There was a flag pole in front of the church and pine trees. As I slowed down, I read, 'St. John's Presbyterian Church'. From what the policeman had told me, the Chandler River was nearby and then the turnoff to Jeogla.

I pulled over. The people were all were carrying umbrellas. This time I brought mine and approached them.

Before I said a word, one from the group ran forward and motioned for the others to go back to the house. I saw that he was wearing a clerical collar. He shook my hand.

Come out of the rain, he laughed. You must be the new school teacher at Jeogla. I asked how he could tell. You look lost, mate – and miserable – he replied, continuing to laugh.

On the veranda everyone put down their umbrellas and stared back uncomfortably at the rain; it struck the tin roof of the veranda with the sound of a snare drum.

In my mind the word "Wollomombi" tumbled and I forgot its pronunciation. My mind wasn't moving backwards or forwards. I was lost in the present moment. Time had stalled.

A car and then a lorry sped down the highway, back towards Armidale, the spray from both vehicles obliterated by the rain as it became airborne. All this in the space of a fraction of a second before the voice spoke again.

The man in the clerical collar was speaking with a Scottish accent and introducing himself as the local minister.

Alex Clark's the name. Hiya.

He introduced his wife, Jill, and the other couple, both of whom also spoke with Scottish accents. The other man was a professor newly-appointed to the Classics Department of the University of New England. This was the Presbyterian parish of St John, and the minister was a home missionary. Where we stood was on the veranda of the manse, and they were all going off towards the coast to get a good view of the Bellinger in flood when I arrived. I had no idea where the Bellinger was – although I thought I knew the coastal rivers of New South Wales – so I nodded as if I knew, shivered, introduced myself and smiled, then asked about my school.

This time the minister's wife smiled, but without an underlying meaning to it, more in the way of sympathy

She spoke softly, coughing. I'm from Sydney myself – Normanhurst – and I know exactly how you must be feeling. At least I was married when I came here – a year ago – and I still haven't got used to the place.

I immediately liked her sincerity. Her eyes were bright and her smile was warm. A thin woman with a tremulous voice, and slightly stooped, she turned her back to the rain disdainfully.

The minister lit up a cigarette and motioned towards the

door. I'm sorry, I said, but I feel I should keep going. Maybe I can visit you later?

Again he laughed. Mate, I think we'll be seeing a lot of you. Your landlady is Carrie Sloggett. She's been boarding the teachers since the year dot. Husband's Elmo. Son's Gerald. Her mother, Granma Williams, lives with them. You can't miss their place – it's just before the cattle grid, opposite the hall. The school's about a mile further on.

There was something about this man that didn't add up to the image I might have had of a church minister. Of medium height, with an Elvis Presley hair style, shiny and swept back, his neck was long and his Adam's apple stuck out. He drew deeply on his cigarette. He seemed too young to be a preacher. As if he'd read my mind, he said, I'm new at this game. Used to be in the merchant navy until I saw the light. God called me across the prow of a ship one morning. 'Come follow me', and I did.

No one else spoke a word. The rain fell and the sodden landscape around us looked as miserable as I felt. I'd better go, I repeated. Another motor vehicle sped down the road.

Why don't you give yourself a few days to settle in and have dinner with us on Wednesday night? Mrs Clark said. Say, six o'clock. We can talk and eat. Carrie won't mind, I'm sure.

I accepted her invitation and said goodbye to them all. Enjoy your trip.

You, too, mate, Alex laughed. Oh, by the way, you should also meet Bill Higgins as soon as you're able. He's the teacher here – at Chandler Public. Married with a bunch of kids. You might see the school residence just before you cross the river and turn off to Jeogla. Good luck....Oh, yes, I'll also be coming up once a week to take Scripture classes.

I drove off into the rain that continued falling in sheets from low clouds sweeping in from the east. There were no other cars in sight. Before I crossed the Chandler I slowed down on the bridge and looked at the running water, bouncing off rocks and boulders, swirling in parts, disappearing downwards, into a chasm, into the darkness of undergrowth and trees that could have been an entrance to Middle Earth.

Turning right at what appeared to be a sheep station, I looked back to where I'd come from, surprised at how elevated Wollomombi was above the dip on the road and how far the river ran below the bridge.

What I saw was an indication of what lay ahead – a series of rises and falls, followed by snaking bends and stretches of road, all without bitumen – that I was now travelling on, but the policeman in Armidale hadn't said how far Jeogla lay from the turnoff, and I hoped that at any moment it would come into view.

The rain was easing off, and visibility becoming clearer. Livestock in paddocks were my only companions – as well as magpies and rosellas that would burst from a clump of trees or out of a forest on one side of the road and disappear into another. Rabbits ran across the road – or alongside it, startled, stopping, starting up, their white tails bobbing in the grass.

On a stretch of yellow road, travelling downhill, I saw a bridge in the distance. No one had mentioned a bridge. The rain had stopped and I pulled over, curious to investigate. A bridge meant water. What water? To my left, the sign read OAKY RIVER

The wind whistled about my ears as I got out from the car. How high was I above the river? Fifty feet? Sixty?

The view took away my breath.

The river was expansive, wide, with vegetation growing above its level; it looked nothing like the fast-flowing Chandler.

A flock of ducks appeared in the distance, coming towards me, flying around a bend. Straight towards me, under the bridge, disappearing, then reappearing on the other side. I crossed the bridge to watch.

Dead trees stuck out of the water. I heard the immensity of silence surrounding me, of distance and elevation, even though raindrops fell from trees and the beating of wings echoed above me, accompanied by duck noises. Rain clouds moved directly overhead, hanging low and looking ominous. They reminded me of zeppelins. On a steel plaque, bolted to the side of the bridge, I read in capital letters DMR. Below them, in smaller letters 1955. Further back a short distance, on a faded red sign by the roadside, in white letters:

NEW ENGLAND COUNTY COUNCIL
OAKY RIVER HYDRO ELECTRICITY SCHEME
SHOOTING AND FISHING
STRICTLY PROHIBITED

My spirits felt buoyed. I no longer felt so isolated. Maybe it was the fresh air, the temporary absence of rain or the wind blowing in the trees? Or maybe it was the silence I heard above everything else? The silence was an element itself, untouched by the weather, existing purely as a welcome after my long drive. A sense of freedom flowed past me, around me, seemed to lift me. I became acutely aware of my own breathing and how it had slowed down.

Leaving the bridge I drove uphill, levelling out and continuing to drive for another five minutes. I drove past a dark wooden farmhouse on my right, close to the roadway, then past a sign that read JEOGLA STATION. A road ran off the main road towards this property. In the distance, through the trees, I could make out a homestead beside a windbreak of pines.

Further ahead, a truck had been parked on the right side of the road, its tailboard down. A man in a raincoat and hat, with a small dog by his side, was disentangling a sheep caught in fencing wire. I pulled up opposite him. Bringing my umbrella, as it had just started raining again, I approached him.

Excuse me, sir…

You must be the new teacher? He turned around and held out a hand. Diamond's the name. Call me Ron.

Yes, I am.

We shook hands. I told him my name.

The little dog started barking. Oh, you be quiet, Suzie, now. Don't be jealous… Ignore her.

Some kind of short-haired terrier, Suzie was one of the ugliest dogs I believe I'd ever seen. Her bottom teeth stuck. Her coat was shaggy. She looked disgruntled, frowning, like she'd never been happy in her life and would bite her own tail out of spite. I always thought Suzie was a pretty name. So I asked, Why did you call her Suzie?

She reminds me of a girl I knew during the war.

The cigarette dangling from his lips didn't fall as he spoke; nor did it go out in the rain that spattered his face.

The sheep at his feet started bleating.

Bloody sheep! He spat out the words. They wander off. Get lost. Tangled up. This one's about to drop her lamb. If we stand here long enough, she might just do that…Ah, shaddup, Suzie, or I'll sell you – you beautiful bitch.

Suzie growled.

I asked, Is Jeogla nearby?

Jeogla! Strewth, mate…you're standing in it. See that cattle grid. Go over that and in the blink of an eye you'll be leaving Jeogla.

Thank you.

No need to thank me ….Oh, by the way, see that house down there…That's where you'll be staying. With Carrie and her family…Jeogla…Huh! Don't look so long in the face! Why, you couldn't've come to a nicer place.

He'd grunted and managed to heave the bleating ewe onto the back of his truck, slammed the tail board shut, locked it and waved goodbye to me. Come on, Suzie. Come with daddy.

The little dog growled at me and barked. She turned around arrogantly. Ron held the driver's door open for her and she jumped into the cabin. He followed her. The cigarette continued dangling from his lips.

Thank you, I said again.

See you around, he called back.

I returned to my car.

The jeep started up, its wheels spinning out of the grass by the roadside and off it went, down the road of yellow dirt and mud, drumming over the cattle grid.

A pair of rosellas burst out of a tree and flew across the road, dipping and rising in flight as they did.

*

I wonder what the Slogget family thought of their new boarder as he drove into their front yard and, carrying an umbrella, left his car and approached them with a nervous smile?

You must be the Sloggets?

They all nodded.

I introduced myself. One by one, they replied.

G'day.

G'day.

G'day.

All except the old lady, sitting in a wicker chair, who smiled at me, lifted a hand, and nodded.

Don't mind Granma, she's deaf. I assumed the woman who spoke was Carrie. I'm Carrie, yer landlady. I'm also the school cleaner. She introduced the others. This 'ere's Elmo, me husband. That's Gerald, our son. Gerald stood to attention, against the wall, as if he'd been reprimanded. Taking off his hat, he nodded and clicked his heels. He looked frightened. Elmo and Carrie looked curious. Granma looked amused. We all shook hands.

Here I am at last, I said, after such a long drive from Sydney.

Yer must be hungry, then. Are yer? Carrie asked, leaning forward.

I hadn't eaten since breakfast at the motel in Tamworth; it was now well after lunchtime.

I am a bit.

Come inside, said Carrie. I thought yer'd be here about now – so I cooked extra; then we'll go and have a look at the school.

I'll just get my things, I said.

Don't bother, she said. Gerald can help yer with them later. First, yer gotter eat.

She reminded me of my mother.

I followed her into the house.

As all this was happening I heard a dog – or two dogs? – barking outside.

In the blink of an eye I thought I saw a white cat dart out of the shadows of a room we were walking through, cross the corridor and disappear into another room.

A rooster was crowing and ducks were quacking.

You have ducks? I asked.

Carrie laughed, and replied… Gee, I don't know. Yous people from the city, can't yers tell the difference between a goose and a duck?

So you have geese?

They keep the foxes away.

We sat down in the kitchen to a meal of roast beef and vegetables, covered in gravy, strongly tasting of dripping. I took a deep breath before starting to eat. I say "we" but really it was just myself who ate. The rest of the family, apart from Granma, sat at the table and watched me. Carrie opposite me, Elmo to my left and Gerald between his mother and father. They never took their eyes off me. Our conversation consisted of talking about the rain – and how important it is to farmers – and the drought that had broken recently, the likes of which this district hadn't seen for decades. I knew nothing about it, but I listened, and agreed with them, as they told their story.

Nothing like it.

Not for a long time.

We can always do with more rain.

Always.

The weatherboard house sat snugly around us, offering warmth and cosiness, the kind of sanctuary that travellers traditionally look for when they're journeying and in need of a roof to come under, out of the rain, and a place at table where they might welcomed to a meal.

After lunch Carrie and I drove up to the school. As we were leaving the house she said, Here's where the school keys're kept – and pointed to a nail beside the telephone on the wall, to the left of the door separating the lounge room from the outside corridor. One's mine; the other's yours. Yer don't mind drivin', do yer?

Jeogla Public School

The Slogett's home

The School

The sky was grey and the landscape was grey, the school building was painted grey and I felt grey inside when I saw the school that was my first appointment, its name painted on the front wall, as well as its year of birth.

JEOGLA PUBLIC SCHOOL
1925

It stood nearly a mile from the Slogget homestead. Made of weatherboard, with a shelter shed, a water tank and ablution block at one end, its four large windows and one smaller one gazed out on to a world as they had been doing for more than forty years. A small tin chimney poked up from the roof.

A pair of sheep greeted us in front of the gate, their woolly coats soaked. One had a broken horn. Bleating pitifully they stared at us with their yellow eyes, and stopped eating the roses that were growing through the wire fence.

Ignore 'em, Carrie said.

A track ran off from the main road into a semi-circle and became what might be called the driveway to the school. Anyone visiting the school for any reason would have to take this track and stop at a yellow gate. From here, a path ran down the side of the school and joined up to a concrete assembly area that faced the back veranda and the entrance of the school. At the end of the veranda was the fuse-box. To reach it, one would have to stand on a ladder or on the top veranda railing.

Rabbits ran across the yard.

The yard was covered in large and small puddles; two toilets and an incinerator were located at the bottom; basketball goal-posts stood at either end. A row of pines grew along the western side, green and majestic, like the spires of cathedrals. Pine cones were scattered under them, as well as logs and a wood pile, stacked in the furthest corner.

Carrie saw me looking at a farmhouse beyond this corner. Smoke rose from its chimney. That's Ron's place. Yer might' er seen the turnoff on the way here.

The rain stopped.

The wind blew through the pines with a whispering, surf-like sound as if it was telling a story. Their peaks swayed. Their scent was cool.

Standing on the veranda, Carrie pointed out to the paddocks beyond the school that belonged to Ron. To our right, on high, was Bob Frizell's farm. In the immediate foreground, on the right was the school's sheep paddock with a creek running through it. Down the bottom there's a couple of sheep, she said.

Sheep? I asked

They get shorn and the money from the wool goes to the school. Never thought you'd be lookin' after sheep, did yer? An' you won't have ter shear 'em.

She must have seen the surprised look on my face, and added, Don't worry. They look after themselves. She gave the same mischievous laugh that she did back at the house when referring to ducks and geese. The grin on her face spread; the twinkle in her eyes shone.

I smelt damp wood, earth, vegetation, mildew, rock. Yet we were standing inside the school, completely dry. Why did I feel that I had come to a very old place – that I might have been standing inside a thatched cottage, a dwelling, a cave in a hillside? It was like standing on the roadway, back at Wollomombi, in the rain, trying to sort out this sense of displacement.

The corridor had several cupboards, large and small, along its left wall. At the end was the small window I saw from the road. Inside the cupboards were school supplies – spelling books, English books, Mathematics books,

Singing books, exercise books, lead pencils and coloured pencils, bottles of ink and ink powder, nibs, pens, pen holders, a Fordigraph duplicator, art and handcraft materials, chalk, spelling books, singing books, a film projector, ropes, tennis balls, medicine balls, basket balls, cricket equipment, softball equipment, shelves of cane for basket weaving. Carrie opened each cupboard and displayed its contents.

What about that one? I asked, pointing to a blue cupboard.

Just old copies of the "School Magazine", she replied. All the teachers keep 'em there once they've finished with 'em. She opened the cupboard and that smell hit me again. It was as if the cupboard was the entrance to a mysterious cavern. I was intrigued by the stacked magazines.

Come on, Carrie prompted me.

At the end of the corridor was a door, on the left, that opened into the schoolroom – one single room that was the heart of Jeogla Public School. I took a deep breath and said, So this is it, eh?

Sure is, Carrie replied. You like it?

Standing to the side, I could tell she was looking at me, waiting for my reaction. Our inspection of sheep, paddocks, pine trees, puddles of water paled by comparison to what my response would be now. At that precise moment, my success or failure as a teacher at Jeogla Public School – and as a boarder with the Sloggets – depended on my answer. I knew it.

I shook my head in amazement, disbelief, Isn't this amazing? I said, throwing up my arms. Fantastic. Imagine being out here in the middle of a forest, in the New England ranges – and having all these shelves of books under a tin roof. I pointed to the bookcases at the back of the room. Mrs Sloggett, I said, this is wonderful...I'm sure I'm going to love it here...And you've been doing a great job as school cleaner, I can tell. The place is immaculate.

Yer gotter start calling me Carrie, she said seriously. None

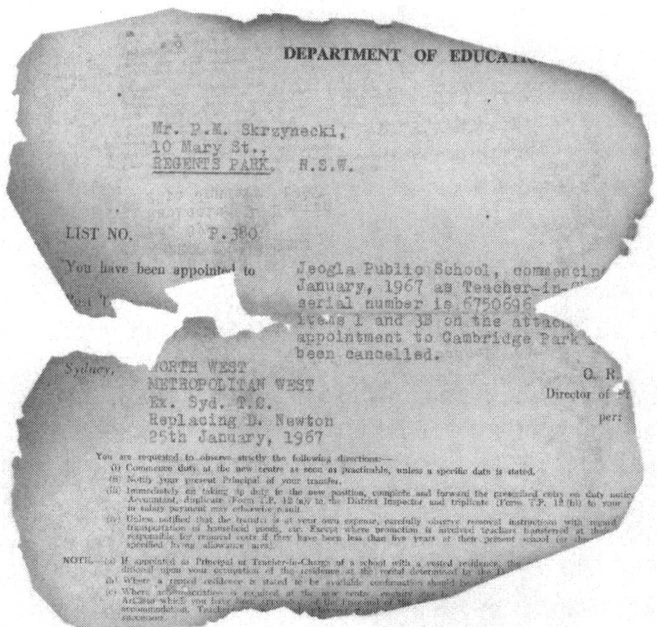

DEPARTMENT OF EDUCA[illegible]

Mr. P.M. Skrzynecki,
10 Mary St.,
REGENTS PARK. N.S.W.

LIST NO. P.380

You have been appointed to Jeogla Public School, commencin[illegible] January, 1967 as Teacher-in-[illegible] serial number is 6750696[illegible] items 1 and 3B on the attac[illegible] appointment to Cambridge Park [illegible] been cancelled.

Sydney, NORTH WEST
METROPOLITAN WEST
Ex. Syd. T.C.
Replacing D. Newton
25th January, 1967

O. R[illegible]
Director of [illegible]
per:

You are requested to observe strictly the following directions:—
(i) Commence duty at the new centre as soon as practicable, unless a specific date is stated.
(ii) Notify your present Principal of your transfer.
(iii) Immediately on taking up duty in the new position, complete and forward the prescribed entry on duty notice [illegible] Accountant, duplicate (Form T.P. 12 (a)) to the District Inspector and triplicate (Form T.P. 12 (b)) to your [illegible] in salary payment may otherwise result.
(iv) Unless notified that the transfer is at your own expense, carefully observe removal instructions with regard [illegible] transportation of household goods, etc. Except where promotion is involved teachers transferred at their [illegible] responsible for removal costs if they have been less than five years at their present school (or [illegible] specified living allowance area).

NOTE.—(a) If appointed as Principal or Teacher-in-Charge of a school with a vested residence, [illegible] ditional upon your occupation of the residence at the rental determined by the [illegible]
(b) Where a rented residence is stated to be available confirmation should [illegible]
(c) Where accommodation is required at the new centre, enquiry [illegible] [illegible]

Fragment of letter of notification of appointment.

School mailbox

of this Mrs Sloggett stuff.

Whatever you say.

I'm not posh, yer know. I'm not one of those people – like some aroun' 'ere I could name – them that likes ter spread the jam real thick.

She ran her a hand across a desk, showing me there was no dust.

What now? I asked.

You'll probably want ter come back termorrow by yourself and have a better look. Stay longer. Darryl's left a letter. She pulled open the drawer of the "teacher's desk". A sealed envelope lay inside, addressed to the "Teacher-in-Charge / Jeogla Public School." When I received my appointment the telegram from the Education Department stated that I was replacing one "D. Newton". I guessed that "Darryl" was my predecessor.

Was he from Sydney too? I asked.

No. He was a country boy. From Mullumbimby. By golly, he was a nice boy...Never complained about nothin'...Ate everything I cooked. Always askin' fer seconds. Best teacher we've 'ad fer years. Not like some other mongrels I could name.

Maybe I was yawning too much or maybe she saw my eyes closing, but she said, Okay, I think that's enough fer now. Yer've had a long drive...Let's get back, get yer car unpacked, have some dinner and yer can have an early night.

I'd like to send my parents a telegram to say I've arrived safely, I said. Or phone to let them know.

Post office's closed. Termorrow's a public holiday. Yer can do it Tuesday.

I looked at her, shrugged my shoulders, and replied, Okay.

I followed Carrie to my car and closed the gate behind me. Yer gotter wire it closed, she said, otherwise them blasted sheep will push it open – and there'll be no flowers left.

Flowers? I'd seen the roses growing against the front

fence but failed to notice the dahlias growing down the side footpath.

Yes, I said, Keep them sheep out. I promptly looped the piece of wire hanging on the gate around the fence post.

Watch the road, she warned, as I sped up too quickly, out of the turn-off, tyres slipping in the mud, nearly colliding with a post on which a kerosene tin was nailed on its side. What's that I asked?

School mailbox, of course."

Mailbox?

School gets mail; it's gotter have a mailbox.

How often does the mailman come?

Three times a week. Picks up the mail from Wollomombi and goes down the Kempsey Road as far as the Big Hill."

Where does the postman live?

Same place as you. Gerald's the postman.

Before the homestead came into view I slowed down and asked her about rent. How much a week will I pay?

Same as Darryl, if yer don't mind. She mentioned the amount. We agreed that I would pay her every fortnight when my pay cheque arrived from the Education Department. But yer don't have ter pay today. Wait till yer get yer first cheque; then we can fix it all up.

The car's wheels drummed over the cattle grid for the second time that day. Once again the rapid series of bumps made my insides bounce. That'll take some getting used to, I said.

No it won't, Carrie said. Best to drive over it fast. After a few days yer won't even notice it.

*

Gerald and I barely spoke a word to each other as he help me unload my suitcases and boxes of books, a small portable record player and two boxes of records, LPs in one, singles and EPs in the other. He'd been told by his mother to hurry up with helping the teacher and *no two ways about it.*

He was tall, sinewy, strong, freckled, with brown curly hair. The sleeves of his shirt were rolled up. He seemed suspicious of me.

I asked him how old he was. He replied, Old enough to drive a car.

And how old's that?

Why do you want to know? Don't you believe me?

So, I said, changing the subject. Despite all this rain, Jeogla looks like a great place to live.

Reckon? I suppose so. The unloading of my car was just finishing. Hoo-roo, he said. See you at dinner. He disappeared into the room, opposite mine, across the landing, slamming the door behind him.

My room consisted of a single bed, a bedside table, a chair, a wardrobe and dressing table, a washstand behind the door with a basin and water jug. One window. No bookcase or stand where I might put my books and record player. It felt cramped. It must have been ten by twelve feet. The lino was grey; walls were painted blue; the ceiling was yellow. As I opened and closed the door, I noticed the gap between the bottom of the door and the floor was large. A towel hung from a hook on the back of the door. A single globe, with a milk-white shade, hung from a black cord directly over my bed.

I closed the door and washed my hands, face, neck: refreshed myself. I felt thirsty and took a drink from the water jug. I took off my shoes, changed my clothes, hung on my shirt and trousers on coat hangers I'd found in the wardrobe; these I hung from the ends of curtain rods; then I lay down. The bed-spread under my back felt warm and comforting. It was four o'clock; there was time for a 2-hour nap before dinner. This was the Australia Day long weekend and tomorrow was a public holiday. The obligations of my appointment would start in earnest on Tuesday when children arrived for classes.

Lying down for a nap, the road before my closed eyes was grey, divided by lines that were yellow and white, broken and unbroken; it travelled in a straight line, up and down hills, turned corners, straightened out. My hands were empty, yet they were gripping a steering wheel. The car's engine was purring. I knew exactly where I was travelling yet I had never been there before. The open sky welcomed me, as did the mountains in the distance, long and unbroken, green and blue at times, grey and hazy at other times. This is where my appointment lay, in the sky beyond the mountains.

Motor vehicles that I encountered along the way ceased to exist once I caught up with them. I passed them, one after another. Cattle, horses, sheep. Farms, small towns, villages. I saw them all without having to look. They were familiar. I knew them – along rivers and willow-lined embankments, protected by the shoulders of hills, overlooking highways and deep in the heart of valleys – without having been there previously. They all welcomed me. I was never lonely. Birds flew across my windscreen, that swooped and disappeared – magpies, crows, galahs, white cockatoos, rosellas, hawks, wild ducks, water hens, even pelicans that lifted off awkwardly from rivers and lakes – or an eagle, circling like a speck in a hot blue sky – all these were my companions. That too, I knew, without anyone telling me. I dared to ask, Where's all the rain? And knew the answer. The rain was there, waiting for its time to fall, in the clouds that were rolling in from the Southern Ocean and moving up the coast, swelling and darkening, heaving against the hot winds, preparing to flood the coast and move inland to the ranges, to fill all the thousands of water tanks, all the dry dams, giving relief to the land and animals, to the farmers and country people from the drought that plagued the countryside the year before my arrival. I continued dreaming and steering, driving into the strange but familiar landscape, falling deeper and deeper into a sleep that my body craved, as I slept on a strange bed, in a strange house, under a tin roof that rain drummed on, creating a rhythm that had descended into a whisper.

Wake up, teacher, dinner's ready! Wake up!

No, let me sleep. Let me...

Y' c'n sleep after dinner. Come on, teacher, dinner's on the table. We're waitin'. The voice was followed by another knock on the door, hard and solid. The voice was Gerald's.

Coming, I called out. Just a sec.

We sat at the same places as before. Granma sat in the lounge room in front of the TV set, eating her dinner off a tray on her lap. The picture was fuzzy and the voice distorted.

I commented on the reception.

Best we can get in weather like this, Carrie said, as if I'd offended her. We don't get much reception from Armidale. What we get comes mostly from Coffs Harbour. Even with the big antenna we got, it's pretty bad in wet weather – an' when it blows a strong wind. I s'ppose yer used to gettin' a good reception in the city.

Yes, it's pretty good where we live; but we don't have the fresh air that you've got – or this fabulous scenery. Too many houses and factories shut out the sky.

Dinner consisted of lambs chops and vegetables. I asked if there was any soft drink. No, Carrie replied. S'ppose we could get some lemonade in....Here, have some tea instead.

I'd watched Elmo make the tea. Warming an empty tea pot, he put in the tea leaves, poured boiling water, closed the pot and covered it with a crocheted cosy. He turned the pot three times. Only way to make tea, he said.

I asked for milk and Carrie brought a jug from the refrigerator. We got a cow, yer know...Keep 'er across the road in a paddock that belongs ter one of the farms. If yer hear someone leavin' the house early in the mornin' that'll just be me, goin' up ter milk Peggy. By golly, but she's a good milk cow. Best I ever had, anyhows.

Carrie and her cow Peggy

They asked me about my family and I told them; what my parents did for a living and where I went to school. I told them that I'd trained at Sydney Teachers' College and was looking forward to teaching in their school; but I said I was surprised to have received an appointment so far from home and, to be perfectly truthful, would have preferred one in the city or, at least, closer to home. My friends had received city appointments.

Yer got somethin' against the bush? Carrie asked.

Or the people that live there? Hope not. Elmo added.

Nothin' wrong with us, Mr Teacher, Gerald said. It was the first time he'd spoken during the meal. He was bolting down his food.

No, I tried to argue. Jeogla's a long way from my home. That's all.

Yer got a lady friend?

Before I could answer, Elmo interrupted. No, Mum, that's the teacher's business. Would yer like some dessert? We got rice pudding tonight.

An' some peaches, Carrie added.

Her question prompted me to ask, What do I do to ring Sydney or make a phone call locally. I noticed there wasn't a phone in the school.

Yer come here – yer new home – Carrie said proudly. Ring the local exchange – and she mentioned the family in the district who ran the exchange in their home – and they connect yer to Armidale. Tell the operator who yer want and they'll connect yer. No call before nine o'clock or after nine o'clock. Not unless it's an emergency.

After dinner I offered to help wash up. Not on yer first day. Gerald can do it tonight. Just watch an' learn. Hardest part's the separator. Yer gotter take it apart and wash all the pieces, one by one.

I watched as Elmo and Gerald wiped what Carrie washed in greasy, grey water that smelt of milk. The separator's inner rings, disassembled, looked like the rings from a child's toy. Termorrer morning when it's dried I'll put it back together, Carrie said, by way of explanation.

Everything else was put away, cutlery into a drawer, plates and cups into a cupboard; the wet tea-towel hung over a handle of the stove. Granma had brought in her tray and left it on a sideboard; this would be her part of a nightly ritual that I observed for as long as I boarded with the Sloggets. Goodnight, she smiled in my direction, as she disappeared into her bedroom. The door clicked shut.

Gerald called back, Goodnight, Jack.

Show respect, Carrie chided her son and punched him on the arm while he continued to scoop the last of his rice pudding and lick the spoon clean.

Jack? I wondered. His grandmother?

Nothing was offered by way of explanation.

I'd showered the night before at the motel in Tamworth, and now ventured to ask about taking a bath or shower.

A bath? Elmo asked, surprised. We don't have a shower. We take baths here once a week. Friday night. Before we go to town on Saturday morning. Do you really need one tonight?

Taken back by his question I didn't have time to think. I blurted out, No.

Make do with a wash each night and I'll show you how to work the chip heater next Friday evening when I get back from Nowendoc; but I'll tell you now, the golden rule is don't make the fire too hot and boil the water otherwise you'll disturb the rust at the bottom of the heater, an' have rusty water. We need a new heater but not just yet.

I thanked them for their hospitality and said I'd like to go to bed. When I enquired about the toilet I was shown outside, to the outhouse by the chook yard.

The dogs started barking instantly. Don't mind 'em, Carrie comforted me. You'll all be friends in no time.

A weak light lit up a pit toilet. The smell was a combination of phenol and human waste. Toilet paper consisted of newspapers cut into squares, hanging from string on a nail.

Before returning to the house I stood under the small awning at the back steps, under a light, and looked around me, up to the sky and to the paddocks and hills in the distance; they were merely silhouettes in the darkness, in the rain that drizzled, as if allowing me the luxury of absorbing the night landscape. Thick, rolling clouds hid the stars. A few lights twinkled, to my left and right, through the watery darkness and I took these to be neighbouring farmhouses. By now Blackie and Brownie had stopped barking and stood in the rain, wagging their tails.

I washed my hands and cleaned my teeth in the bathroom and said goodnight to the family.

Hoo-roo, said Gerald, and off he went, out the back. I'm goin' over to Jimmy's for a while, he called back to his parents.

Mind how yer drive, his father said. There's been a lot of rain. Mind them corners.

Standing in the kitchen with Carrie and Elmo I felt isolated and yet comforted. Here I was, in the middle of a foreign landscape, dependent on these people for my immediate survival, at least, having become part of a family for the next three years, as my contract with the Education Department stipulated – that I should serve out three years of "country service" and go to where I was sent.

Rain fell as I tried to go to sleep, in vast sheets – that I pictured sweeping over the weatherboard house with its tin roof – and intermittent, solitary falls with the silence in between punctuated by drops falling from the tree outside my room as the wind swept through it. It took a long time to adjust to the darkness, the strangeness of a new bed and what was a totally alien environment to me. I could sense the strangeness. At first I shivered, but then became warm under a doona, tartan blankets and a bed spread. I thought of my parents farewelling me, back in Sydney, as they stood in their garden, against a backdrop of roses, and waving goodbye. Now they would be waiting for a telegram or telephone call, informing them I'd arrived safely.

Was that a car's engine outside? Were those Gerald's footsteps outside my room, across the corridor that separated us? I thought I heard a bull bellowing, crickets singing outside my door and a cat meowing under my bed. I got out and looked under it. No, there was no cat. Back in bed I heard it again, a cat's meow, several cats at one stage. Was all this a dream? My body started to feel like it was made of lead.

Ullum

Gerald and I met each other in the corridor as we were coming out of our rooms. The rain continued, slowed to drifting showers, but then it stopped. A wind blew. The air was clean without the sun being visible.

Good morning, I said. Maybe it was my imagination but I think I heard cats under my bed last night.

Huh? With that he opened the front door and yelled triumphantly, Hey, mum, I know where the white cat's had her kittens. Under the floor of the teacher's room!

I sat in my allotted place at the table and ate as if I'd never been fed in my life. Boiled eggs. Toast. Butter. Marmalade. Tea. Cereal if I preferred it. All laid out. What a feast!

Don't mind the cat, Carrie said with a reassuring smile. She'll try an' move 'em soon enough. Always does. So we gotter get them out from under the house before their eyes open.

Why?

She looked at Elmo who continued eating. Gerald said nothing. Grandma was in her room. I have to take 'em down to the dam…If yer know what I mean.

No.

I gotter put them into a sack.

A sack?

With a brick in it.

You mean….?

That's right. We can't afford cats runnin' all over the place.

But why before their eyes open?

Oh, after that it'd be cruel. When the eyes are still closed they have no idea what's goin' on.

Discussing the life and death of kittens put a different coloured hue over breakfast. I'd eaten, was still looking for a second slice of toast, but no longer felt hungry.

Did we put yer off yer breakfast? Carrie asked.

No, I replied. I guess I wasn't expecting your answer,

that's all.

Come on, eat up. Yer gotter keep yer strength. Have that other bit of toast. Do yer like my homemade marmalade?

After breakfast I unpacked the rest of my belongings and told the Sloggets I was going up to the school; by then the rain stopped but Carrie insisted on showing me around the house and yard first. I also told her that after the school I was going to drive back to Wollomombi to ring my parents from the public telephone and tell them I'd arrived safely. Waiting to send a telegram on Tuesday was too long.

Carrie explained that Gerald's room was opposite mine on the landing in front of the house. As I'd figured out, a small corridor separated us. Entrance to the main part of the house was through a door that opened into the lounge room, with coloured plastic strips hanging over it, as a precaution against flies. From there, one entered the kitchen/dining room area, bathroom and the other two bedrooms. Carrie and Elmo's bedroom was behind mine, Granma's was behind theirs. Towards the back of the house, behind the kitchen complex were two other rooms, "guest rooms" Carrie called them. One with a double bed, the other with two single beds.

The laundry was a separate building from the house, so was the toilet. A large undercover car port was attached to the back of the house and I was told if I wanted to I could park my car in there, on one side, behind Carrie's, although the tail of my car jutted out, not quite undercover. On the other side was a tractor with Gerald's ute behind it. A jeep was parked further down the yard and that belonged to the Forestry Commission; it was Elmo's work truck. She said that sometimes it had a trailer attached if he brought home leftover wood. Elmo was the foreman with a team of timber workers in Nowendoc, past Walcha.

That's a fair drive from Jeogla. Elmo arrives on Friday afternoons and leaves very early Monday mornings.

Beyond the car port was a wood heap and two dog kennels behind it. Brownie and Blackie were both kelpies. They were tied by chains to a long wire run, a kennel at either end, and when they barked and ran they would meet in the middle. Beyond the kennels, up a rise, lay a dam where the geese hissed and honked in warning as we drew closer, their necks waving and weaving in the air. Above the carport, on a platform of heavy timber, stood the main water tank. Below it, a smaller one. Next to it, an empty aviary.

Gerald used to keep budgies in there, when he was younger. He bred some beautiful birds, she said sadly. By golly, they were beautiful birds. Snakes got 'em in summer. We can't keep canaries, of course, it's too cold, Carrie explained.

There was also a third water tank was on the other side of the house, next to my room, towards the front.

Carrie kept on talking. That one's mostly fer doin'the laundry and havin' a bath; it's not drinkin' water. At the very bottom of the yard, behind the toilet, was the chook run, closed in by chicken wire and containing a henhouse and trees where bantams and white pullets roosted in the branches. Foxes used ter be a problem, Carrie said. We baited 'em and the dogs and geese keep 'em away. Now our biggest problem around here are the dingoes. They mostly go fer the sheep.

As we left the yard and walked up to my car, a bantam rooster started crowing from a branch, its metallic coloured feathers shining in the light, its neck elongated, straining, announcing to the world that he was king of his castle.

*

The school had a damp smell of wood and earth that I'd picked up the previous day.

Standing on the verandah, I looked out over the paddocks. The rain had stopped. Cattle stood around in groups. Smoke rose from the chimney on Ron Diamond's property just like yesterday afternoon. I wondered when I might see him. I stretched out my arms and took a deep breath. Like the bantam rooster, at the age of twenty-one, I was king of the castle; but that sense of displacement, that I felt at Wollomombi less than twenty-four hours ago, remained.

Inside the school, I opened the envelope left by my predecessor. I read his letter of introduction, his welcome and his account of the various families who sent children to the school. Eight families currently sent their children to the school with their numbers totalling fourteen; another family was due in the district within the month and two more children would attend. Total: sixteen. That was a good number for this year. The letter explained how, to stay open, the school needed a daily average attendance of nine pupils. Anything less would attract the attention of the Education Department, and the recommendations of the District School Inspector as to the viability of the school would most likely be followed. Sixteen was a good number and the school's future was secure.

I looked through the different cupboards and bookcase at the back of the room with their dictionaries, readers, arithmetic books, their "Let's Use Better English", SRA Reading Lab., spelling, music, and a general library ranging from books on colour words, sound words, animals, birds, nature study, social studies, and a range of HOW TO reference books; there were also Biggles and Famous Five books. Two shelves of one cupboard were stacked with ABC music books that catered for "Let's Have Music" and "Let's Join In." There were records, too, LPs and EPs of fairy tales, stories like Peter and the Wolf, Instruments of the Orchestra and excerpts from the classics. All this supplemented what I'd seen the previous day in the cupboards in the corridor as we'd come in.

On the left side of the room, below a double power point,

was an old dark-red bakelite wireless attached to a record player that someone had built into a wooden box that made it easy to lift and move around. I plugged the wireless in and quickly found Radio Station 2AD. At another end of the band I picked up classical music on what sounded like the ABC; apart from those two, all I could hear was static and crackling, whizzing sounds that made it sound like the set might blow up. I returned to 2AD and heard a rural report, preceded by a choir singing "God Save the Queen", bagpipe music and Scottish dancing. I figured that to connect the record player you plugged it in to get a power source, flicked a switch at the back of the radio and plugged in a short cable running through a hole in the side of the wooden box. The loudspeaker in the radio served as a speaker for the record player. I wondered who had devised this basic but efficient system. To the left of the record-player/turntable, and below it, was a Warmbrite heater. An empty box, presumably for logs, was next to it.

I spent the next hour putting spelling lists on the blackboard and arranging arithmetic books for each grade. I also wrote out multiplication tables onto a separate blackboard that stood on an easel at the side of the room. That should be enough for tomorrow morning, I figured, and then I could play it by ear for the rest of the day.

Back in the corridor I opened a blue cupboard where copies of the "School Magazine" were stored. There must have been several hundred.

I brought a pile out and sat on the bench that ran the length of the veranda. Less than a day at Jeogla and I already loved this view – overlooking the paddocks, the sheep and cattle, the gradual slopes of rising hills, partly wooded. To my left stood the windbreak of pines with its continuous wind-whispering sound like a distant sea surge. The sight of those magnificent trees impacted on me more than yesterday; behind them the silver roof of Ron's property gleamed in the sun. Rosellas burst from these trees every few minutes, flying low and high, calling their "clink-clink" to each other as they swooped beyond the school paddock where the school's pair of sheep wandered; or a pair of crimson rosellas would appear out of the sky and sit on one of the branches, making their crystalline bell-sounds before disappearing into the camouflage of pine needles.

Taking the first magazine from the stack I thumbed through until I found the first poem; it was a stanza from Judith Wright's "Legend" and I read it twice.

When I looked up there was a bull standing on the other side of the school fence, across the yard, directly opposite me.

I walked over and called out, What's up? What do you want?

The bull started shaking its head and pawing the ground.

Go on, go away! I waved my arms and stamped the ground, moving forward as I did – like you do to shoo away a dog. Go on, get!

A mighty bellow came from the bull's throat, as if it was in pain, followed by a snort; it shook its head angrily, lowered it, and took several steps backwards.

I did likewise, and ran, because it suddenly it occurred to me that the bull was intending to charge me – or the fence, at least. But what chance did a wire fence have against a beast that size? I ran back to the veranda and watched to see what would happen.

The bull ran forward to the fence and stopped, still pawing the muddy ground, throwing its head from side to side angrily; it did this three or four times, then stepped back and stopped. Maybe it didn't see me from a distance or maybe it sensed that the danger was gone: that there was no one or nothing else to challenge it.

Returning to the veranda I resumed going through the school magazines – but still kept an eye on the bull that was now standing still, facing the fence. Several times I was prompted to imitate its call, to see what the reaction would be but decided not to tempt Fate.

A voice interrupted my reading. I looked up and saw Ron Diamond striding towards me from under the pine trees, that ugly little dog at his heels.

How's it going? he asked. Nice to see a bit of sunshine.

It's going good, thanks, Ron.

Have you done something to upset poor Ullum over there? I saw him pawing the ground. He nodded in the direction of the bull.

Ullum?

My bull.

I thought he was going to break through the fence.

Oh, he could've done that easily…Except he's as gentle as a lamb.

He started bellowing and….

You must have upset him.

I only shooed him away.

Ah, so that's it…You frightened him.

Not exactly frightened, but…

Gee, I don't know, you blokes from the city, you think you know it all. To understand the country you have to step back ……Watch and learn… See how Mother Nature works. Ullum was only being neighbourly when he came up to the fence…He was just saying g'day…

I started to say something and turned suddenly towards Ron, as I did Suzie growled, coming between us, as if to say: keep away from Ron.

Your dog's pretty protective of you, I said.

Oh, she just cares. Like some women. He drew on the cigarette dangling from his lips. It looked identical to the one yesterday. I thought it might drop off but, no, it stayed in place, as if it'd been glued on. What've you been doing?

Just going through what's in the school – like these old school magazines… Not much point in preparing lessons, really, until I meet the children…A meet-and-greet day. I suppose parents will be arriving too.

How's it at Carrie's?

No complaints. I take it she's bit of an institution in these parts?

You could put it like that…Larger than life…Doesn't miss much and the school's her love. Boards the teachers and keeps the school clean, although she tends to get a bit possessive – but that's better than not caring…Someday someone might even write about her… But I've even seen her do her lolly – and then she becomes a force of nature, if you know what I mean.

Sure.

One of my daughters started teaching this year, by the way. Joan. Over in the Newcastle area. We've got four daughters. Has Carrie told you that yet?

No.

She will. Wendy's the eldest. She's married to Frank who works up at the university. Our twins, Sue and Jill, board in town with them.

Twins.

Identical…Most people can't tell 'em apart. They come out here on weekends because they like riding their horses… You'll meet them. We'll, that's about it from me…You've met Suzie and Ullum. That only leaves Dof – Dorothy – my wife. You've got to come over and have a meal with us when you get settled.

Thank you, I will.

Come on, Suzie, let's go and do some real work. He turned around and was gone under the pine trees and through the wire fence. Keep away from Ullum, he called as he turned around. You mightn't be so lucky next time.

Suzie barked.

Kangaroos and Cockatoos

I put aside several school magazines that contained the work of poets I was especially interested in and prepared the classroom as best I could for tomorrow – putting out chalk, pencils, rulers, exercise books and readers. Arithmetic books for all grades, spellers and paints for an afternoon lesson on art. I thought it best not to put out ink for the first week. Children could use their own biros if they had them.

Magpies watched me, heads cocked to one side, as I walked along the footpath, passed through the yellow gate and wired it shut; then they resumed poking in the wet ground. Roses and dahlias grew along the footpath and, with the roses along the front fence, added a domestic touch to the front yard.

Getting into the car I heard falling sounds and saw what looked like small pieces of timber and leaves hitting the ground. Looking up, I saw several black yellow-tailed cockatoos ripping into the bark and seeds of one of the eucalyptus trees that grew over the small track leading from the main road to the school. I could hear the harsh, grinding sounds they were making, as they flapped from branch to branch.

I drove away and I saw a blue house perched on top of a steep rise, overlooking the main road, just past the turn-of to Ron Diamond's place. Carrie had told me that David and Marie Williams lived there, and I'd be teaching their son, Wayne, who was in the Juniors. After that a smaller house, with a wide, spacious front yard and a garden around it. An extension, an annexe of some type, had been added to it. Carrie had pointed it out as the local post office. The Witherdins live there, she said.

As my car approached the cattle-grid just before the road down to the Sloggets I remembered what Carrie had said yesterday about driving over it. *Don't slow down; it's better fer yer tyres to go over it quick.* I accelerated and heard a rapid *brrummp* sound, like a muted drum-roll. Passing the Slogget's house I could see Carrie sitting out the front, on Gerald's side of the landing. She waved to me and I waved back. I decided to make the phone call to Sydney and come straight back, in time for lunch.

The sun was out and I saw the countryside in reverse from yesterday. What looked like a hall stood back from the road almost directly opposite the Sloggetts. With my window wound down I thought I could see black swans on a waterway. On the Sloggetts' side of the road, also, several hundred yards along was a small brown house with a silver roof, not far back from the road. Further along was the sign to Jeogla Station. All this looked magical, as if the rain had dissolved overnight to reveal a completely different world than the one I drove through yesterday. Gone was the grey sky, the bleakness. Features stood out distinctively, fresh, cleanly-washed, delineated from each other. Greys and greens were individual colours. Brown, yellow, khaki, olive. The watercolour wash that rain had created over the entire landscape had vanished.

Approaching the Okay River bridge it was too tempting not to stop and have another look. As I pulled over, a big grey kangaroo appeared from out of the bush, stopped, stood up and stared towards me. Nonchalant, majestic! Its ears swivelled in all directions, stopping, starting, as if it was putting out receptors; its paws hung forward, then, realising there was no danger it bounded across the road, over an embankment and into the bush. Before I could get over my surprise, another kangaroo appeared. Without stopping it bounded across the road and followed the first.

Noises from the sky made me look up and this time a flock of black cockatoos flew over the treetops, sweeping low over the river, their mournful cries sounding like a dirge. They seemed to glide effortlessly, with slow wingbeats.

Unlike the flock of ducks yesterday they didn't disappear under the bridge but flew over it, climbing slowly to the forest on the other side and disappearing over it.

As before, the view was breathtaking but this time even more spectacular because of the added visibility. Again, I couldn't help noticing the number of dead trees sticking out of the water; but it was the expansiveness of water that I marvelled at, how swiftly it swept around a bend from the east, passed under the bridge and flowed out of sight, as if being drawn towards a precipice. Waterbirds had come out to hunt for food. Ducks, water-hens, grebes, grey herons poked about in the mud and wet grasses. Kookaburras were laughing. Crested pigeons started up in a flock, bursting into the sun. Magpies and blackbirds eyed me from the side of the road. I thought how good it would be to jump off the bridge and allow myself to be carried along just to find out where the water flowed.

The more I looked up the more the scenery me held: it was like standing inside an open-sided cathedral, where a structure of trees grew from out of the side of the mountain and arched overhead before leaning towards the river. I saw a forest growing out of a mountain, felt the wind blowing through trees and saw leaves being lifted into the sky, falling into the river, the roadway, and back into the forest. I became conscious of surrounding birdsongs, from birds that I could see and those that I couldn't. I was surrounded by a music that I couldn't understand but felt was entering me, shutting me off from one moment but opening up my senses to the next, as I absorbed it.

Looking down onto the river and wanting to jump in seemed a natural thing to want to do.

Ringing Home

At Wollomombi I rang my parents from the public telephone. At first there was some difficulty in getting through to the operator in Armidale; and then I had to wait because the lines to Sydney were all busy.

When the connection was finally made my parents were overjoyed to hear that I'd arrived safely. My mother cried and I repeatedly assured her that there was nothing to worry about. I told her I would write and they'd probably get the letter within the week but mail was delivered to Jeogla only three times a week.

Are there many shops? my mother asked.

There are no shops, Mum, but there's a general store in a place called Wollomombi. I'm ringing outside it now...There are plenty of shops in Armidale and I'll be going there on Saturday.

All this was getting difficult because I had to say a lot in three minutes in Polish; then I was told by the operator I had to insert more money for the next three minutes. I had enough silver for that but not beyond. Again, I spoke as quickly as I could while allowing my parents, who took it in turns to speak, to have most of the time.

Very quickly I told them about the Sloggett family, what nice people they all were and I was warm at night and getting plenty of food. I also told my mother to call P and tell her not to phone me at Jeogla – and that I'd phone her from Armidale on the weekend. Going through two telephone exchanges to conduct a private conversation with a girl I was going out with in Sydney was my not my idea of privacy. As the pips ran out for "time up" the last thing I heard was my mother telling me she was praying for me.

Dusty Slides

In the general store I met the owners, Mrs & Mrs Robson. Mrs Robson wore an apron over a floral dress. She was short, big-eyed and seemed to be out of the conversation but you could see she was taking in every word. Frank, also short, with receding black hair was also the local postmaster.

The mail's sorted in Armidale, brought out here and Gerald picks it up and takes it to Jeogla and down as far as the Big Hill, he said.

They knew I was the new teacher because word had spread from yesterday and a description of my car had been given by the minister. Also, he added, laughing, *You'd be looking like a lost lamb.*

I couldn't wait to get out of the place.

I bought a few bars of chocolates, a bottle of coke and a packet of potato chips. The chocolates would do if I got peckish at night and the coke and chips were for now. When Frank asked if I needed petrol I thanked him and said no. I had enough petrol in my car until the weekend.

Seen my slides in the window? he asked. I got some beauties.

Of what?

The countryside…especially the Falls.. The slides are for sale, if you'd like to buy some.

What…?

Wollomombi Falls…Don't tell me you haven't heard of them?

Sorry. Can't say that I have.

They're really close by…Just through Wally Edgar's property.

Okay.

Ask Carrie…She'll know.

What's so special about them?

One of the biggest in Australia…. And this is the best

time to see them. After we've had rains like we've just had. The amount of water going over has to be seen to be believed.

I said goodbye and was out the door before you could say "falling water." Passing the windows of the store I saw racks of dusty slides on sale for 20c each, just as Frank said; they showed the countryside, mountains and slopes, but most were of a waterfall, taken in all kinds of weather, at sunrise and sunset, with water cascading over it like a dam; in other slides of the same waterfall there was barely any water.

Teachers Before Me

I returned and had lunch with the Sloggets, sensing a rebuke from Carrie when she said, Didn't think you'd be gone so long. Didja get lost?

No. I stayed at the school as long as I needed. Ron came over and we talked for a bit…He told me about his daughters, and so on. He asked me over so that I could meet his wife; then I went to Wollomombi and rang home.

Are yer parents okay?

Yes, but my mother cried.

She's only worried that you got here safely. Mothers worry.

Then I met the Robsons and Frank told me about the waterfall; he suggested I go and see it because we've had so much rain. Do you know where I go? To get to Wally Edgar's property.

Nice man, Wally. Yer wouldn't meet a nicer man. Lets people drive through his place without charging a cent… Doesn't mind, long as you close the gates. He runs sheep… That's a rule out on the land: remember what I told yer before – yer gotter close the paddock gates.

You really do know everyone here, don't you?

Why shouldn't I? Spent me whole life here…Born and bred, as they say.

And so am I, added Elmo, though I came from the other side of the Styx River bridge, me and me brother Eddie and sister Laurel.

How long have you boarded the teachers, I asked.

Oh, dear me, ever since I can remember, Carrie sighed. Way back…Before you there was Darryl, then Bob Tickle, then George Comino, then Ron Loudon, then Winston Sutors, then Eric Wallis, then Arthur Parkes….During the war years it was the women, Doreen Musgrave and Kate Frizell.

I said to her, Amazing.

Why didn't yer think I could remember back that far? She asked with that same quizzical look on her face that she did when I arrived; she watched like the proverbial hawk.

*

Granma continued eating in silence, smiling at me whenever our eyes me. She was the first to leave the table, and shuffled off on her walking stick to sit out on the front landing in the sun. Her hair was snow-white, looked as soft as eider-down, and seemed to flower under the straw hat she wore. She wore glasses for reading, and there was a pile of TV and women's magazines on a small table out front. Elmo and I helped Carrie clear the table and Gerald said he was going out to do some work on his ute.

A sense of inertia settled over the remainder of the day: it was like a lazy Sunday afternoon, with families having a picnic lunch out on the grass somewhere, in a park or by a river, except here the grass was wet and the rivers were swollen, some had overflowed their banks. Mud squelched beneath my shoes and the light was watery; but I could smell the scent of eucalypts in the air, blossoms from a forest that surrounded the small acre property where the Sloggetts lived.

By the way, I asked, Who lives in that house up the road from you –quite close to the road, the brown house with a silver roof?

Oh, Carrie said, them's Ron's parents – old Mr and Mrs Tom Diamond. Ron looks after them real well...Added that new roof for 'em not long ago...Good son, Ron. Came back from the war a hero.

Really?

You might hear more about it ...but not from Ron. Never talks much about the war.

Do you mind if I go for a walk around the place? Up to

the dam and maybe across the road to the hall?

Do what yer like? It's a free country...The hall's closed up and you won't see anythin' there...Look out fer snakes...

I thought I saw swans nearby...Maybe they're still there?

Maybe there are....Oh yes. Yes they are... Beautiful creatures. They look so peaceful...There's a big dam and they often come after the rains... Mind where you step up there. The grass is high and there's lots of potholes, fallen timber, most of it rotted.

What about your geese?

Oh, they're used ter humans...If you disturb 'em too much they'll give you a piece of their mind. They'll honk an' hiss. Try to chase you away, they will, just ignore 'em, that's the best thing to do.

*

The track from behind the woodheap was worn and easy to follow. Blackie and Brownie strained at their chains and barked but stopped when Elmo yelled at them. I wanted to pat them but decided against it – at least for now. Even though they'd barked, their tails wagged madly.

It wasn't possible to sit down because of the wet ground, but I thought how peaceful it would be at this spot in summer: watching the dam, trying to incorporate as much of the landscape into a single view, despite the hissing and honking of the geese which had already started. Did they recognise me as a stranger? An intruder into their kingdom?

It was a small dam with brown water and bulrushes growing out of it, fringed by tall grasses, and it was from out of these that the geese emerged, full on, as they stormed towards me, their necks waving, dipping and lunging forward, hissing like snakes in a Greek myth. Carrie had told me to ignore them but Carrie wasn't here and if they called my bluff and I ran away, what would they do next time I came to the dam? I took extra long strides as resolutely as I could, straight towards them, trying not to be intimidated...One, two, three...They separated into two columns and reformed behind me, continuing their protests, honking and hissing, their necks weaving, still striking out, but as I outdistanced them and got closer to the dam they dropped back, sensing that danger had passed. Carrie told me that next time she feeds the geese I should come with her. That way they'll get to know yer, she said.

There was a bench against the aviary where Gerald once bred budgies, facing the west, and when I sat down I understood why: it afforded a view over the dam, the paddocks and forest behind. Behind me and beside me, separated by the walls of the garage I could hear Gerald working on his ute and Elmo loading up his jeep in preparation for his early departure for Nowendoc in the morning. Carrie and her mother were inside the house.

It's a nice place to come and sit in the evenin' an' watch the sun go down. Carrie's head appeared from around the corner of the house. Anyways, I'll leave yer to it.

Had she been watching me? Or did she know I'd come to this spot?

When I walked over to the hall I found it closed up just as Carrie said; the doors were locked and the windows had curtains drawn. I was surprised to see at how big it was and how trees hid it from the road. Undergrowth had been cleared on all sides, allowing a path around it. Toilets and a water tank stood behind it, and when I turned on the tap water ran from it slowly, foul-smelling and discoloured. Not far behind the hall, over towards the hills in the background was a watercourse, a lake or dam, where I'd seen the swans. Approaching it, ducks flew up, but no swans.

I was gone for about an hour. When I returned Carrie and Granma were sitting outside on the front landing. Carrie was knitting.

Well, Carrie asked, Didja find what yer were lookin' fer?

You look pleased with yerself.

I wasn't looking for anything in particular. I was just looking around.

S'ppose you found a treasure? she said giggling. Granma smiled as if she'd heard.

I found the hall. I found out that old Mr and Mrs Diamond's place is called "Overdene"...and...

There's a sign on the front gate. We could've told yer that?

But I found it out for myself. That's why I feel pleased.... And I found a big property – well back from the road. The one you called Jeogla Station; but why does it have V2V painted on the roof.

That's the "Wallamumbi" brand of cattle...Herefords. P.A. Wright runs them over at Wollomombi...an' his son, Bruce, owns Jeogla Station.

Wright? Wright? The name was ringing a bell in my head. I asked, By any chance, are they related to the poet Judith Wright?

Yes they are...P.A.'s her father an' Bruce's her brother.

I sat down with Granma and Carrie and was quiet. They seemed to know that something was stirring in my mind and I needed time to sort it out. Are you sure? I asked.

Hee-hee. Of course I'm sure. Told yer I've lived at Jeogla all me life. I should know.

Granma kept nodding her head and laughing, too, as if she had suddenly acquired her hearing and was sharing in the joke about my ignorance.

Do you know her well?

Sort of – but not since she moved ter Queensland. Best person aroun' ter ask is Ron. They were real good friends since before he went off ter war.

Ron's name being mentioned didn't surprise me.

All this is just too amazing to take in, I said. I still find it hard to believe.

Why, yer don't think we'd lie to yer?

No, I don't think my friends back in Sydney are going to believe this.

Well, then, write an' invite them up 'ere – hey Mum. We wouldn't mind some of the teacher's friends visitin' us, would we?

Granma giggled and got up, supporting herself on her cane, and left.

Mum gets tired real easy. Even long conversations make 'er sleepy.

But she's deaf, isn't she?

I guess you could say that...But she still manages to understand what's goin' on.

What happens here on weekends?

On Saturday we all go into town.... I got two sisters livin' there, Dawn an' Olga, and I take Mum in ter one of them...I do shoppin', Elmo an' Gerald might get their hair cut or they help with the shoppin'...Then we all go back ter where Mum is an' have lunch with the whole family. We get back aroun' dinner time, have a meal, watch the TV an' go ter bed. On Sunday we go to church at Wollomombi or once a month the minister comes 'ere and we have a service in the hall. Olga an' Dawn might visit or we have visits from the nieces an' nephews an' their families... It's a busy life. Someone from the city mightn't think so, but it is...We're not backward, yer know.

Apart from being the mailman, what does Gerald do?

He gets work on the properties aroun' Jeogla – mendin' fences, blackberry sprayin', dippin' sheep an' such...He's good at fixin' tractors an' farm machinery.

That's impressive.

He's an epileptic an' takes tablets...It was the epilepsy that stopped him from learnin' much at school; but once he left school an' got his driver's licence he was able to learn on the farms. That came naturally to 'im...You might hear people sayin' things about him but he's a good boy an' means no one no trouble.

She continued talking about her family without me asking questions: it was like a vein of gold had been unearthed by running water, as she shared her life, talking slowly, deliberately, at times her voice dropping to a whisper, then she'd sigh, take a deep breath, and continue.

What about you?

I continued the conversation with her from last night's dinner, but told her I had no brothers or sisters; how I'd come to Australia after World War II with my parents, that we lived in the western suburbs of Sydney. My parents were originally from the land, my father in Poland, my mother in the Ukraine. They were and still are working class people. I went into teaching because I enjoyed books and had studied to be a high school teacher but it didn't work out and I ended up in primary education. Jeogla was my first appointment. Did she know that?

I guessed as much, she said laughing, with a winkle in her eye. You look lost...Never mind, we'll look after you...Tell yer mother an' father not ter worry...Promise?

I promise.

Sydney Teachers' College December 1966. Author at front left.

Poetry and Poets

After leaving St Patrick's College, Strathfield, at the end of 1963, I studied Arts at Sydney University with the aim of becoming a high school teacher of English and History. I failed everything except English but, as disappointing as it was at the time, in retrospect, it had benefits I would never have anticipated. It was at university that I discovered the work of the Moderns in English literature: Yeats, Eliot, Beckett, Hopkins, Dylan Thomas, Joyce, Lawrence…I also met P, the girl whom I was still dating when I was sent to Jeogla, who did pass her courses in 1964 and was continuing her studies in social work.

And it was in 1964 that I began writing poetry.

I had been following the TV career of Frank Partridge VC, on Bob Dyer's Pick-a-Box quiz show. This man had returned from war a decorated hero and had taken on champions such as Barry Jones. He was one of the contestants who'd won all 40 boxes. He met a nurse, they married and had a baby son. With his prize money he was building a home for them on the North Coast, but was killed in a motor vehicle accident in March of that year. His wife and baby son survived.

I began asking that eternal question, *Why?* Why did a man who was a war hero have to die when he had come into his own? I asked it over and over. Did I expect to hear a voice from the sky? To see an answer blazing in flames across the night sky? I don't know what I expected, but I wrote a poem called "The Guaranteed Clock". Today, I only remember the first four lines:

We all see happiness and we all see sorrow
written on the face of a clock –
the hands are carriers of life and death
but never complain of their burden.

I was also writing romantic poetry to P, poems – or verses – of passionate longing and late-teenage angst: poems influenced by the Romantics, expressing undying love while comparing her to a beautiful flower or a star or a goddess in Greek or Roman mythology. She was Inspiration, part of Creation itself, Life, Immortality. We existed in a union I never understood nor cared to understand.

Afterwards, when I transferred to Sydney Teachers' College and enrolled in a General Primary Course, I continued writing poetry. One of these poems, dedicated to P, even won a $5 first prize in a poetry competition run by the students' union. "Puppets' Chorus", another of these early poems, was included in *Drylight 1966,* the annual magazine published by the college.

A special debt of gratitude is owed to several people who encouraged me with my efforts at poetry. At Sydney University I had Professor Derek Marsh as a lecturer, a man whose interpretation of Shakespeare was second to none. I would stop taking notes in the Wallis Theatre and sit there listening to him, awed by his knowledge and presentation; it was like watching an actor on stage and, with its heavy red curtains draped on either side of the stage, the Wallace Theatre seemed an appropriate setting for him.

I'd made an appointment to see him because I wanted to get an opinion about my poetry, and I left several poems in a folder with his secretary. Climbing the steps to his office, for the scheduled meeting, and looking over the Quad of the main building, I felt as if I was climbing into a sandstone castle that once belonged to the kings and queens of England, but felt that I was out of place, and that neither my poetry nor I belonged there.

The secretary apologised for Professor Marsh not being available but gave me an envelope marked "Mr Skrzynecki". Inside was a letter, still in my possession, it read:

English Dept.
9/4/64

Dear Mr Skrzynecki,

I've just remembered that there is a meeting of the Faculty of Arts which I must attend this afternoon, so I won't be able to meet you as we'd arranged. I think you have something to say in these poems, but that your technique is not yet equal to saying it. I'll be pleased to discuss this in more detail with you. The poems as they stand aren't very good, but they're not hopeless either and I think it worth your while to continue. Tomorrow at sometime between 10 and 11 or 11.30 and 12 would be a good time to see me.

Yours sincerely,
Derek Marsh.

The meeting with Professor Marsh was tense, nerve-wracking. He sensed my unease and was "non-academic" in his reference to my poems, pointing out where their faults lay and how they might be improved. He encouraged me to read as widely as possible, and not confine myself to those texts set for study. Returning my folder of poems he wished me good luck for the future, and said that all aspiring poets needed to go through trials of doubt.

At Sydney Teachers' College, I was fortunate to find support for my poetry from several English lecturers: Frank Davidson, Jack Allison, John Rowland, Una Wilkins and Bill Gunn. It was here, in their classes, that I began to see for the first time the connection between poetry and other forms of literature – whether we were studying Shakespeare, Synge, Orwell or Hemingway. As small as they were these "connections" often revealed the underlying theme of a play or novel. For me, a poet could sum up in a line or couplet what a novelist took a chapter to write or a playwright took a scene to explain. For me, poetry was a condensation of human experience like nothing else; other literary forms were an explanation of it.

P had given me a copy of *Collected Poems 1934-52* by Dylan Thomas. This hardback edition had a black and white photograph of the poet on the front cover, wearing a shirt and bow tie, with a cigarette in his mouth. On the one hand he is there as a separate illuminated image, on the other hand he is part of the darkness beyond the non-existent smoke. There was something mythic but also spectral about the photograph, and it only added to the mystique that had built up around the poetry as I read it. "The Force that Through the Green Fuse Drives the Flower", " In My Craft or Sullen Art", "Should Lanterns Shine" and "Fern Hill" became my favourites. I read them repeatedly. The last poem, especially, about Time holding the poet while he is "green" and "dying" was and still is, in my opinion, the greatest modern poem of lost youth, comparable to John Milton's "Lycidas".

Apart from Th*e* "Penguin Book of Modern Australian Verse" I was reading from "The Faber Book of Modern Verse", ed. by Michael Roberts and various other anthologies I'd bought. I wanted to educate myself in Australian and English poetry, as well as European and American. At first, spare time was poetry time but very quickly it grew into the fabric of every hour and minute of every day and into the night. Lines of poetry ran through my head it. I carried a book of poetry with me on the train and on the bus, to and from classes. I read poetry, I wrote it, I thought it, I dreamt it, I lived it.

*

I helped with washing up after dinner and excused myself, saying that I wanted an early night; school started tomorrow and I needed to prepare myself by getting plenty of rest.

Sitting up in bed I first wrote three letters to Sydney, one to my parents, one to my friend Kevin Coates and one to P. To my parents I was full of confidence and reassurances. I had a writing kit with me and, sitting on my bed, told them much the same as I did in our telephone conversation.. There was nothing to worry about, I said. The people were hospitable where I was boarding and the food was great. The school was close by. Armidale was less than an hour's drive away. I promised to write to them every week. Three years' country service here would pass quickly – not convinced this was totally true – but I said that I was happy, was living with a good family and looking forward to my first day of teaching. I reassured them that I would telephone and write regularly. I was probably less enthusiastic with P, telling her that I missed her and advised against expecting telephone calls from me at Jeogla. I disliked the idea of going through a local telephone exchange, unless it was an emergency, and said I would ring from Wollomombi or Armidale where I could use public telephones.

I also wrote two short letters, one to Frank Davidson and one to William Gunn, both of whom I knew had experience living and teaching in the country: Frank was from the New England area and Bill Gunn had had experience in a one-teacher school.

Kevin had been a friend since 1961 when he came to St Patrick's College, Strathfield from the De La Salle Brothers in Bankstown. He was a fervent Labor Party supporter and vowed that one day he would become Prime Minister of Australia. He lived at Mount Lewis, in the Punchbowl district, and we travelled by train on the Bankstown line, to and from school, along with others who lived in the area.

Kevin and I sat for the Leaving Certificate and, although we passed in four subjects, we failed to matriculate. So we repeated in 1963, passed six subjects each this time, and both did Arts at Sydney University. At the end of the year we both failed. I passed English, Kevin passed Anthropology. To this day, we laugh how, between the two of us, we managed to pass two subjects. So we enrolled in General Primary at Sydney Teachers' College, and this time graduated. When our first appointments came out, Kevin received a posting to a city school, mine was to Jeogla.

Over the years I'd visited Kevin at home and his parents welcomed me from the outset. His father was a bank manager and, in my family's eyes, that was a prestigious occupation. Whenever Kevin came to our home, my mother cooked meals for him and insisted he eat them to the last morsel; one of his favourites was beetroot soup. Whenever she served it, he'd licked the spoon clean and ask for a second serve. My mother said that if I'd had a brother he couldn't've been nicer than Kevin. She nicknamed him "Kevinovski".

Like myself, after we graduated from teachers' college, Kevin continued with his studies and became a school principal, serving in various schools in the Sydney metropolitan area.

I was in bed, wrapped in a blanket and sitting up, writing with the pad on my lap. It was only 8 p.m. when I finished but I didn't feel tired. I carried stamps in my writing kit so I addressed and stamped the letters. Tomorrow, after school, I'd drive over to Wollomombi and post them – or maybe Gerald could take them when he went to pick up the Jeogla mail.? There'd be mail tomorrow to make up for the Monday public holiday when there was no mail. Tomorrow would be a momentous day in my life, my first day as a teacher in my own "small school". There was a strangeness in the term, even though I'd heard it and spoke it many times since I received the telegram from the Education Department. Never, in the two years at Sydney Teacher's College, did I entertain the idea that I really would receive an appointment such as Jeogla.

My books and records were still packed in boxes along the walls of my room – as was my old Globite school case in which I kept the poems I was writing, some were in folders, others in foolscap books.

My method of writing and recording these efforts at poetry was to write them in longhand, keep the original in a folder, and then, when I was happy with the final draft, to write it out in my best longhand in one of the foolscap book or type it up on my Remington typewriter that my parents gave me when I completed teacher training. However, I was discovering more and more that the final draft resembled the original, and I was not rewriting much. I wrote quickly, usually in a burst of emotion – often after an experience had left me troubled, elated, indifferent or pondering about something for a time, long or short, and writing poetry became a way of making sense of that experience.

Flicking through them I read poems of protest, of issues raised against the order of the universe; they were poems of philosophical argument, abstract and agitated; they were highly pretentious, derivative, clumsy – as if it had become my duty to solve the problems of the world. They were drivel, but, if these poems had a redeeming feature, at least they had become a legitimate outlet of expression for me, and they were a beginning.

II

First Day of School

I woke and heard magpies singing outside my room; looking through the curtain I saw a family of them on the lawn, poking in the grass for worms, flying to the pine tree outside my window, and then flying back to the grass – gliding, more than flying, for their wings hardly moved once they became airborne. One, in particular, just stood there, head thrown back, carolling its round vowels of song that sounded like they were coming from a flute and rising into the morning sun. The garden and the countryside beyond it were flooded in light.

Packing up the poetry books and folders around me on the bed and floor, I dressed and went out to the kitchen to get hot water for a shave, establishing a routine that would remain as long as I boarded with the Sloggets at Jeogla: attend to all morning necessities, return to the kitchen and have breakfast. Carrie was already up and dressed, Elmo had left for Nowendoc, Gerald was about to leave for Wollomombi to collect the mail and start the mail run; Carrie explained that it would be around lunch time when he went by the school.

Excitin' day fer yer, today – I mean, like it's yer first day at the school. Are yer nervous?

I suppose I am.

What're yer thinkin' about?

Magpies.

There's plenty of them aroun' ...They sing the most beautiful songs when the sun's comin' up...An' after the rain there's lots of worms in the garden.

I could have listened to those birds all morning, I said.

Gettin' back to business, remember you're the teacher up there – don't go takin' no nonsense from no one...I could name a few – even though I'm related to some of 'em – but I won't...An' by that I mean parents too. Most of the kids will be comin' from the Oaky Dam. A feller named Max drives 'em in....The rest'll be from all directions.

We finished breakfast. Gerald went off to do his mail run. Granma appeared out of her bedroom, aided by a walking stick, nodded to me, smiled and sat down. Carrie put breakfast in front of her.

I collected the apple, sandwiches and thermos of hot tea that Carrie had packed for me, made sure I had everything I needed in my briefcase and drove off – full of hope and bewilderment at what lay ahead, wondering if Kevin had left home yet.

The yellow gate was open when I pulled up in front of the school, yet I couldn't see anyone in the yard. It was another hour to bell time, but surely there'd be someone here by now?

The front of the school faced the east and the sun was so bright it made the grey paint of the building look white.

No sheep at the front fence to greet me, no bull at the back fence, but suddenly from around a corner three boys appeared, all of them barefooted, and stood before me, eyes wide-open, half smiling, unsure what to say or do. I felt exactly the same way.

Good morning, I said, My name's Mr Skrzynecki. I'm your new school teacher. Pleased to meet you.

They all stepped back.

I'm Wayne Moult. He looked and acted as if he was the eldest.

I'm Allan. He said he was the youngest. Some of his front teeth were missing, and his hair was cut in a mop-top style. Mouth wide-open, he squinted into the sun.

And what about you? I said to the middle boy who'd stepped back, nervous, fidgeting with a shirt button, reluctant to speak. He was almost as short as Allan, but stocky, solid. What's your name?

He's our brother, said Wayne, and he's shy....His name is Ian. I sensed that Wayne was embarrassed to have to speak up for his brother.

That's a nice name, Ian. I thought I'd change tack, be extra friendly, and approach the conversation from a different angle. What are you going to do when you grow up?

Burn down the school.

Goodness! Why!

Because I don't like school. I'd rather stay home and play.

What class are you in?

This year I'm going into Fourth.

Oh, you'll learn that school can be fun.

Will I?

Yes.

See, said Wayne, I told you he'd be okay...Let's go and play chasings.

By the way, boys, I asked, how did you get here?

We walked, sir. It's only four miles, said Wayne.

The three brothers ran off, yelling and whooping, as if the school holidays had just started, not the other way around.

I opened up the school and watched them running around, breathless, happy, throwing glances at the new teacher in his suit, white shirt and tie, dressed just as he'd been instructed at teachers' college, remembering he was representing the teaching profession and must always be a credit to himself and the Education Department.

As I was opening the windows a Land Rover pulled up outside, children came spilling out, reclaiming the school after a six-week break. As soon as they ran into the yard the Land Rover drove off, back down the muddy road towards the Oaky Dam. Carrie had told me he'd be back at 3.30p.m. on the dot. *Punctual, that's what Max is – to the very second.*

No sooner had he left than a truck stopped outside the gate and a man and three children came down the side path. I walked out to greet them. He wore a white, short-sleeved shirt, brown felt hat and grey trousers. His face was ruddy, unshaven. His eyes were watery. The rest of the school seemed to have forgotten that I existed and continued running around, laughing and talking among themselves. The three children started to run towards the others, as if drawn by a magnet, but were quickly called back by their father.

Come back, Christine, Susan, Bruce! Where are your manners?...I'm so sorry, sir, he said, holding out his hand to shake mine. These children have forgotten their manners over Christmas....My name is Wallace – Wally – Frizell, and these are my children. My wife's name is Joyce and we live on a property called "Copper Rocks", down the road, towards the Styx. He took off his hat and nodded in the direction they'd come from. As he spoke a timber lorry went speeding down the road, out of Jeogla, and in direction of Armidale. It was the first timber truck I'd seen.

I told them my name and welcomed them to the school – and agreed that it was important to have good manners. After we all exchanged formalities, and he welcomed me to Jeogla, Wally told the children they could go and play – but if he heard a bad word about them from the new teacher they'd be sent to bed without any supper. Christine, the eldest, was in Sixth Class; Susan in Fourth and Bruce would be in Second class. Wally appeared timid, held his hat by its rim but looked me in the eyes and said, We want what's best for our children and going to school everyday is so important, don't you think, sir?

But of course, I replied, Why, do your children truant?

No, no, heaven's to Betsy no, but there are those that do and they could be a bad influence on those who don't.

Where would you go if you wanted to truant? I asked. There's no much out here except the bush.

But you never know, do you? Never know what's out there – I mean, the bush…They could be out drinking, smoking, getting up to all sorts of mischief. Be firm, don't you think so, sir? Keep an eagle eye out for your children's sake….Now, you'll report to me, won't you, sir, if my children misbehave, if they forget their manners.

Yes, I will, Mr Frizell.

Oh please, call me Wally….How's Carrie? Is she looking after you?

She's well, thank you, and she is looking after me.

I'd better be going now…Off to town, collect the goods and groceries, and be back in time to collect the children… By the way, that's my brother Bob's farm, over there, past the paddock where the school sheep are kept..... Bob lives on his own. Bob's a real character. You'll hear about him, I'm sure. His wife and children live in town. Goodbye, sir.

Was it because he couldn't pronounce "Skrzynecki" or was he showing good manners, like he insisted his children should be doing, that he kept calling me "sir"?

Wally disappeared around the corner and I stopped to take count of the pupils that had arrived. If I was correct, there were twelve, with two more to arrive. I decided to wait another ten minutes and then blow the whistle for assembly, when, a man and a woman appeared, walking down the footpath. Two boys ran ahead, one younger than the other; they saw me waiting and skirted the footpath, the older one giving me a suspicious look, the younger one smiling and waving.

The man introduced himself as Noel Williams and his son was the older boy, Darryl; the woman introduced herself as Marie, and her son was Wayne. The boys were cousins. Marie's husband was Dave, who couldn't come this morning, while Noel said nothing about Darryl's mother. Noel was short, sinewy, with black slicked-back hair. He wore his sleeves rolled up. They seemed taken back when I told them my name and I could see the same questioning look in their eyes as I saw in Wally's – as if asking, *What sort of name is that?*

So I said, The name is Polish, and I gave them the phonetic pronunciation. See, it's not that hard.

Marie said that she and Dave lived in the blue house, just past Ron's place, while Noel pointed in the opposite direction, "Towards the Styx," he said. By now I'd heard that expression about the Styx so many times in the last few days that I made a mental note of going to visit it. Why was it named after one of the Rivers of the Dead in Greek mythology?

I'll come and pick up Wayne, Marie said. Trim, petite, looking like a school girl herself, she wore make-up and kept looking sideways, as if she expected to find someone looking over her shoulder.

Darryl will make his own way home, Noel said. It's not far to walk – or he can get a lift with Wally.

They left and it was time to start the school assembly, to bring together the children and introduce myself formally, to remind them of school rules, attentiveness to personal welfare, respect towards others, our country, Our Queen.

It was right on 9.30. I brought out the school bell, held it by my side, and rang it as hard as I could. The children came from all directions, from around the buildings, and out of the shelter shed; they converged on the concreted area in front of the veranda and fell into two lines as if they'd rehearsed it Infants/Juniors in the front row, Seniors behind them. They all stood at ease, feet apart, hands behind their backs.

Had we been taught at teachers' college how to take a school assembly, its format and what should or should not be said?I couldn't remember. So I decided to apply common sense and would ask, at the first chance I got, from a local teacher, what should be done?

Sixteen faces looked up at me as if I was the Man in the Moon come to Jeogla. Their expressions said, *Huh? Who are you? I wish I was still on holidays!*

My mind went blank, as clean as a blackboard that'd never been written on. I thought I saw chalk dust floating up into the clouds, becoming cloud-dust, disappearing. Maybe I was disappearing? Say something, I said to myself, or otherwise they'll think you're stupid or scared or both and that won't do you any good. Remember what Carrie said, *Don't take any nonsense. You're the boss!*

Words starting coming out of my mouth and I almost blurted out her advice, but stopped myself and said, instead, Good morning, children.

They all replied, Good morning, sir.

The sixteen blank expressions didn't seem quite as blank. Signs of life began to appear – a smile, a light in the eyes, a shift of the head, a cough. Even standing at ease seemed more relaxed.

Welcome to the new year at Jeogla Public School. My name is Mr Skrzynecki...although some of you might already know that... I told them the phonetic pronunciation of my name and asked them to repeat it. "Shen-esk-ki".

See, it's not hard at all. I told them that I was from Sydney and was boarding at the Sloggetts. You know the rules of the school better than I do, and if I make mistakes today I won't make them again tomorrow. You must help me during these early days – but I also have the help of your parents, and people like Ron Diamond and others like Mrs Sloggett –

Pupils.

people who keep an eye on the school – because the school's here for you. I knew that what I was saying made sense, and was correct, whether or not my procedure was correct.

I continued with general rules of good behaviour, manners, having respect for the school and what it represented in the district. I reminded them to play on the grassy parts of the school yard, and to avoid the wet and muddy parts. Remember to wipe your shoes on the mat before you come into the school.

I finished what I had to say with, Attention. As one, they brought their heels together and their hands to their sides. Then, I said, School, turn, forward in. Again, as one, they turned, and marched into the school, Seniors following the Juniors. I followed them in and found them standing behind desks which must have been their allocated places. In three rows, with six double desks in each row, they were grouped as Kindergarten – Second Class, Third-Fourth, Fifth-Sixth Class. The desks could sit thirty-six places, and we had fourteen pupils in the school. My predecessor had drilled them well and, to his credit, they'd forgotten nothing over the Christmas holidays. From bell-time to when I said, *Sit, please* must have taken fifteen minutes.

By recess we'd covered basic spelling, times tables and some number work with the Infants and the same with the Juniors/ Seniors, except numbers was called Arithmetic. In that first hour and a half I learnt that the secret of this kind of teaching lay in preparation, as thorough as possible, with the teacher doing face-to-face teaching with one group while the others were given work from the blackboard or from books. Several subjects, such a singing, social studies, physical education, art, and natural science could be combined – as could handicraft and music appreciation. I wasn't sure what to do about scripture classes but remembered what Alex Clark had said coming to the school. The work I'd prepared yesterday was invaluable and actually carried us through to lunch time, except that I gave the Juniors and Seniors a poetry lesson based on the "Legend" poem by Judith Wright while the Infants coloured in some stencils I'd found in a cupboard. I'd brought the copy of the "School Magazine" back with me in case I needed it.

Why do you think it's called that? I asked.

No one answered.

I read the poem again. Think about what he's going to do?

No answer.

With folded arms on desks they all stared at me.

Rivers get in his way, cobwebs tangle his feet and branches get in is eyes, trying to make him blind. The poet says the boy can *swim rivers* and he can stare out spiders. He's talking to his dog and his rifle.

Michael Burleigh, one of the boys from Oaky Dam spoke, He's being brave.

He's not afraid of danger, said Christine Frizell.

That's right, I said. Now we're on the right track...The two things that will protect him are his dog and his rifle. He's not scared. Do you think you'd be scared – going off like that – into the wilderness.

No, the whole group answered.

Why? I asked. Why wouldn't you be scared?

Because there's nothing to be scared of, said Ian, the boy who said he would burn down the school.

Nothing scares you, Ian?

Nup.

The whole school laughed.

That's disgraceful, I snapped back. All of you, apologise to Ian.

Sorry, Ian.

Alright, let's return to the poem. Listen. I'll read it through one more time.

While I was reading I could hear some deep sighing. I knew it was a sign of exasperation or boredom but I wasn't prepared to look up and spoil the narrative of the poem. So, let's try again. The boy is going out on a dangerous adventure, taking his dog and rifle with him. Why did the poet call it "Legend"?

A voice spoke softly, almost demurely, it was Roslyn Turner, who was in Fifth Class, another pupil from Oaky Dam. Because none of this really happened. It only happened in the poet's mind.

Very good, Roslyn.

She beamed, lowering her eyes, and the whole school applauded her.

That's right. A legend is a traditional story or a myth… And this is a story that's been going around a long time. It doesn't matter whether it's true or not. It happened in the poet's imagination and what's true for her also becomes true for us. That's why there's a poem.

Sir, Judith Wright used to live around these parts, said Christine.

Yes, so I've learnt…Who knows, maybe she was even writing about a boy from Jeogla?

Lunch time was at 12.30 and I had a full hour to regather my thoughts: to decide what lesson or lessons I could set for the last two hours of the day. The ground was still too wet for cricket or any kind of ball games.

Siting at my desk, listening to the radio and finishing my cup of cup and sandwiches, a group of children, Seniors and Juniors, came running in, Sir, can we have art this afternoon? Roslyn Turner asked.

Art? Why didn't I think of that? Of course, what a clever idea, I replied. I'll get out the paints and paper. Give me a chance to set it up.

We know what to do, said Christine. We used to help Mr Newton…We know where everything is kept.

I'll spread the newspapers, said Susan Frizell.

I'll get the jars of water ready, said Leanne Wunch.

Back verandah of school where Art and Handicraft classes were held.

I'll get the brushes, said her sister Marie.

Can I help? asked Alan Moult.

Help me with the newspapers, said Susan.

Before I knew it the whole school came running in, excited about having art.

Yes, you can all help but first go and finish your lunch, I said. I'll ring the bell at 1.30.

*

What an inspiration it turned out to be!

Spread out on the veranda, their faces set with concentration, and given the topic

Paint whatever you like, the whole school became a hive of creativity for the next two hours. Trees were painted, paddocks with cows and horses, trucks carrying logs, rain falling from grey clouds, the new school teacher in a suit, holidays at the beach, Father Christmas stuck in a chimney, a kangaroo jumping over the moon. Someone had even half-drawn, half-painted the boy in Judith Wright's poem, running towards a river, a rifle slung over his shoulder and a dog at his heels. Spider-webs in the corner of the painting, ready to entangle him, bring him down.

Look at mine, sir.

Hey, that's not what a horse looks like. The head's too big. Your horse looks like an elephant without a trunk.

How can it be an elephant if it doesn't have a trunk?

Sir, look at my picture of the Sydney Harbour Bridge.

That's very good. Have you ever seen the Sydney Harbour Bridge?

Only on TV.

I have, sir. Our family went to Sydney once when mum got real sick and had to go to a special hospital....That was sad. We all cried but mum got better.

Their words, my words, our words, mixed up in an afternoon where formal lessons from teachers' college about colour and shape were forgotten, and children had a period of free expression. First poetry, and now art. They were loving it and I was loving it, sitting on the floor with them, mixing colours and not caring whether what I was painting made sense or not. The children could see that I was enjoying myself. I could see they were having a happy time. It couldn't have been a better ending to the first day at school. When I said, There'll be no homework tonight, they clapped and yelled, Yippee!

By bell-time the cleaning up was finished and the children pinned their paintings to the display board at the back of the schoolroom, with many of the paintings still wet, but nothing mattered in that respect except to see the finished products hanging up in a room that had become an art gallery. They all beamed with pride as they stood back and admired their work.

Next art lesson, I said, we can talk about your paintings.

And paint some more? asked Roslyn Turner

When I was dismissing them the children told me there was no need to ring the bell. Through the windows I could see the Land Rover from the Oaky Dam waiting, as was Wayne Williams's mother's car and Wally Frizell's truck – although there was no sign of Wally; but as we rounded the corner there he was – coming down the side of the school, hat in hand, Well, I hope my children were well behaved?

They were Wally – and so was the whole school. I'm lucky to have such fine children to teach.

Go on, all of you then – into the truck. I'll take the Moult boys home too.

Wayne Williams went running past, Come on, Darryl, Mum said you're coming home with us.

For some reason Wally seemed reluctant to leave, and while we spoke he kept putting his hand up to his mouth. Was that beer I could smell? His eyes were red and he continued holding his hat, turning it around and around, as if looking for an imperfection in the rim. I sensed he wanted to say something badly, but couldn't bring himself to spit out the words.

Is there something wrong, Wally? I asked.

No, no, sir…but if I'm ever late coming to get the children, just let them go home will you? They know the way and it's safe…Everybody along here knows everybody. They often walk with the Wayne, Ian and Alan. They all get on well… Except my Brucie, he's a bit shy, keeps to himself, drags along behind the girls…Now, dear me, I'd better go, otherwise I'll be rambling long into the night. Besides, if Carrie finds out you're late getting back because of me, I'll really cop it, you know. She can be something else when she gets mad… Goodbye, sir.

As he was leaving I noticed a dead rosella by the roadside and walked over to have a look at it; it had probably been hit by a timber lorry speeding down the road. I also saw mail sticking out of the letterbox. Gerald must have come during the afternoon. I brought it indoors and was surprised at how much there was – mostly official envelopes, small and large, from the Education Department, newspapers of various kinds as well as mail-outs from educational companies. Every item was addressed to The Principal or The Teacher-in-Charge. There was no personal mail.

A Visit from Bill

By the time I returned to the Sloggets' house it was four o'clock. Carrie had made a pot of tea and laid out date biscuits that she'd made.

Thought you'd got lost, Carrie said.

Don't be silly, I laughed. How could I get lost?

Yer never know, a young feller like you from the city, might go gettin' strange notions in his head – goin' off to explore the bush – hopin' to find a treasure....So, how was your first day?

She sounded like she was trying to sound funny – or make a joke about me being late. I decided to ignore it. I said, Wonderful...I met some of the parents, Marie Williams and Wally Frizell.

Wally can be a perfect gentleman. She nodded her head emphatically.

I didn't meet Max from the Oaky Dam – he just came and left.

Max works to a pretty tight schedule. Droppin' off and pickin' up the kids is only one of his jobs...He work pretty late hours an' yer gotter respect that, don't yer think. He's got a family to support. Lives at Wollomombi.

Yes...I wasn't complaining.

Now I must tell you that I start cleaning the school at 4 o'clock. That means you should be back here as soon as possible after school finishes. Unless I'm away, a cup of tea an' biscuits will be waitin'. I'll go up and clean the school. I'll be back in an hour an' start on gettin' dinner ready. Any questions?

This was a side of Carrie I hadn't seen – sharp, bossy. No questions. I replied, No.

Then I'm leavin'. Be back in an hour.

Shortly after she left, the dogs started barking madly. I was still having my afternoon tea when there was a knock on the door.

I went out the front and saw a car parked on the rise, above the house, to the side of the road. A man came walking towards me. Of medium height, balding, he had a moustache and was smoking a pipe. Puffing deeply, lost in thought, he looked like an academic.

G'day, he said, extending his hand, Bill Higgins is the name. I'm the teacher at Chandler.

Pleased to meet you, Bill. Come in.

I made him a cup of tea, and he said. We better go outside, otherwise my pipe'll smell out the house. Mind if I take a few biscuits?

Sitting on the bench between Gerald's room and mine, he looked at me and smiled, then laughed: the same sort of smile that the policeman in Armidale and the minister in Wollomombi smiled.

How'd the first day go?

Good...I'd like to think... I got through it.

That's the shot.

The programming is going to be a challenge. I said. At teachers' college they never prepared us for running multiple classes like you've got to have in a small school.

Once you get the hang of it, it's a pushover. Use the ABC's music and health programmes whenever you can ... Combine certain subjects..... Use the SRA Reading Lab. Daily spelling, multiplication tables, drill them over and over....Come around to the school and have a look at what I'm doing. I can give you some old timetables.

I heard you have a residence?

That's because I'm married. Isabel and I have a few kids. The eldest two go to Chandler.

Bill proceeded to give me a run-down of the district. Not much escapes your landlady. She's been boarding the teachers for ages and keeps an eagle-eye on the school. She thought the world of Darryl. You'll have to be good to live up to her estimation of him.

I'm not from the country and I think that's a minus to start with.

Have you met Ron Diamond yet? He's pretty important in these parts...War hero and all that...Shire president. Don't be fooled by the rough and gruff manner or that cigarette that he's always smoking. Underneath it all is a steely mind, sharp as a razor

I find the silences awesome – especially those paddocks that the school overlooks– or that view from the bridge over the Oaky River.

They might be awesome but you'll go crazy if you spend all your time out here. You should get into town as much as possible. Armidale's got a lot going for it.. theatre, art gallery, if you like that sort of thing...It's got the Capitol – a picture show at the end of Beardy Street...Have you heard from Harry Harris yet?

No, who's he?

Local inspector of schools.

When will I see him?"

Could be any time. He might just drop in unannounced. They like to do that, catch you off guard.

Oh?

Bill seemed surprised by my reaction, and laughed. Nothing to be scared of. Just keep doing your job and smile. Because you're a probationary you'll be inspected before the end of the year – but I'm sure you'll meet Harry Harris before then.

They never told us about school inspectors at teachers' college. I wonder why?

Probably didn't want to turn you off the course. Know the funniest thing about school inspectors when they come out to places like Jeogla?

No.

There's a protocol they follow; and they all say the same thing when they're inspecting you. It'll be, *Just carry on, Mr*

Skrzynecki, as if I wasn't here. And all the time you're scared out of your wits that you might be doing the wrong thing.

Bill's pipe smoke was starting to make my eyes water. I got up and walked around the garden.

So what happens tomorrow?

Make sure you fill in your Entry on Duty form. Schools like ours are officially called Fourth Class Schools and the form is a T.1. 3 (a).... Why don't you come around tomorrow and I can show you? Also, check your mail. There should be a copy of this month's "Education Gazette". There's a calendar in there that's easy to follow. It has all the dates, week by week, month by month, of what you have to fill in and where it's got to be sent. Once you get the hang of it, it's easy.

I'm going to the Clarks for dinner. I could stop in. What about five o'clock? I'd also like to ask you about the correct way of taking school assemblies.

Perfect. Tomorrow. Come straight up to the school. I'll still be there. By the way, you know this area is all Country Party, don't you?

Why was Bill asking me about political parties? No.

Just be careful what you say and who you say it to. The trees have ears around here – and if the locals get wind that you're anything but one of them, life could be made difficult, especially if you're Labor supporter.

Okay, I'll remember

I'd better be going, said Bill, puffing on his pipe. Time and tide and all that stuff.

When Carrie returned and I told her that Bill Higgins had visited she became tight-lipped, curt in her responses. You don't like him? I asked.

Not that I don't like him; it's just that I feel sorry for his poor wife and all them kiddies. She works so hard, bless her heart.

Kiddies? How many have they got?

Three and another on the way. She's stuck at home and he's in that school across the road, being a school principal, smokin' on that smelly pipe.

Smokin' on that smelly pipe!

So that's what was upsetting her! Bill's pipe!

After dinner I drove up to the school to put up some lessons for tomorrow and try to find an Entry on Duty form and check the mail for the *Education Gazette.*

This was my first visit alone to the school at night.

Once over the cattle grid the road became a tunnel as it disappeared into the forest. Lights blinked from the McCrae property on the hill, along the Williams Road on the right and from the Witherdins house on the left. Further up, on a rise, was Marie and Dave Williams's house and a short distance further on, well back from the road, Ron Diamond's property; then there was nothing. Unless you looked for it, you could drive right past the school.

Pure black. Pitch black. Call it whatever-kind-of black you like. With stars overhead, mere pinpricks of light, glimpsed through the overarching trees. The headlights from my car illuminated the road ahead. It was spooky. It was only a mile's distance but, *Look out fer kangaroos*, Carrie had warned me. *The blighters'll jump out of the forest, wreck yer car and you, if yer not careful. Possums too. Their eyes shine red in the dark.*

Whether I subconsciously followed the path of other cars that I'd seen parked in front of the school or whether it was instinct, but I drove straight into the side track, off the main road, that led to the yellow front gate. By parking exactly next to the gate, I was able to open my car door, lock it, and reach out and open the gate. By staying on the path that ran down the side of the building I rounded the corner, climbed the steps of the veranda and was able to open the door. I could also climb on to the veranda rails, reach the switch beside the fuse-box and turn on the back light.

Standing inside the school felt different than it did during the day; it was something about the timber, the warmth of wood, perhaps, offering an intimacy that wasn't there during the day. I turned on the radio and found a station playing Sixties pop music.

I put up reading, spelling and number work on the blackboard, as well as some written expression topics for the upper grades.

In the teacher's cupboard I found some concertina files and brought them out. Starting with one, I went through the compartments alphabetically. There was nothing here that I could remember being shown at teachers' college during my training. There were white forms, blue forms, green forms, pink forms. There were forms for milk returns, forage allowance claims, organizations that had used the school, travel allowances, applications for additional pupil record cards, bursary applications, evening college applications, returns for classes for slow learners, altered numbers of the "School Magazine", altered numbers of the "Education Gazette". Then, when I'd just about given up hope, I found the T.I. 3(a), Entry on Duty forms. The original to be sent to the District Inspector of Schools, the duplicate to the Area Education Office. I also found forms for Term Returns of Enrolment and Attendance and made a mental note of where they were kept. In a large envelope, separate from the files I also found the Pupil Record Cards. Confidential information was recorded on these cards and I'd heard during Practice Teaching periods that these were never to be removed from school premises unless a pupil was going on to high school, or transferring to another school. Blue cards for boys. Pink cards for girls.

I went through the pile of mail that had arrived and found the "Education Gazette". In black and white, neatly-squared, sixteen faces of girls and boys, from all grades, adorned the cover. I expected to read their names and perhaps the schools they were from, instead, on the inside of the cover it read: *The beginning of the school year – new faces, new teachers, new classes, and new pupils.* There were several articles in the gazette, ranging from "The Duke of Edinburgh's Award Schemes" and "Readability Studies" to the "Individual Mathematics Programme." On page 27, however, I found what I was looking for. "The School Calendar, 1967."

When I finished going through the concertina files and the "Education Gazette" I didn't look to see what time it was but I knew I'd had enough. Packing up everything, returning it to the teachers cupboard and locking it, I turned off the light and radio and went outside.

The night was warm. There was a lot of cloud-cover. Maybe tomorrow there'd be rain?

Staying on the footpath, I walked back to my car, through the yellow gate and closed it behind me. As I reached out for the door handle, a heavy breathing confronted me. Deep, deep. Inhalation and exhalation.

I stopped, frozen to the spot.

Again, the breathing.

I was terrified. I started to whimper. Who's there?

No reply.

Just that deep breathing. Deep. Deep.

I managed to get my hand to the door handle, opened the door, closed my eyes, and literally jumped into the car.

Clicking the door shut, I turned on the headlights.

Between the car and the fence stood a cow.

A cow!

I tooted the horn but it refused to shift, then it backed off and stood directly in front of the car, shaking its head and making mooing noises.

I reversed the car, up the track and turned back onto the main road.

A cow!

I had the life scared out of me by a cow.

First Poem

The Sloggets had gone to bed by the time I got home. It was after ten o'clock. Parking my car alongside my room, I tried to make as little noise as possible, still a little shaken from the encounter with the cow.

The white cat ran across the garden.

A Willy-wagtail began to sing in the pine tree when I came into the house and switched on the light in my room. I listened to its sweet, happy song and I got ready for bed, wondering what could be making it sing at this time of night. My room was warm and I settled into bed as quickly as I could with images from the day running through my head. Accompanying the images were songs from the radio – songs by Donovan, The Beatles, The Rolling Stones.

I lay awake for a long time and could not get to sleep.

That same feeling of unreality that had come over me as I was leaving the school returned: a feeling that a new life, or voice, had entered my body and was now living inside me. Among the images of the day, children's voices, echoes of songs, parents' faces, and that "something else", a voice was trying to speak but could not articulate itself. Switching on the bedside lamp, I took pen and paper from the dressing table and wrote:

Fortunately you are not the last of your kind –
lying there without a tail!
Doubled over with a cracked beak,
biting the yellow mud.
An ant walks onto your half-open eye,
then stops.
And the wind blows down the hill,
vainly moving your crimson wings.

I called it "Rosella" and put it away. The image of the dead bird on the road had been captured, as well as the feelings I had about it, whether those feelings were consciously perceived or not. My only spontaneous reaction to it was that I liked it – not because it was an outstanding poem, but because it was simple and direct, clean, uncluttered by emotions.

The poem was proof that my poetry had found a new place of living, here, with me at Jeogla. If I could write one poem here, maybe I'd write more? If the poems in the past had been born of a discontent or conflict I felt about a person, place or situation, perhaps there was a life beneath the surface, as plain or ordinary as it seemed, at the end of the highway that had brought me to my first teaching appointment? What would the policeman at Armidale say, now, if he knew I'd arrived safely and got through the first day? Would he still be smiling?

Six weeks earlier I'd gone into Head Office of the Education Department on the corner of Bridge and Loftus Streets when I received my appointment and objected on personal grounds. After a lengthy wait and a very short interview, I was told I'd be notified by telephone of the decision made by the Primary Registrar. Next day, I was told I must go.

When the realisation of this set in at home, my parents became philosophical and told me it would turn out for the best. If things were not turning out favourably, and I was unhappy in teaching, my parents offered to pay off the bond that was owed for teacher training and I could reconsider my future. I told them *No*. I'd see out the three years, whatever happened. As slight as it was, this small poem about a dead bird – as trivial as it seemed – became a refutation of my parents' proposed solution. A justification for me, also, that poetry might become a way of understanding or coming to terms with expressing this "other life" whose existence I was becoming more aware of.

Dinner at the Manse

Carrie explained to me over breakfast that the Willy-wagtail sings by moonlight, so that when I switched my light on last night it was the light through the window that set him off.

You haven't forgotten that I'm going to the manse for dinner tonight?

No. I'm not that forgetful.

You know the Clarks?

Can't say I know 'em, but I've met 'em. And when he comes to Jeogla once a month for the church service in the hall we always stop and talk. Fer a minister, I must say, he's a bit fancy. She's a real nice lady, kind, though, always helpin' wherever she can. Her health ain't the best, I think you'll find.

Why, what's wrong?

Dunno. Never been able ter find out.

I'm also stopping in to see Bill Higgins – but first I'll be home for that cup of tea and date biscuits.

So, you like 'em, eh?

Must be the best in all of New England.

I thought you'd say the best in the world.

Where's Gerald working today?

Inbetween doin' the mail run he's got a job fer a few days...Doin' some blackberry sprayin' over at George Gray's place.

George Gray?

He's a farmer down the Styx...Like Ron, he's a cattle-breeder. Been here all his life...Nice man...He done a lot for the school in the early days...Raised money for the P & C. He's bound to stop in at the school and say hello...Known 'im all me life.

I'm off, wish me luck.

Remember, no nonsense from any of 'em.

No sooner had I driven up to the front fence and parked

under a cover of trees, than a truck came from the opposite direction and pulled up alongside me.

A man approached. He was balding, wore glasses, was solidly-built and, from all appearances, I would say he was very strong. He walked with some exertion, with what appeared to be a slight imperfection, lifting his right leg extra high. He was sweating from the effort. His mouth was pulled to the right and seemed swollen or larger than the left side of his face. His left eye also seemed to droop.

I'm George Gray, he said. His speech sounded slurred. I have a property down by the Styx called "Roxburgh" and I was educated at Jeogla Public School. So was my brother Bruce and my five children.

Pleased to meet you, Mr Gray. We shook hands and I told him my name. I supposed you've seen lots of changes at the school?

It used to be called Jeogla Provisional School – did you know? – and was at a different location. He laughed at my question about changes and said yes, there'd be too many to talk about now but he'd like to welcome me to Jeogla. Carrie'll look after you like you were her own. If you ever want a history of the place I can give it to you. I live on my own now that my wife's passed away. One day, when I retire, I'm going to record my life and the history of Jeogla for the Armidale and District Historical Society. He added, laughing, Who knows, you might even read it one day?.

He saw me looking up at a flock of noisy birds that came swooping from out of the trees, as if parking our motor vehicles where we did had disturbed them. They began creating the noisiest racket imaginable – raucous, high-pitched piping calls that sounded like they were coming from peewits and were fighting among themselves. I'd seen them around the school in one's and two's but not in such a large number.

What are they? I asked.

Noisy miners, George said. They're also called soldierbirds. There must be a nest nearby.

Motor vehicles began to arrive and George returned to his truck, smiling and waving to everybody as he drove off. The children waved and called back, Hello, Mr Gray. He seemed chuffed by the attention he was receiving.

The start of the day was much as the day before. I saw the same parents, the same children, the same time spent before the bell was rung before line-up. The Moult boys were the first to arrive and Wally Frizell dropped his three children off next. This time, instead of driving to Armidale, he returned home.

Too many chores waiting to be done. I must confess, I 've fallen behind with my chores. Oh, goodness me. You know what it's like running a farm.

Of course I had no idea what it was like running a farm but I smiled, and nodded, feeling an instant liking for the man. He was plainly honest. Ron Diamond. George Gray. Wally Frizell. I felt I could trust them all.

I dispensed with the formalities of an assembly and decided to wait until I spoke to Bill Higgins about the correct procedure.

During lunch time I took Ian Moult aside and asked to him about his spelling problem.

What makes you stop trying when it comes to spelling?

Dunno.

Do you have trouble sounding out the parts of a word?

Nope

Tell you what, let's make a deal.

Okay.

If the fourth class list is too hard, why don't you try the third class list when we have spelling in class?

Nope.

Why?

Others will laugh at me.

I can promise you they won't. Why don't you go in and copy out the third class list now. No one needs to know. Tomorrow or next day we'll go through it, just you and me, and you can tell me if you found it hard or easy. Don't even try to spell the words. Just sound them out for me...Break them up, one by one, into parts.

I had no idea why I tried this approach with Ian. The rest of the school was running around, playing chasings – Juniors and Seniors mixed, as if they were all in the same class. There were sufficiently dry patches of grass in the yard now. Since the playground sloped downwards, away from the building, the water ran off into Ron's paddocks or the school's sheep yard where there was creek at the bottom. Feet and shoes squelched and could be heard separately from the children's voices. In two days I had come to rely on those voices as a sign of security. If they were nearby I knew all was well. If I couldn't hear them, something was wrong. Either they were lost or I was lost.

Now, Ian go and copy the Third Grade list into your spelling book. Try and learn to spell as many of those words as you can tonight.

Yes, sir. I'll try.

I spent the rest of lunchtime refilling the Fordigraph duplicator and making some stencils for a nature study lesson I wanted to give the next day. Insects would be the topic. There was a collection of them and small reptiles preserved in methylated spirits in jars at the back of the room.

In the last half hour of the day I decided to read them a story.

Has anybody read *Treasure Island* by Robert Louis Stevenson? I asked. No one put up their hand. Has anyone heard of it?

Roslyn Turner put up her hand. It's about pirates.

And buried treasure, said Michael Burleigh.

That's correct! Pirates and buried treasure! Lots of strange and interesting characters…Exotic places, foreign shores…A man with one leg and a parrot on his shoulder. Anyone else want to say anything? I asked. Anyone? Well, I thought that by way of doing something different, maybe in the last fifteen minutes or so of each day I'd read you a chapter from it.

I began the story of *Treasure Island*, and when it came to the part of the sea-song,

> Fifteen men on the dead man's chest –
> Yo-ho-ho, and a bottle of rum!
> Drink and the devil had done for the rest –
> Yo-ho-ho. And a bottle of rum!

I asked the school to repeat it, as a song, and, to help them get into the mood of the story. I asked them to swing their arms across their chests, as if they were holding a baby, swaying from side to side. Every child loved it.

Afterwards, as the children ran out of the gate to the waiting motor vehicles, I could hear some of them laughing and singing out, *Yo-ho-ho, and a bottle of rum!*

*

When I entered the grounds of Chandler Public School there was no sign of Bill. There were some children still playing, and I figured they were waiting for their parents to come and collect them.

Glad you could make it, said Bill, appearing from a room. Come into the office.

You have an office?

Chandler used to be a Third Class school. It had an assistant, now it's just got me and has been reclassified to a Fourth. Numbers are good – and will grow next year. That's why it's got the office and the residence across the road…So, how've things been?

I'm settling in slowly.

Bill saw me looking at the pyramid of papers on his desk, Don't worry. There's order in the chaos.

Order? It's a mess.

Here, let me make you a coffee, he said, lighting up his pipe.

When we were both settled and drinking coffee, he said, He's adopted, you know.

Who?

Gerald. The Sloggett boy. Did Carrie tell you?

No.

And he's an epileptic.

Yes, she said so...But what's it matter if he's adopted? I have an adopting father – and you couldn't have asked for a nicer man.

A lot goes on here, you know, below the surface. You think it's all quiet. There're dramas and intrigues of all sorts. Wait till you hear about who got caught with whom in the bedroom by the woman's husband – and then the woman and the boyfriend both had to leave the district and now live in town.

Actually, Bill, I wanted to ask you about how to take an assembly correctly – and about programming.

Bill reached under the pile of papers on his desk and pulled out a folder with a number of programmes in it. Here, borrow these. Copy what you like – adapt it to your own school or whatever ideas you've got. Modify it....

Thanks.

Assemblies....Well, you have one big or main one on Monday morning. Salute the flag. Sing the national anthem. Go through the school rules. Have a civic or patriotic theme – like loyalty to the flag, what it stands for and why we should be proud of it. Tell them a story of heroism if you've got one. They're madly patriotic out here. It's all Country Party, federally and at the state level. From their hats to the soles of their boots. Country Party. You'll soon hear about the New England New State Movement. Voting's soon. Everyone'll tell you why we should have it. No one is game to say why we shouldn't.

You're pretty keen on politics, aren't you?

Aren't you?

No.

Why not? With your European and – I assume – working class background, surely you're a Labor voter?

I've just turned twenty-two. I've hardly had time to think about politics.

What about the Vietnam War?

What about it?

Where do you stand?

I'm against it. I was in the very first National Service call-up but was found to be medically unfit. My voice had suddenly become edgy, tense.

That's the shot, Bill cried gleefully, sensing the change of tone in my voice. Now you're getting riled. Now you're starting to show your true colours. Of course you're a Labor man. So am I! Put it here. Shake hands, mate!

We shook hands and, as far as I was concerned, that was the end of politics and political parties; but beneath that proverbial slap on the back and professional bonhomie, I sensed Bill wasn't finished with me yet. There was a directness in his approach, but there was something else that I could not put my finger on, just yet. If I had to respond to a gut feeling, I'd say that he had a higher design for me: something that would elevate his sense of personal dignity and convert me to a cause. I wondered what it would be?

After he showed me around the school, I said I had to leave. The Clarks will be waiting. Besides, I asked, shouldn't you be going home across the road, to your wife and children?

Soon, soon, he said. Isabel's fine over there with the kids.

They know that I've got work to do here...Sure you wouldn't like another coffee? He stuffed more tobacco into his pipe and drew on it deeply, gazing up at the sky. Ah, isn't life beautiful? Smell that fresh air. What more could a bloke ask for?

⁕

I knocked on the door of the manse and a big black dog came bounding from around the back; it stood back from me, playfully, woofing and jumping up and down, as if inviting me to play.

Back Cassie, get back! The Reverend Alex Clark appeared following the dog and ordered her to quieten down. Excuse Cassie, will you, she's just excited and wants to play. Here, this'll do. He picked up a tennis ball and threw it far into a paddock next to the manse. Go, fetch, Cassie...And off Cassie bounded, like a kangaroo. Now, let's get inside before she returns.

By this time Mrs Clark had came out onto the front veranda. Hello, welcome to the manse. Come inside. Take off your coat and I'll hang it up. Dinner's not quite ready but we can have some refreshments... Here, into the lounge room. She spoke in that same, careful tone of voice that I heard when she stood in the rain on the day I arrived. This time her eyes were bright, not showing the disdain that she showed when criticising the cold weather. The three of us sat on lounge chairs, around a coffee table on which peanuts, chips and pretzels had been laid out. Mrs Clark poured each of us a soft drink and proposed a toast to my stay at Jeogla. Cheers, I hope it'll be happy one, she said. And please call me Jill.

Me too, I replied – and thank you both for your hospitality. I feel I'm meeting people at the other end of the road, so to speak, the road between Wollomombi and Jeogla. One group of human beings live at one end, where I live, another here.

And the rest of civilization lives in Armidale, Alex added, oblivious to us – whether it's carrying a beacon for the Education Department or God's Word. Do they know we exist? Would they care? Lighting up a cigarette, he asked, Would you like something stronger? What about a whiskey? I think I'll have one. Enough of this insipid soft drink!

He got up, walked to a glass cabinet, poured a whiskey, held it up to the light and proposed a toast. To Cassie, may God grant Cassie – a dog looking for a tennis ball – a long life.

Now, dear, you're not preaching in the church now. Stop being ridiculous… You must excuse Alex, he takes his calling very seriously, she said to me. God, the Bible, the conversion of sinners…it's all in his calling, isn't it,? But he does like to have a whiskey before dinner and a cigarette – even though he knows he mustn't fill the house with smoke.

I'll just have a few puffs, Jill. With that he drew on the cigarette, long and deep, and stubbed it out into an ashtray.

Tell us about yourself, mate, Alex said. Are you a Papist by any chance?

A what?

A follower of Rome?

Never been to Rome in my life. How would I know?

What's your religion?

Catholic.

So you are a Papist. Listen, mate, give it up. All that sin and guilt and telling sins in the confessional. It's all a con – a trick to save your so-called immortal soul. In the Presbyterian Church we don't have any half-way house. You talk straight to God. No black curtains or absolutions in Latin.

That's enough, Alex. We have a guest in the house and you'll behave correctly. No preaching, no showing off. If you want an audience, go outside and talk to Cassie.

I was lost for words. Once again, rattled out of my comfort zone by a stranger. First it was Bill Higgins with an inquisition about politics; now it was Alex Clark interrogating me about my religion.

That's alright, Jill, he can say what he likes. Thanks for having me to your house, by the way. It's nice and cosy. Did you furnish it or was it a predecessor's work?

Ah, come on, matey, I'm only stirring you to get a response. Alex came over and ruffled my hair. Young bloke like you – you have to take it on the chin. No offence taken. Have you ever thought of running for parliament? I think you'd make a great demagogue?

No. What about you?

Come to think of it, I have – yes. Upper House of New South Wales. Though I'd have to join the Country Party first and seek preselection. Would you vote for me?

No.

That's enough you two, Jill rebuked us both. She must have sensed my rising antipathy towards her husband. Would you like to go to the bathroom and get refreshed? she asked.

Refreshed? That would be so good. Then I added, Last time I showered was in a Tamworth motel four days ago. We can't bathe or shower except once a week at the Sloggetts'. On Friday night. Before we go to town on Saturday.

Oh, I wasn't implying you had to have a shower – just for you to get refreshed. But, by all means, have shower. Our water tanks are full. Here, let me put out a towel for you.

Yeah, matey, Alex added. Come here once a week and have a shower. Middle of the week or anytime you feel like it. He seemed to have become accepting of me being a Papist. My mother would have turned on him like a tiger if she'd heard him telling me to stop being a Catholic.

I had a shower before dinner, mindful that this was not on the agenda when I accepted an invitation for dinner, and that, by accepting the offer to have a shower, I was probably holding up dinner. I could have stayed under that hot water for an hour. I luxuriated in the steam and the hot water running into the pores of my skin. When I dried off I rubbed my skin extra hard, making sure the blood circulated as much as possible.

During dinner we exchanged our stories. The Clarks were newly married and being sent to Wollomombi as a home missionary was Alex's first appointment. He was from Kilmarnock in Scotland and Jill was from Normanhurst on Sydney's Lower North Shore. During the meal she would stop and cough, or stop, and catch her breath. I thought she might be an asthmatic. They both said that they were looking forward to this phase of their lives. Alex was doing "God's work", but I heard Jill mutter under her breath that a warmer climate would have been nicer. She helped out with charity work in the district and also took needlework classes at Chandler Public School when Bill's wife wasn't able to. Sometimes she even came to Jeogla for needlework classes. When I asked about Scripture classes, Alex said that Tuesday afternoons he would come to Jeogla, but that would be varied if he was called away to other parish duties, such as funerals.

I told them much the same as what I'd told the Sloggetts about my background. Maybe I sounded anxious, or maybe they just sensed that I wasn't that comfortable at having received a posting away from Sydney.

Just think of it as a challenge, Alex said. Like I did when the church sent me here.

There's a reason for all that happens, mate. You mentioned something about writing poetry – maybe that's it: maybe you'll find your footing here as a poet. This landscape might inspire you – like it did one of the locals, old P.A's daughter, Judith. You've heard of her?

Of course.

There you go. Mind you, she and her family are part of New England's history. You're a stranger – a wog, as they say, without meaning to denigrate you.

Even though I'm a Papist.

Ah, now, you see. You're being too sensitive. You can be a Papist and still write poetry.

Jill interrupted him, That's enough, Alex. Stop.

Seriously, mate. Did you know Gerald's adopted?

Bill told me, but I don't see why it's such a big deal. It's like you're telling me something I'm not supposed to know. Adopted and an epileptic. Are they taboo words around here?

That's right, said Jill. You'd think that two educated men, a school teacher and a minister, would know better than to make a point of conversation about something like this? All that it needs is for Frank Robson to be here. Talk about a bunch of three old gossiping women. Why don't you all form a sewing circle?

The three Fates, I said. That'll use up all your spare time.

Saving souls, mate, that's full-time work.

Jill also told me that her parents sometimes came up from Sydney and stayed with them – as did her sister Sandy.

And so do my parents, mate...Do you think your parents would visit you?

Not in a million years. My parents work and, besides, where would they stay? I'm going home for Easter and then it'll be the May holidays...Then September holidays.

It's the middle of the year that'll drag, mate. Cold and frosty. You'll wish you had someone to snuggle up to. Oh, by the way, has anyone told you that at the end of February we're having the New England New State elections? Your school's going to be the polling booth. You might be the Returning Officer or at least the Polling Clerk. Have you heard of the New England New State Movement?

Bill mentioned it.

It's been brewing for decades. The Country Party is behind it. They want a part of New South Wales to secede and form a new state called New England. This is the referendum. If they win, it must then go to the rest of New South Wales for a vote. One of the leaders in this area is an old farmer called Lex McCrae from Jeogla. You probably haven't met him yet but you will. You'll know it's him because he rides a horse – and he'll be up at your school to leave his credentials behind: his viewpoint which is inflexible and his attempts to try and convert you if he senses you're against it. Trying to get him to change his mind is about as easy as trying to get water to run uphill. Ah, mate.. You'll certainly earn your stripes by working out here.

But still, a new state! Sounds exciting.

Listen, just don't get too caught up in it. You're here to teach, not try and convert people to political ideology. You're younger than Bill – and me – and still too impressionable not to be swayed.

Like with my religion?

Mate, I've already figured you out. We can argue till the cows come home – but you'll stay a Papist and I'll stay a Presy.

A Protestant.

A Presbyterian.

By now we were having our coffee. Alex had a whiskey because he said it makes him dream of home. I knew that shortly I'd be stepping out into the darkness and returning to Jeogla but wasn't looking forward to stepping out of the warmth of the manse.

When they saw me to the door, they invited me back to visit them anytime. You're always welcome here, Jill said.

And have a shower, Alex said grinning. We even let Anglicans and Papists use the shower.

Go on, you, get inside, Jill said laughing, and pushing him indoors. Ignore him, Peter...Have a safe trip back.

I drove back to Jeogla feeling elated. There was no traffic in either direction. Turning off at the Chandler River was done as an automatic response, and then, with the headlights on high beam, I negotiated the turns back to Jeogla, stopping only on the Oaky River bridge. Turning off the car's engine, I stepped out into the chill night air to look at the same scene that had earlier given me the feeling of being inside a church. The awe returned. Night sounds. River sounds. Crickets. Frogs. More than I could have imagined. The river was breathing its own life into the sky and talking to it, reflecting clouds and stars, branches of trees, masses of shadows I couldn't comprehend. A fish leapt from water. Ripples broke out towards the banks and disappeared. There was barely enough moonlight to see them but there was enough. And, at one place, where there were no clouds to conceal it, the moon lay reflected on the river.

Going to Town

When I returned from school on Friday I found that Elmo was home. He left his base in Nowendoc earlier than usual and was unpacking when I arrived. We sat in the kitchen and drank tea together, as well as the customary date biscuits Carrie left out while she went up to clean the school.

As I said before, Friday night is bath night here, Elmo said. So I'd better demonstrate how to light the bath heater. He led me to the bathroom and brought in a box of kindling and wood chips. You might remember I said we can't afford to make the water too hot, otherwise it disturbs the rust at the bottom of the heater. So, just feed the chips in slowly, down here, a few at a time – after you got the fire going with twigs an' newspapers. Water heats up down 'ere…Don't let it boil – otherwise you'll disturb the rust an' end up with rusty bath water…

Who bathes first?

Granma always goes first. We get the water ready for her an' Carrie helps. After that it don't really matter. Tanks are full. We got plenty of water and there's plenty wood chips in the box out back.

What about going into town? What time do you leave?

Right after breakfast. Early. Not long after the shops open we're there. Of course you can go whenever you like…Sooner or later than us. That's up to you.

Any advice where I should go or what I should see?

No…Elmo was thinking deeply, it seemed to me, or maybe he was just tired. He spoke slowly, taking off his glasses several times and wiping them. Take your time. Walk up an' down Beardy Street – that's the main street. Go up to Central Park. That's real pretty…Buy whatever you need. Of course there's no need to buy food to bring back because you pay rent an' that includes food. Have a nice day in town…

Buy some lunch. Plenty of places to choose from…Tomorrow we'll go out to the Falls, Carrie an' I were thinking. Show you one of the real wonders of the world.

At dinner I mentioned how many rabbits I'd seen. Are they a problem? I asked Carrie.

Not like they used ter be.

Shoot 'em all, I reckon, said Gerald. Get out the .22 – and pow! Right between the eyes.

I'd watched Gerald sit down and, as he did at every meal, take tablets from two brown bottles that Carrie put on the table. After he took the tablets she'd remove the bottles. She saw me watching, and said, Them's fer his epilepsy. If I don't put 'em on the table he fergets.

Gerald's face went red. He lowered his head and ate in silence.

How was yer week? Carrie asked, turning to Elmo? Anythin' excitin' happenin' down at Nowendoc?

Some big shots from the Forestry Commission come down. Had a look, filled in some forms and were gone. We're going into new areas for clearing…Timber's in big demand.

I said to them that I was excited at the idea of a trip to town. My first big trip away from Jeogla since I arrived at Jeogla.

What about banking? Carrie asked.

What about it?

Have yer got enough money?

I think so. What should I be doing?

The other teachers'd take their cheques in on Friday after school and cash 'em or bank 'em. That's when they did the school bankin' too.

School banking?

The Commonwealth Bank'll send a person out soon enough to give them a talk about savin' money. Yer job'll be to take the money to the bank and get their pass books stamped.

Thanks for telling me…No, I'm right for money at the moment. When my first cheque arrives I'll go in and cash it. I'll pay you what I owe you. I haven't forgotten.

Never thought you did, she said, giving me a little smile and raising an eyebrow.

⁕

That night, trying to fall asleep, I thought of the drive from the Upper Hunter to Tamworth. I remembered how the landscape changed once I passed through the township and left the Peel River behind. Gone were the flat paddocks where crops were grown and livestock grazed in open spaces and how, once I passed through the villages of Kootingal and Moonbi, the landscape became more rocky, the gradients steeper and there was something foreboding, even Gothic in the landscape of these two giant hills. Boulders were huge, bigger than houses, prehistoric, resembling skulls, fists and knuckles, shoulders and backs that pushed up from the earth. Cold. Dead. Inanimate. Yet trees and whole forests grew out of them. And what must the landscape look like in reverse, coming down from the top, how awesome must that look? I wrote :

Moonbi Hills

Over the northern rise
you feel an air of dampness
settling on to your shoulders like a cape –
and nineteen hundred feet of skyway
point to a horizon of grey, dotted hills.
Sloping paddocks and a brown river
become reminders of a warmer season,
a different country perhaps.

Southward, the plains – mauve edges
of a torn hat covered in dust and pebbles,
blades of grass, peppercorns and wheat –
unroll at the foot of corrugated spurs.
Coming from the top you move
to the left as the sun gathers
momentum behind you: make way
for an avalanche of trees and rocks
that falls and falls, but never leaves the sky.

Two hills: a bridge of rock,
bitumen and guideposts between climates,
winds you can pass through in the same breath –
volcanic deposits of snow and lava:
hideout for centuries of people and years,
unknown like fallen stars.

When the last diamond of snow
is mined, polished, cut and sold,
who will remember the hand that stole
fire from out of the sun:
formed two hills like rings on a broken knuckles;
and when rivers stained the tips of leaves
settled a little further into the earth?

Going to Town (II)

Sounds coming from the rest of the house woke me, and I could tell the Sloggets were up and about. After writing late into the night I would have preferred to sleep in, but remembered what day it was and why I had to get up.

I quickly joined them at breakfast.

No need to hurry, Elmo said, take your time. We'll be gone in half an hour.

Dinner's about the same time's always. I can warm it up if yer late getting' back, Carrie said.

I might run into you all in town, I said.

Yer never know what might happen, but I doubt it. Town's pretty busy most Saturdays. We'll be going up to one of me sisters fer lunch. Others'll then come over…It's really nice ter have the family all together in one place, don't yer think so?

Don't know, I said. We have no relatives in Australia. Only friends from the camps and others nearby where we live.

Boo-hoo, don't cry, said Gerald.

Carrie lashed out with the tea towel and hit him across the head. Mind yer manners! Hear? Now, apologise ter the teacher or yer'll stay home all weekend.

Sorry, teacher. I didn't mean it.

Now, Carrie, said. Get to yer room and get yerself ready. We'll go without yer, if yer not ready.

When Gerald left he kitchen, she said, It's all them tablets he has ter take. He don't mean nothin'. The tablets help his epilepsy but they make him go funny sometimes.

Ignore him next time, Elmo said.

Granma kept eating her toast, moving her dentures around as she did. I thought I saw her smiling – as if she'd seen it all before.

*

The air was warm, the day would be sunny, with maybe rain towards evening. Carrie and Elmo made the forecast, but again it depended on the coastal winds that blew in. They told me to have a good day, to look around and enjoy myself.

Stop yer from getting' too homesick, Carrie said by way of saying goodbye.

The Sloggets left before I did and on the drive into Armidale I thought of the incident with Gerald at breakfast. Was there something different about him that made Bill Higgins and Alex refer to him in the early stages of our conversations? His comment was so unexpected, so brutal, and yet, did he sense something in what I was saying that made him interpret it as an answer that required an honest response – as rude as it was? And that response, to him, would not have seemed rude but genuine?

I didn't stop on the Oaky River bridge, nor at Wollomombi, as much as I wanted to. It was only as Baker's Creek that I slowed down to look at the homestead and woolshed I was passing. The scene was idyllic, a direct contrast to the granite boulders strewn across inhospitable acres of yellow and grey weeds. How did stock survive on that? Baker's Creek, on the other hand, was fringed with weeping willows on both sides, as far as the eye could see – soft greens, glowing after last week's rains and warmed by the morning's sun. I promised myself that one day I would pull over right here and walk down to the creek. I'd also calculated that it was exactly ten miles from Jeogla to this concrete bridge over the road that now ran straight as an arrow with an unbroken yellow line and broken white lines. This is where the policeman had mentioned the road straightened out. I had to remember that these would be the last ten miles whenever I was returning to Jeogla.

By now the Sloggetts were probably in town. I decided to park in the vicinity of Central Park and begin my discovery of Armidale from that point.

*

A week ago the park was shrouded in a pall of rain. Trees and shrubs were dark blurs, shadows wherever I looked, and there wasn't a human being in sight. Now, people walked around me in all directions and children ran ahead of mothers, while an old man walked a dog. Colourful small plants and flowers had been planted around the park's perimeter and created small avenues. I hadn't noticed the rotunda or fountain in its centre – nor the paths that crossed it diagonally from the four corners of a square placed within the park's circumference. I had seen diagrams of mandalas in a book by Carl Jung. Was the park a mandala? And why did it draw me as it did? Was it because I'd been told by the police officer that it was where I should turn left to continue my journey to Jeogla?

From where I stood I saw three spires and walked towards them in a clockwise direction, through summer colours that flowered in circular and square flowerbeds. The air was warm but also crisp, invigorating, pleasant to suck in and fill the lungs.

Masses of roses were in bloom – pinks and reds, golden like the Apollo variety my mother grew. Scarlet salvias grew like a fire around the fountain on which, around its base, bronze plaques were inscribed with the names of the war dead. On closer inspection, I saw that the fountain was a war memorial, designed in three layers like a wedding cake. Crepe myrtles, pinks and reds and mauves were blooming. Camphor laurels, oak trees, prunus, spruce, weeping willow, varieties of pine trees and foliage I didn't recognise threw up canopies and offered shade. Bird sang from all directions, oblivious to who was walking where, whether children were laughing and squealing and playing games – or whether a barking dog was chasing another dog. Families were carrying shopping bags. Other families sat at park tables, eating and talking. Mothers were pushing prams. A man sat on a bench, smoking a pipe and reading a newspaper.

Directly in front of me stood the largest of the spires, and a painted sign proclaimed this was the Catholic "Cathedral Church of St Mary and St Joseph." I found the door was open, and walked in, blessing myself at the holy water font in the vestibule.

Is this what was called Gothic architecture? The arches and sandstone columns, the marble high altar and sanctuary, the stained glass windows? There was a choir gallery and pipe organ. A baptistery with a marble font. The roof was timber and supported by steel brackets and metallic " rods" that somehow, to an amateur like myself, seemed to stop the structure from collapsing. Statues of the saints lined the walls on both sides, down the side aisles, and there was a small chapel at the end of each of these. Blue and white tiles, set as mosaics with a fleur-de-lis motif, ran down the centre aisle of the nave. The pews were a dark-red wood, soft to the touch.

I knelt and prayed, whispering and mumbling prayers from childhood, trying to concentrate on where I was, closing my eyes but opening them. No one else had entered. Were the doors open because there'd been a Mass? It was cool and I liked that because, whatever the season, warm churches always tended to make me doze. Should I make the effort tomorrow morning and drive out from Jeogla? Go to Mass. I said to myself that I must, but knew deep in my heart that I wouldn't. Surely God understood? Of course, God understands, my mother would have said if she were here. There is nothing beyond God's understanding. Forget what "smart" people think they know. They know nothing. Have faith.

Blessing myself, I left the cathedral and walked to the next spire. This was the Anglican "Cathedral Church of St Peter, Apostle and Martyr". Built of a bluish-brown stone, with its square tower, it reminded me of drawings and paintings I'd seen of Norman castles in England, the sort I'd associated with Robin Hood and the Sheriff of Nottingham. This cathedral had stained-glass windows. When I tried to open the door I found it was locked. From its design, I thought that maybe the cathedral had been envisaged as a fortress for God?

Passing the Town Hall, opposite the park, further along, in the direction where I'd parked my car, was the Presbyterian "Church of St Paul". Not a cathedral, but like the other two, it also had a spire. When I tried to go inside, I found that it, too, was locked. Smaller than the other two, there was a thrift about this modest building that contrasted with the opulence of the other two.

Asking directions to the post office, I was pointed away from the park. I asked a man. He said, Across the road, mate – straight down. On the corner.

Preparing my coins, I dialled the operator and waited for the connection to my home in Sydney; it rang and rang but no one answered. I asked the operator to try again and waited. Pity, but never mind. I would try later in the afternoon, before returning to Jeogla.

When I rang P her mother answered but said she was out. She asked about my welfare and said how good it was to hear my voice. She suggested I call back after lunch. She also asked about my parents. I told her they were fine but were anxious about my survival at Jeogla. Everyone in Sydney they told about my appointment said they'd never heard of the place. She said that she'd taught in a one-teacher school many years ago in Western Australia.

Did you know that?

No.

Well, you must get P to tell you. Alright, dear…Look after yourself. Goodbye.

Even though I hadn't spoken to anyone that I'd wanted

to in Sydney, on the telephone, it felt good to be here and to have tried.

This is what I was missing at Jeogla….People. Human company. I'd come from the city to a very small village. I had grown up in Sydney and was used to having people around me. This is what the park and the city offered: human companionship. Even if I never spoke to anyone, being here was enough.

I stood in one of the arches at the front of the post office, opposite the court house. Turning back a few steps, up the street where I'd come from, I noticed two buildings – one was the folk museum, the other was the lands office. Both buildings had magnificent wrought-iron verandas. Closer to where I stood, almost behind the post office was the library. The Imperial Hotel stood across the road, also on the corner, decorated with wrought iron lacework, arches and urns.

This was exciting! I'd discovered new landscapes around the Jeogla countryside, and now these buildings in Armidale itself – plus the feeling of isolation was gone. There were people here, walking up and down Beardy Street, just like people walked up and down the streets of Sydney.

A shining silver dome on top of a large red-brick building caught my eye and I walked towards it – passing a long row of shops that included a chemist, bank, Pidgeons Newsagency, Tattersalls Hotel, the New England Hotel and the IXL Café. Crossing the street, I stood on the corner of Beardy Street and Dangar Street, below the name on the building's frontage: 1842 J. Richardson & Co. Ltd. I continued walking west, past the Capitol cinema and the Mun Hing Chinese restaurant, past the public baths and technical college, turning left and right, without actually knowing what I'd find, but continuing to walk, without feeling the heat or getting tired, although I wished I'd worn a hat or cap. When I reached the district hospital I sat down in a park opposite and watched a game of cricket.

The scene was reminiscent of an English village, the men in whites, playing in a park surrounded by a white picket fence, against a green background of trees and hills, among which houses, brick and weatherboard, had also been built. Asking a group of people where the best place was to get a view of Armidale, they pointed north and said it was from the Apex Lookout in Drummond Park, but warned it was a steep climb and it would probably be best if I drove. I decided to walk a few more blocks west until I reached Drummond Public School. By now I was well out of the immediate city commercial zone and into a residential area. I was also starting to feel hot and thirsty, and hungry. I turned north, turned right into Dumaresq Street and found myself crossing a stone bridge over a creek.

A steep hill rose to my left and I figured that was where the Apex Lookout was located. Yes, it was far too steep to climb. I kept walking and found myself, still in a residential area, on the corner of Faulkner Street. Southwards, I thought I could see what looked like the edge of Central Park in the far distance. So if I walked south I'd be back to where I started from. Good! I began to think of food and drink – and the only place that I could remember where I'd wanted to eat in the first place was the IXL Café in Beardy Street.

Back I went, walking neither fast nor slowly but tempted by the food I was going to buy and go back to Central Park to eat. What a little adventure I'd had. I wondered what Kevin would have said? *Didn't know you liked walking so much, Pete?* And he would have laughed. P might have sighed and said, *Always the adventurous one!*

A hamburger with the lot, hot chips and a bottle of coca-cola never tasted so good. I wished I'd bought an ice-cream as well, but it wasn't too late.

My face and arms felt hot and sunburnt. I was tired. Choosing a spot between a row of bushes in a corner next to St Peter's cathedral, I lay down, promising myself to have only a catnap, which would refresh me before I made my telephone calls to Sydney and drove up to the Apex Lookout. My arm under my head served as a pillow. I turned my back on the track that cut diagonally across the park. Facing the corner of the park, screened by the bushes, I had privacy.

My fingers were touching grass and soil; I could smell and taste it. I heard a bell tolling. All I could see was the wall of green foliage in front of me. Gradually, it turned dark, then black. I closed my eyes. A cloud had entered my head and was overwhelming my thoughts. Whatever or whomever I was thinking of, lingered and faded, was absorbed into the cloud. I was floating, now a part of the cloud that had absorbed me, over the city, revisiting the places where I'd walked. A wind blew me away from the Apex Lookout, towards the city's outskirts, over the stony paddocks, creeks and gorges, cattle and sheep, back towards the Grafton Road, over farms, forests and gullies, the green and blue ranges that were part of New England. I was being blown in the direction of the Kempsey Road, and then I was hanging over the Oaky River. Now I was dissolving, turning into rain, falling over the river, falling, falling, until I was nothing, until I no longer existed.

A magpie woke me, singing from an araucaria, prompting me to get up, finish doing what I still wanted to do before returning to Jeogla. The tiredness left me, although my face and arms still felt hot. Before going to the post office to ring Sydney, I first went to a chemist and bought some sunburn cream.

*

When P answered the telephone I was overjoyed to hear her voice. I had filled my pockets with plenty of silver coins for both calls that I intended to make.

How is Armidale? she asked.

Oh, it's a fine city. I think I could live here.

Live there?

Yes.

Are you feeling okay? You haven't been out in the sun too long by any chance?

Funny you should ask that.

Seriously, though. How's it all going?

So I told her about the Sloggets, Ron Diamond, the Clarks and all the other people I'd met. I described my school and my pupils. I told her I was missing her like crazy and I was missing Sydney. I was missing the comforts of home but, if she spoke to my parents, she wasn't to let on. She had to promise me that. Okay?

Okay.

I said I'd most likely be coming into town each Friday afternoon and Saturday. The school children's banking would have to be done – and then I wanted Saturdays and Sundays to myself. She was fascinated when I told her there were no shops in Jeogla but the open spaces of the countryside compensated for that. You had to be here to believe it, I told her.

When I asked her what her news was, she said, I'm moving out of home.

Where to? I asked.

Forest Lodge. To a boarding house. It's on Parramatta Road, right across the main gates from the university.

What do your parents think of that?

Dad's being more supportive than mum. You know what she's like.

She's a nice lady.

She's so old-fashioned. She thinks I belong in suburbia forever.

Oh, but you could do a lot worse than where you live.

I know, but I've had enough. I need to start my own life.

This was her dream and she was determined to live it. Finish her education, travel, and work for social and just causes. One of her sisters was living and working in Dublin and P often spoke about going to Europe.

Oh, well, I said. We can talk about it more when I come home at Easter.

Alright.

We talked for another ten minutes, then she said she had to go. She said she was going to a party with some girlfriends and had to go and get ready.

We spent another five minutes saying our goodbyes. I promised I'd write or ring from Wollomombi or from Armidale next time I was here.

When we hung up, I sensed something hadn't been talked about that should have. It was like one of us wasn't game to admit something, and the other wasn't game to ask.

Then I rang my parents and my mother answered. She started to cry as soon as I said, Hello, Mum.

How are you? I've been worried. Every night and morning I pray that you are well, that Our Lady will look after you…We've sent you a letter but I've also baked a cake and will send it. At the post office, Frank and Darcy said to put it into a strong cardboard box …Are you sure you're getting enough to eat?

Mum, I'm really fine. Apart from missing home and everybody in Sydney there's nothing wrong. Can I speak to Dad, please?

He's not home yet. He had to work today. They're doing a big job out at Green Valley and there's lots of overtime…You know what the Water Board's like.

That's okay. I understand. Tell him I love him and I'll try and call on a Sunday next time – or after school during the week.

Why don't you call and let us know when the cake arrives. It's a fruit cake. Like I make at Christmas. You can share it with the family you are boarding with…That Mrs Sloggett sounds like a nice lady.

She is, Mum. She really is…They're all very nice.

What have you been up to?

I've met people who live in the district. A minister and his wife; another school teacher and a store keeper and his wife...A farmer called Ron and his little dog called Suzie. She has a temper and growls most of the time.

Be careful of strange dogs: they're not all nice like our Bobby.

No, they're not.

I'm safe as long as Ron is around.

What are you doing tonight?

Before I leave Armidale I'll drive up to a lookout; then I'll come home. I might have a bit to eat before I leave. Save me eating later. I walked around a lot and got a bit sunburnt; but I bought some cream and it's already helped. It wasn't much of a sunburn...I'm just being careful.

Are you sleeping well?

I sleep like a log. I'm getting some reading done – and I've even written some poetry.

Poetry? Goodness me? Still, if it's what makes you happy...Enjoy yourself. Don't strain your eyes by staying up too late. Eat well, and sleep well. That's what I've always said. Haven't I?

Yes, Mum....I'd better go now. I'll write or ring during the week and certainly ring next time I'm in town. You'd like it here, Mum...Lots of farms, animals, hills, mountains...

I'm sure they're not as big and beautiful as the Carpathians in the Ukraine.

They're beautiful in their own way.

I never meant to say anything wrong in what I said.

I sensed this conversation had taken a different turn from the main reason for my telephone call, and my mother would persist with what she had to say until she said it; she was a strong-willed and determined woman. The English language had never been a barrier for her and she expressed her opinions forcefully. I never told her how much I admired her for the number of languages she could speak: Ukrainian, Polish, Russian, German and English. She read whatever she could get her hands on – even rail tickets, while we travelled on a train, teaching herself English in the process.

Of course, of course… Mum, I think I'd better get going. It'll be a while before I get back to Jeogla. 'Bye, Mum. I love you…

Drive carefully. Tell Mrs Sloggett I said thanks for looking after you. I'll tell your father you're well and we'll be in touch. We both love you. We've written you a letter and, remember, there's a cake in the mail.

I drove up to the Apex Memorial Lookout in Drummond Park. There was no one else there. I stood behind the stone wall and looked south, down onto the city. The temperature had dropped and I felt a chill wind. The sun had started to set and long black shadows from trees on the hillside were falling across the park. From this perspective, the city didn't look that remarkable. I recognised the cathedrals and other landmarks that I'd passed by. One building, however, caught my eye. It stood out, high on a hill, opposite me, far off, rectangular, massive. Had it been a prison or hospital, situated as it was above the city?

A white obelisk stood on my right, as I'd driven up the hill. Turning my back on the city, I now walked towards it. Situated in the centre of the lookout, it was a giant white needle, that resembled a spire, pointing to the sky, threading its way from earth to sky, carrying a message in the form of a poem inscribed in gold lettering on a marble tablet at the centre of the monument:

DREAMER OF DREAMS! WE TAKE THE TAUNT WITH GLADNESS
KNOWING THAT GOD BEYOND THE WORLD WE SEE
HAS WOVEN THAT WHICH COUNTS WITH MEN AS MADNESS
INTO THE FABRIC OF THE YEARS TO BE!

I read it and reread it, thinking it must be from one of the Romantics, maybe even from a later period, Tennyson or even Yeats. Whoever the poet was, the lines resonated with me and I memorised them while I was standing there; then I noticed the small grey moth, above the inscription, flattened against the marble, as if it were escaping the remaining heat of the day.

*

No sooner had I walked into the kitchen than Carrie asked me, Well, how did yer day in town go? Thought we might've run into you?

Oh, I did what I'd wanted to – like ringing home and walking around the town. I did some sightseeing, and went up to the Apex Lookout in Drummond Park.

Looks like there's a bit of sunburn on yer face.

Just a bit, but I bought some sunburn cream and rubbed it in. Be as good as new in a few days.

Next time take one of the hats out the front there – where Granma an' me sit.

They're ladies' hats.

They're straw hats. Don't matter, anyways. They'll keep the sun of yer face. Stop you from gettin' sunburnt. Sun don't know if yer a man or woman. Sun burns both.

I said I'd go and freshen up and come out to the dinner table.

Not much was spoken during dinner. After washing up, we all moved into the lounge room where the TV was on, and where Granma always ate her dinner on a tray.

How did the day go for all of you?

The picture on the screen flickered, and the volume was a bit woozy – as if the speaker was drunk – but we were enjoying the show, an American comedy. Granma laughed more than any of us. I thought she was deaf but maybe she was just reacting to the situation on the screen. The laughter and applause were canned.

Gerald looked sullen – almost resentful at being there. Maybe he'd been reprimanded over something and had been forbidden from going out. A few times during dinner I thought I smelt beer on his breath but he ate with his head down, avoiding everyone's eyes. When the meal was over he said he was going to his room.

Stay with us, I suggested. Relax and laugh for a while

TV's stupid, he said. Hoo-roo. It's Sat-dee night. I could be out havin' a good time.

He strode out of the room, pulling the door shut behind him.

Granma laughed. Carrie said, Let 'im go. A good sleep's what he needs.

Who was Drummond? I asked.

Mr Drummond was a politician, Elmo replied. Our local state member…A long time ago now, wasn't it, mum, but he was the nicest man.

Oh, I said. I guessed it must be something like that?

Started off as a farmer, Elmo continued – ended up being minister for education and going on to Canberra. We wouldn't have the university in Armidale today if it weren't for Mr Drummond. A very clever man, let me tell you.

Elmo's little speech praising "Mr Drummond" surprised me. He normally didn't speak as much as Carrie, nor did he speak as quickly, but when he did it was slow and deliberate, as if every word counted, and was intended to make a point. He reminded me a lot of the way my father spoke, often using his hand like a teacher to emphasise a point. So the information that he shared about Henry Drummond was essential, it seemed to him, to anyone who wanted to know who the man was – but also, what he represented, what he stood for.

When Granma got up to go to bed, she turned to me and said quietly, Sleep well. It was the first time in a week she'd spoken to me.

Then Elmo went to bed. It only left Carrie and myself, and a TV set with the volume turned down. Carrie said, That's it. We're all turnin' in a bit early tonight, Peter. Termorrer after lunch we'll take you out to Wollomombi Falls. It's not always like this, getting' an early night. Some nights, after goin' ter town some of the locals an' us might go up ter the school and have a game of euchre – or drive ter Hillgrove if there's a dance on…I go leastways, an' Gerald will go, but Elmo don't do much dancin' anymore, not since he got problems with his blood an' arteries an' such – that slows him down a fair bit…Yer couldn't help but notice his walk, a bit slow, an' ter one side, sort of…

Yes, I said. If you don't mind me asking, what exactly is wrong?

No, I don't mind yer askin' – yer a nice enough fella… Elmo suffers from a hardenin' of the arteries… He's got tablets; but in the end it'll kill 'im mostly likely. Elmo works very hard all week, but he needs to rest when the weekends come…So no more dancin'…

We all said goodnight and I went to bed, but took a long time to fall asleep. I felt as if I was still walking around Armidale. My legs were telling me: you should have kept walking, past the city, and followed the highway into the mountains, where there was no burning sun, only forests and waterfalls, the green shade of giant trees, and a river that flowed into another river that flowed into another river that flowed into the sea, and there you could have stopped… So my mind went, back and forth, up and down, following signpost and names on buildings, standing in front of cathedrals, marvelling at spires and stained glass….Then the steep drive to the lookout, standing over a city to which I was a stranger. As I waited to fall asleep, I thought of the moth on the obelisk.

Wollomombi Falls

After lunch next day I drove out to Wollomombi Falls with Carrie and Elmo. Sitting in the front passenger seat, at one point, winking at Elmo, Carrie exclaimed, Golly, this is so posh. I feel like the queen being driven like this – suppose I should start wavin' to all me subjects, 'cept there's no one but sheep to see us – eh, Elmo, doesn't it feel good?

An' the gum trees. Ha-ha...I think you should drop her off here, Peter. The whole thing's gone to her head. Elmo sat in the back of the car, hat off, continuously scratching his head, like he was wondering, What am I doing here?

We all laughed.

The few times I'd driven to Jeogla or from it, I'd missed the sign that said "Wollomombi Falls". No further than ten minutes driving from the Jeogla turn-off, going towards Armidale, it lay to the left, the narrow road passing through a property owned, as Carrie said, by Wally Edgar, a life-long friend, who allowed sight-seeing through his paddocks, to the edge of the waterfall. We drove over a grid. Signs on gates requested they be kept closed at all times.

Don't make no difference to some people, them signs, Carrie said accusingly. They leave the gates open, like they can't read or want to be smart.

After driving through a number of paddocks and bumpy circular paths through a dark wooded area, I parked my car at what seemed an unofficial parking area, away from a small viewing platform and fence that overlooked what I knew by now were "the falls". The day was overcast, and there were no other visitors. Maybe Carrie and Elmo knew it would be like this, or maybe we'd just chanced on what seemed a perfect time to arrive. A man coming from a farmhouse had waved to us earlier, as we drove past some sheds. *There's Wally*, Carrie said, but the man continued walking, followed by a pair of dogs, towards one of the sheds and ignored us.

He doesn't know the car, Carrie said. *Musn't've seen it was us. Wally would've stopped if he'd known it was us.*

Nothing that I'd seen in the slides in the general store prepared me for I saw now. A cavernous grey-green opening in the ground, forming what seemed like a deep valley or abyss but with another massive outcrop of rock rising from the centre – a pointed missile – with a water rushing down it from two sources, one directly in front, the other further back, towards the right, also with a huge downpour of water, but smaller, and both converging onto the centre piece of rock, turning it black. Water and spray shot up, formed about the centre pinnacle and fell again, creating a rushing, echoing noise that barely allowed us to hear what were saying. A pair of ducks flew across our view.

Elmo motioned for us to step back so we might hear what he was saying. That's more 'n a thousand foot fall. The main source of water's the Wollomombi Falls; the one further back's the Chandler. They run down and join up with the Oaky an' the Styx... Then they flow down to Lower Creek and into the Macleay...and onto Kempsey. Pretty rough country, down there...I've worked in the timber camps along the way. Some places you couldn't get a team o' horses down to haul the timber up to the mills. There used to be one at Jeogla, down near the Styx. We'll take you down sometime.

It's a good place to go an' pick blackberries, said Carrie.

Why is it called the Styx?

Dunno, said Carrie.

In Greek mythology it's the name of a River of the Dead.

Oh crikey! I can believe that, said Carrie. Plenty o' ghosts down there.

I haven't seen anything like this before, I said.

We have, said Carrie. Lived 'ere all our lives, haven't we, Elmo? It's been bigger 'n this in the past. Sometimes when you stand 'ere the wind'll carry the spray over in your direction. Hard to believe that when there's a drought there's barely a trickle o' water comin' through....It's real pretty, don't you think, Peter?

Walking back down to the rail, I was lost in silence, unable to stop looking at the amount of water pouring into the chasm, creating "the falls". The water rushed angrily, poured over the edge, then, almost in a suspended motion, fell gracefully until it hit the bottom of the gorge, reformed into rushing water again and became a river. The longer I looked, the more my eyes became used to the scene and I started to see individual trees through the mist, leaves on branches, outcrops of stone, ledges, different shades of green and grey, everything washed by the water, being made clean.

Incredible, I said.

It's been goin' on like this fer millions of years, said Carrie. Long before human beings came along an' clocks were invented.

While we stood and talked silently, almost in a whisper, another car appeared out of the dark wooded area, followed by a van. Children came running down to where we were standing, yelling excitedly.

Time ter go, said Carrie.

On the way back, after the last gate, we saw Wally Edgar again. Carrie told me to stop the car. Let's go over an' say g'day.

He walked towards us. The two dogs ran forward, sniffing at my car.

G'day, Carrie...Mo.

G'day, Wal...said Elmo. Peter, this 'ere's Wally.

Hello, Wally.

G'day, mate, said holding out his hand and shaking mine.

Peter's the new teacher at Jeogla. We thought we'd show 'im the sights.

Not much to see, said Wally. Unless yer count that bit o' water runnin' over the Falls.

So what's new, Wally? said Carrie. Haven't seen much o' yer lately.

The three of them stood and talked as only old friends can talk, seemingly not saying much but probably saying enough. It may have sounded like small talk to a stranger, but it was the essentials in their lives they touched upon.

While they talked I looked around, trying to take it the surrounding farm, situated as it was, on the western side of the falls. I imagined what the coast, another hour and a half's drive away, might look like, the ocean, beaches, seagulls, breaking waves, surf.

Sheep bleated and nibbled at grass, and a few head of cattle grazed in the background. Wally's farmhouse and sheds were painted pink, paled and weathered, with the grey of the timber showing where the paint had flaked away. Another car crossed the grid and drove on, and that meant more visitors.

You should start chargin' 'em, Wal, crossin' yer land like they do. Don't seem right…

Reckon so, said Wally, seemingly nonplussed…Well, I'd better get movin'…This bein' Sunday, I'd better go an' put me feet up fer the rest o' the day.

*

When we returned to Jeogla I dropped off Carrie and Elmo, got the key for the school and drove up. Most of what I wanted to write down was in my head and I'd been repeating it to myself, as we drove. As soon as Carrie had made the comment about the age of the falls, I knew I had a poem; it needed an ending but I knew that was already in the unwritten poem, and I only had to flesh out the opening lines to find it. Not a long poem, but short, intense, like the conversation between the three people back on Wally Edgar's property:

Wollomombi Falls

More than a thousand feet of rock face
rise slanting through a cloud of mist
and outcrops of undergrowth shadows –
photographed in all seasons, at sunset and in flood,
dusty on a rack of slides in the local
general store. Farmers graze sheep and cattle
on the brink of the chasm, and visitors
leave surrounding paddock gates open.

Chipped for specimens and dating, measured
in line with the coast a hundred miles away,
this New England monument, formed deep
into granite and ironbarks – milestone now
for winds and rain: souvenir of time and origin,
sold and bought for twenty cents.

Samurai Sword

Music appreciation might be a good lesson for tomorrow afternoon I reasoned, after basic subjects in the morning and social studies or natural science in the mid-morning.

One of two pieces: either "Danse Macabre" by Saint-Saens, or Mozart's "Eine Kleine Nacht Musik", both of which we'd listened to at teachers' college. I'd brought both from home among my collection of rock 'n' roll records. The children might appreciate listening to a few short classical pieces – or they might not. It was worth a try.

While I was writing up lessons on the blackboard, I heard footsteps on the veranda and there was a knock on the door. Before I could answer "come in" there was a familiar growl and bark and I knew it had to be Ron. Within a two or three seconds he walked in, followed by Suzie.

Me and Dof would like to invite you over for a cup of tea, he said – and so would Suzie, of course. Dof's made some scones.

I'd love to come over.

Not too late in the day for you?

No.

Mind if we drive over with you?

No. I'll just lock up here.

Ron and Suzie slid into the back seat of my car and we drove around to the farmhouse, in what was a short, semi-circular drive that lasted no more than three or four minutes.

It's not really Wyatts Creek here, he said, it's Ducks Gully – Wyatts Creek is further up the road – much further.

So why call it that?

Oh, it's just giving the homestead a separate name from the actual place where most of the livestock's kept. Dof called it Ducks Gully after we were married and moved here. There were ducks all over the place… Here she is, I believe, coming out to say hello to you…Go on, Suzie, out you get.

I stopped the car, got out, only to find myself surrounded by turkeys gobbling and trotting around the car, fanning their tails and pecking the ground.

Must think you've come to feed them, said Ron, waving his arms at them. Silly buggers...Go on, shoo, shoo...

A woman with short black hair was coming towards us, wiping her hands on her apron. Hello, she said. Welcome to Jeogla. I've got tea and scones waiting...Please do come in. How are you finding us, rain and all?

Hello...I introduced myself.

Yes, yes, Ron's told me all about you...I do believe you two will get on really well.

We do already.

He doesn't take quickly to strangers, she said, but he has to you...I think he might even like you.

Ron watched us sceptically, drew on the cigarette hanging from his lips, and said, Well, let's get cracking, shall we, and have that cuppa...Besides, we might even show off our latest joey.

Oh, Ron, laughed Doff. You and your joeys!

A joey? I asked.

Well, this is the latest one...Ron finds them in the forest; the mother might have been killed by shooters or died...Ron brings the joey home and we raise it.

On second thoughts, we can look at the joey later, Ron decided. My throat's dry and I would like a cuppa and some scones. I'm sure the teacher would too.

We entered the rear of the homestead into what appeared to be a glassed and screened-off area, a kind of lounge/sitting room. On one of its walls, to my right, hung a samurai sword and a seascape painting of a tropical scene; waves crashed on to rocks, palm-trees hung low from a jungle. Ron saw me looking at the two objects, but said nothing.

Now, said Doff, bringing in scones, a teapot, cups and saucers, butter and strawberry jam.

It was only then that I noticed Suzie, sitting at the edge of the carpet, licking those thin lips and realized she was joining us for tea and scones.

We ate mostly in silence, making do with small talk. Ron would break off a piece of scone and give it to Suzie. Whenever he did, Dof would reprimand him and say, Oh, Ron, you musn't spoil that dog at every chance you get; then she'd turn to me and say, It makes no difference, does it, what I say, as you can see. Ron's Ron and Suzie's Suzie.

But Ron never took his eyes off me and saw that I wasn't taking my eyes off the painting on the wall – or the Samurai sword. Go on, he said finally, Ask it. You know you want to ask.

Ask what?

Now, listen, Peter, if you and I are going to get on, let's level with one another from the start.

How am I not being level with you?

Because you're pretending you don't know what I'm talking about.

Okay; but if I think it's rude to ask what I want to know. You might say, That's none of your business.

Then that's what I'll say. Don't you want to be offended.

I guess not.

Alright, Mr Smarty Pants, I'll tell you. The painting was done on parachute silk by a prisoner of war in New Guinea. We got him to paint it before we cut his head off with that sword.

Oh Ron, Dof cried out, you big fibber! That's not true, Peter. Don't you dare believe him. Oh, Ron. How could you even think up an idea like that....Cut his head off! Indeed! If you were a little boy I'd make you go and stand in the corner until you said you were sorry...Peter, another cup of tea? Yes, please.

We were all laughing.

By now I was feeling comfortable – even with Suzie

who, having been given piece after piece of Ron's scones, was sleeping peacefully at his feet. There was something wholesome about these people, as there was about the Sloggetts: people one felt at home with, even though their way of life was very different from my own back in Sydney. Sitting here with them, talking and observing – even with Dof reproaching Ron – was like watching Carrie and Elmo having a conversation with Wally Edgar earlier in the day: they made you feel accepted, even though you were an outsider.

Let's have a look at this joey… Poor little blighter is probably fast asleep. Ron sprung to his feet. Dof stood up.

I followed them out into a lounge room where, hanging from the side of the fireplace, was a sack with something bundled inside. Sticking out from this sack was a pair of legs and the tail of a little kangaroo. Here was the joey, sound asleep, just as Ron said. Ron brought the sack over to me, and placed it at my feet, Have a look inside, he said, but it would be shame to take him out, I reckon. Not time for his feed yet.

I peered into the sack and made out the head of a baby kangaroo turned to one side, avoiding the light; its body doubled over; yet it seemed to be comfortable and made no effort to get out of that position. It just moved around a little, like human beings do when they sense the presence of someone watching them.

I couldn't hide my surprise. I asked, What do you feed it?

Milk, of course, Ron replied. Must warm it up first… When the fire's on, I just heat up a poker and the joey's got warm milk… Come to think of it — what do you reckon, Dof – we might take Peter out to Wyatts Creek around March. The pigs will have bred by then and there's bound to be a litter. Ever seen piglets being fed after they've stopped suckling?

No. My mind was going at the rate of knots. Samurai sword. Painting done on a parachute. Joey in a sack. Talk of pigs. Piglets…Suzi walking around me like I was her owner – or rather, ignoring me, as if I didn't exist.

Thanks for showing me all this, I said, and for the tea and scones. I think I'd better get going.

The sack and its contents was returned to its place by the fireside.

Oh, by the way, Ron added. Dingoes are a big problem in these parts, did you know that?

No.

Well, the farmers and graziers in this area have formed a group. We've called it the Jeogla District Dingo Destruction Association. We hold the meetings in the school. First one's due in April but the point is – you'll get a letter in writing and you have to reply in writing for us to be able to use the school. I'm sure it won't be a problem, will it?

No. You didn't have to ask.

Yes, I did. I've had lots of experience with bureaucrats in my time, and there's always a smart bastard, somewhere, in an office – someone who thinks they know best – and will then get you court martialled because of a technicality.

Sure, just send the letter and I'll reply in writing… Dingoes. Wild dogs. There's something romantic in their image, isn't there?

Nothing romantic when you see how they rip the guts out of a sheep – or leave the live ones behind, their throats torn open, and then a farmer's got to come along with a rifle and finish the job.

I said goodbye to Ron and Dof among the turkeys who'd come out to see me leaving, gobbling around the wheels of my car, as if I'd come out to feed them

Say hello to Carrie and Elmo for us, won't you?

Will do. Thanks for the tea and scones…This day's turned out pretty good, I said. You too, Suzi, nice dog.

Suzi didn't respond.

Dof waved from a side gate, standing between the house

and yard, wiping her face with the back of her hand.

Ron had come out of a shed and was about to start throwing handfuls of corn to the turkeys from a tin. By the way, he called out, as I wound down the window of my car. In case you're still wondering about that sword…I'll make sure it gets sent back to Japan when I'm gone…The kids'll do it….Here turkey, turkey, turkey…..gobble, gobble, gobble…

A mass of white turkey fantails and outspread wings encircled a man throwing corn to them – their heads and red wattles bobbing, bobbing, non-stop, massing around him; the sun going down behind the hills, creating an outline around his head, and summer shadows starting to fall over his farm.

From that evening on, it became standard practice for me to write a letter or letters home on a Sunday night; it was mostly a letter to my parents or to Kevin or a lecturer from teachers' college that I'd promised to stay in touch with; then the letters could be posted next day. Gerald would take them to Wollomombi on Monday and they'd be on their way from there, next morning, to Armidale.

I decided to ring P next weekend from town or if I had to go in during the week. From the tone of the conversation we'd had yesterday, I honestly didn't know what to expect or what was happening in that respect back in Sydney.

III

Letters

That week, among all the official school correspondence, I received three letters from Sydney. I laughed like I hadn't laughed since arriving at Jeogla. Tears ran down my cheeks.

Gerald dropped the mail off just before lunch, one of the children ran out and brought it in, and I spent all of lunch hour reading the letters over and over.

I recognised my mother's handwriting and opened that envelope first. Written on a folded blank card, in Polish, with a rose printed in the top left corner, dated a week ago, the letter read:

Dear Peter,

We thank you for your phone call and letter. We don't worry about anything except that you don't worry and slowly you will get used to everything. Ask God and everything will be ok. I am well and wish the same to you. But Dad has a cold and is missing you but that will pass. There is no news here at home. I am working as usual. Today Dr O'Brien gave me my long service pay. 128 dollars and I will take it to the bank. James O'Brien got a scholarship for his last two years and his father is very happy. Last Sunday Mrs Butler came over to visit. Otherwise there is not much else new. We had a very heavy rain and there was some damage in the garden. But now the weather is fine.

With kisses from us both,
Your loving mother and father.

The second letter was addressed to:

> *The Headmistress,*
> *Public School*
> *Jeogla*
> *via Armidale, NSW.*

Flipping over the envelope, I saw that it was from

> *K. Coates*
> *134 Wattle Street*
> *Punchbowl*

The letter read,

Dear Pete, *Fri 10th*
Received your letter this afternoon. Great to hear from you. Your fairy tale existence is too good to be true.

My school was built in1865 and had 87 old boys fighting in World War I. Present school population is just over 100. So we have a huge building with no kids. The school is surrounded by factories. I haven't seen one house yet.

Most of my kids are slow learners. 5 of them have parents who've attempted suicide, 1 has a drinking mother, several broken homes + other problems. Most of the kids have some sort of problem. Besides the Catholics, 3 kids from the rest of the school went to church for Christmas. The C of E has declared it a special mission area, the Salvation Army has given up. It's real funny Pete.

The kids are pretty good hearted. It's a pity, many of them have to go home at night.

I went over and saw your Mum last week. She showed me your letter. She's looking on the bright side of things and told me she's been in touch with P. She said your Dad had been upset for the first few days. I only stayed about ½ an hour but I think she enjoyed the talk.

I heard over the news that Brian Filan drowned while on hols. Q'ld. He was training to be a priest. He'll be in Heaven now.

You ought to go into Armidale during the weekends. See the priest and see what he can do about some genial company for you. Maybe the Newman Society at the Uni.?

Keep the flag flying Pete. Honour your God and serve your Queen. For thine is the K'dom, the power and the glory.

Yell my love to Granma Sloggett. She's a real swinger.

Like from
Kev.

After the children left for the day, I returned to inspect the rest of the mail that had come in during lunch. Sorting through it, I was surprised to find a personal letter that I had missed, addressed to:

Mr Peter Skrzynecki,
Teacher-in-Charge,
Public School,
Jeogla,
Via Armidale, N.S.W.

The punctuation was perfect. This was not a letter from one of my mates. I turned to the last page and saw it was from Bill Gunn, one of my former lecturers at teachers' college.

Feb 12, 1967

My dear Peter,

Your letter was here when I returned from Cronulla where I spent a few days. I am sorry indeed to hear that you seem unhappy with your first appointment. Having had a very similar experience, I know exactly how you feel. You have the added discomfort of feeling homesick but this will pass.

I would endeavour to deter the blowflies with one of the many insecticides available. You will also get used to the food. I had to endure the misery of living with a woman who was dirty and would cook turkeys that had been killed by foxes, prepare food without washing her hands and make butter which would turn your stomach. She even made her own bread which was a dirty grey colour and tasted anything but bread. After a year there I was skin and bones – about 7 stone. Unfortunately she was a widow and needed the money which I paid for board. As a result, no other family would "board the teacher". I meant to tell you to be sure to say "nutin about nobody", as this could make your life even more miserable.

I have not been doing anything extraordinary since you left Sydney. On Feb 4 I went to a wedding and enjoyed myself a great deal. Last night Elizabeth cooked a nice dinner for my mother and me. To-day Liz is taking me to Rose Bay convent to collect my niece and is going to have a mid-day dinner here.

I saw Harry yesterday and told him how things are in Jeogla. He says to tell you to stick to it, otherwise that you'll be sorry later and I feel the same. Peter, Time passes very quickly and you'll look back and probably even remember parts of it with pleasure. Hope you get to see the Crockers soon.

Thank you for sending the poems. I think you have a great deal of talent and you certainly should continue to write. Must admit that I am unfamiliar with Whitman but will remedy this deficiency shortly. I have been reading again my favourite Gerard Manley Hopkins. I enjoy his work tremendously and always return to him with great pleasure. I feel "Heaven-Haven" is probably the voicing of his reason for becoming a Jesuit. Don't think he ever found peace.

Talking priestly things, don't lose your faith, Peter. I know it is easy to feel bitter, forsaken but a trust in God is something very worthwhile and gives a great deal of comfort at times when things would be unbearable, if it were not for this trust.

Well, my boy, I must go now as Elizabeth will shortly ring the doorbell. I want to post this in town en route to R.B. so you'll get it as soon as possible.

Mother, Liz and Harry all send their kind regards and hope that things will improve soon.

All the very best from me too.

Very sincerely yours,
Bill G.

What had I written, on the night I wrote those letters to make Bill give me this advice? God, blowflies, food, say "nutin about nobody"? I seemed to have opened up a can of worms. The letter made me feel happy. Like the other letters, Bill's was from home, from a friend, and its presence helped to shorten the distance that seemed like the distance between Earth and Pluto.

The Man on the Horse

I went outside and saw a man on a horse riding up to the school. He was an old man, stooped, enjoying a pipe. We arrived at my car at the same time and he dismounted, shuffled towards me and held out his hand.

Lex Mc Crae's the name. I'm from "Bixton Park", across the road where you're boardin' with Carrie. They're my horses you stop to look at when they're galloping aroun' in the paddocks.

I held out my hand, introduced myself, and replied, Yes, I like watching your horses. They're beautiful animals.

He seemed to ignore my name, cleared some dirt from a stirrup and started cleaning out his pipe by knocking it against the bonnet of my car. When he saw the look on my face, he turned to knocking the pipe on the mudguard and then finished cleaning the last of his tobacco with a finger and blowing it away. There. That oughter do it….Now, Mr Teacher, we gotter talk about the upcoming New State election. Only a few months away…April... I take it you know what I'm talkin' about.

I do.

You do? You sound like a groom at the altar. Ha-ha.

Yes, I do.

I cleared my throat, and he must have taken it as a response to his joke. Well, You'll be the Returning Officer and I'll be your Polling Clerk. I've done this sort of thing many times, so don't worry… All you've got to do is have the school open an hour before the voting starts an' have the urn switched on. I'll supply the biscuits, tea, coffee, milk an' sugar…There's not much to it, really. The day kind o' runs itself.. If yer know what I mean?

No, but I'll take your word for it. One hour voting starts. When is that?

Eight o'clock.

He pulled himself up into the saddle, clicked his tongue and his horse started off, heading back down the road towards "Bixton Park" on the hill – across the road from where I boarded, and watched his horses running in the paddocks, kicking up their hind legs as they galloped, shaking their manes and whinnying, as if they were immortal creatures in a book of mythology, the ground echoing with the pounding of their hooves. They would charge in my direction, snorting and stamping when they pulled up, then wheel and gallop off, their bodies looking like they were on fire.

When I returned and told Carrie about my visitor she wasn't surprised.

Knew you'd be gettin' a visit from him sooner or later. His Nibs, I call 'im. Livin' up there on the hill. He's okay but likes to run the show on every votin' day. I'll also help with cakes an' biscuits – like I always do – so don't worry about refreshments. He don't own the school.

As we were talking I decided to ask Bill Higgins for advice as soon as possible. Being posted to a one-teacher school was one thing, running a polling booth during an election was something very different. I didn't have the slightest idea what I was supposed to do. Elections? Politics? We hadn't been told about any of this at teachers' college.

The School Inspector

He was tall, wore glasses, had grey curly hair, carried a briefcase and wore a three-piece suit that made him look like a businessman. His look was steely, his presence imposing.

Mr H.T.B. Harris, B.A., Dip. Ed. (Admin.), Inspector of Schools, Armidale, arrived unannounced at the school during one lunch hour. It was the third or fourth week of term and I was eating inside the school. My mother had sent the cake she promised and I was having a piece of it after the sandwiches that Carrie made for me each day. The children were playing outside.

From my discussions with Bill Higgins after our first meeting, I'd come to feel apprehensive about this man. Bill told me that Harry Harris was a Methodist lay preacher and had a reputation for strictness and adherence to departmental regulations. He was both feared and respected.

He knocked on the door and I opened it, exchanging introductions and formalities; even before he spoke his name I could hear children in the background whispering and giggling, *That's the school inspector. Let's hide.*

Once inside the building I hurried to switch off the radio, bringing a chair for him and creating space at the small desk. I watched him looking at the cake.

No, no, he insisted, please don't go to too much trouble. This is not a school inspection. This is just a courtesy call to welcome you to Jeogla and the Armidale district. One of the nicest places in the state that a young man could have been posted to....My, that cake smells delicious.

Would you like a piece?

Yes, I wouldn't mind a piece, thank you.

Here, I said, as I cut him a finger-shaped piece. My mother sent it.

Hmmm...So fresh...

Can I make you a cup of tea?

Actually, I have some. He produced a small thermos flask from his briefcase and poured some into the plastic top. He also unwrapped a sandwich. Lovely, lovely. A sandwich and warm tea from home, followed by a piece of Christmas cake.

He was relishing the cake, I could tell. I bet he never expected a reception like this. I made a note mentally of telling my mother in the next letter home.

So how are you settling in?

I told him I was unsure of many of the procedures that had to be followed, the paperwork, especially, with its duplicate and triplicate forms, but Bill Higgins was helping me with those matters. Also, the programming, where classes could be made to overlap, especially in subjects that were not basic.

For starters, you have the Education Gazette, use that as your guide. I see you have it on the desk. Very good. As for programming, trial and error, he commented. Experience is the best teacher. No school inspector will fault you with that approach. If something works – well and good; if not, try something else. If it's not broken, there's no need to fix it. You've heard that expression before?

Yes.

And what about the locals, the parents and citizens? It's a floating population, as we say, families that move into the district, stay a while and then move on. It effects your enrolments, of course.

They're safe.

For now. What about the end of the year?

I don't know.

We'll keep an eye on it. I'll be back officially later in the year and do a report on the school and yourself, but don't worry, alright?…It's part of the requirement while you are on probation. I'll send you a letter outlining a day when I'm coming – so you are not caught by surprise – and you just carry on teaching like you would on any other day.

While spoke I watched him taking in the room – the artwork and handicraft on the walls. He seemed pleased.

What's your favourite subject? he asked.

English.... Poetry, actually.

That's interesting. You know Wordsworth's famous definition, don't you, that it's "The spontaneous overflow of powerful feelings."?

I've read that one.

Do you agree?

I don't know. Feelings, yes, but also using language....

Would you care to give a definition?

No; but I do like what Dylan Thomas said.

Which was?

Poetry is what makes him laugh or cry or yawn, what makes his toenails twinkle, what makes want to do this or that or nothing.

Hmmm...Maybe you'll write poetry someday?

I shrugged my shoulders.

And encourage the children to write?

I'm hoping to do that...I read them poetry from old copies of the "School Magazine". There's a cupboard full of them.

Excellent. Excellent. Creativity. Enlighten their young minds. Encourage them to reach for the stars.

It started to sound like the start of a sermon, but it was the end of lunch time by now and Mr Harris saw me looking at my watch.

By the way, he suddenly changed the topic. Your predecessor, as I remember him, was very happy with his accommodation. Are you boarding with the same family?

Yes, I am. The Sloggetts.

And how are you finding it.

Very good. No complaints.

These country people are always decent, hard workers, the salt of the earth. They've survived droughts and floods, hardships that people in the city never experience.

Remember that. … Respect them for it

Yes, I'm learning

He continued, drawing himself up in the chair, breathing deeply, speaking thoughtfully, They are good people. Many of them regard it as an honour to have the teacher boarding with them. There's the money aspect, of course, but we have to also consider the social implications of having the school teacher living among them. The teacher has to be seen as a role model – someone who reflects favourably on the teaching profession and the Department of Education. The Department only chooses its best graduates and sends them to these isolated areas. Remember that when you get down in the dumps – as you no doubt have – and no doubt will. I know all this, Mr Skrzynecki, because I speak from experience. Do you know what I'm saying?

I spoke carefully choosing my reply in case I offended the school inspector, realizing now that I had been "a chosen one". Yes, Mr Harris, I said. At the same time, I thought. *Chosen?*

Maybe he saw a change in my face or maybe I saw a change in his face. He stood up, brushed his clothes down, put away his thermos, closed his brief case. Thank you for the cake. It was delicious. I'll have the taste of it in my mouth all the way back to Armidale. Would you please line the children up so I can say goodbye to them.

I rang the bell and the children fell into line at the assembly area.

Good afternoon, children, Mr Harris said. How are we all today?

Good, thank you, came the feeble reply from some of the older ones. They all stood with their hands behind their back and swayed slightly, unsure what was going to happen next.

Do you know who I am?

Michael Burleigh's hand shot up. You're the school inspector, he said.

That is correct. Why do you think I'm here?

No reply.

Any idea?

Dead silence.

Well, never mind...But guess what?

You'll be back, said Christine Frizell.

And how do you know that?

Because you did the same thing last year?

That's right, children. I first come for a courtesy visit – and then I came for a school inspection. That's what school inspectors do. Isn't that right, Mr Skrzynecki?

Yes, Mr Harris.

Alright, children, attention! he said. File into school.

They filed in like little worker ants, lead by the seniors in the back row and the youngest – and shortest – following at the tail end.

Mr Harris shook hands with me. Goodbye, young man. I wish you all the best. You'll be notified in writing of the inspection date with ample time to prepare. Remember, don't despair. You're doing a good job. I can see that already.

Goodbye, Mr Harris.

He disappeared around the corner of the school. A couple of minutes later his car started up and we watched it disappearing through the trees, down the road. The children looked at one another and let out a collective sigh that really meant *Phew!* All started talking, some giggling. It was as if a natural cataclysm had passed over us, spared the school and all the lives inside. The tension was gone.

The yellow- wire gate was closed once more.

Above the murmuring voices the piercing cries of soldier-birds could be heard in the trees.

*

After school I decided to skip tea at Carrie's and drove over to Wollomombi to visit Bill. He was in his office, talking to

Alex who had finished Scripture classes.

When are we going to see you again for dinner, Peter, he asked, what about tomorrow night? Unless you have a better offer.

No, I'd love to come for dinner.

Come early. Have a shower, too, if you like.

Thank you. I 'll say yes to both offers…When are you gong to start Scripture classes at Jeogla?

Next week.

How does it work?

I come at an allocated time. We can break the school up into two groups. The Juniors are given basic activities. Stories from readers that I'll bring. They also do some exercises. The Seniors listen to a story from the Bible. A parable, for example. At the moment I'm doing The Good Samaritan. We discuss it and then we finish off the lesson with a prayer.

I told them about the visit from Harry Harris, how he came unannounced.

Surprised you, hey? Bill quipped. Never mind. All part of the package of being a teacher-in-charge. You'll cope. Here, have a coffee, mate. You two don't mind if I light up, do you? We stepped out onto the veranda, drinking coffee and Bill smoking his pipe. The last of children and parents, leaving the yard, a stillness settling over the playground, the forest and Grafton Road beyond. Rosellas and magpies swooping overhead. The scene could have been at Jeogla, except it was on a larger scale.

How's the company at Jeogla? Alex asked me.

I've met the Diamonds, George Gray, Lex McCrae. Lex told me about the coming New State elections. That should be fun.

It's a done deal around here, Bill said. Though who knows how the rest of the region will vote – Newcastle and the Lower Hunter, for example. If the vote gets carried in all the

New England regions then it'll go to state referendum.

And how will that go?

Can't see it happening.

You take a great interest in politics, don't you? I asked.

It's all about the bread and butter issues of life, mate, that's what it is. Think seriously before you cast your vote… On the day, when the voting's finished, bring the ballot boxes here; we count with scrutineers present and phone the results into Armidale.

Okay.

Oh, by the way, there's an inservice course coming up on the running of small schools. You're entitled to go. Tell the parents there'll be no school on the day…And you'll meet others like you. You should go. It'll be good for you. I might even go.

What happens to your wife and children when you go off, into town? Do they go with you?

No. They all stay here. We do take them into town – just so's you don't think we keep them locked up in the house; but when inservice courses and such are on, I go into town alone.

He drew on his pipe, savouring the taste of tobacco, looking skywards, as if he'd uttered a prayer, I thought.

Amen, to all that, said Alex. And thereby lies a tale, mate.

What do you mean?

I mean: don't let it happen to you.

Huh?

Only joking, aren't I, Bill. You've got a good wife…

And I know it….Oh, the joys of it all…Family. Teaching. Politics.

I better go, I said. Get some petrol at Frank Robson's and back home. See you tomorrow night, Alex. See you, Bill, at the inservice course if not before.

Huh! Said Alex, breaking out into a laugh... Here just a month and already Jeogla's "home". Didn't take long, did it?

You know what I meant, I said.

Bill said, Drop in whenever you want to – have a coffee or if you want some company. I'm up here most of the time.

*

While Frank was filling up my car he saw me looking at the sign of the flying red horse, alongside the red telephone box. Pretty, isn't it? he said. Always flying but getting nowhere.

That's not the point, I replied. That's Pegasus. Greatest of all horses. He's red because he sprang from the blood of the Medusa. He's also the horse of the Muses. He inspires poets.

Are you a poet? he asked, raising his eyebrows in mock surprise.

I don't think so; but I try to write poetry. Maybe one day I'll get published.

Any money in it?

I doubt it.

Have you been out to the Falls yet?

Yes, I have. Carrie and Elmo took me out the other Sunday. I also met Wally Edgar.

Three local legends, Frank said. You couldn't've hoped to meet nicer people.

They're all a bit like that, aren't they?

Oh, there are some that aren't that nice. Always looking for a way out. They're sneaky. There are some who haven't paid their accounts in six months – complain they haven't got any money – yet they go to town and live it up in the pubs. I've stopped giving them credit.

Inside the store I paid my money, bought a copy of *The Sydney Morning Herald* that was a day old and some bars of chocolate.

I asked, When's the weather going to get colder?

Oh, after Easter you'll feel it. If you're going to Sydney for Easter bring your winter woollies back with you. The temperature will drop during April and May, then the frosts start. By August the winds are blowing and you'll really know you're living at Jeogla.

As I drove away I remembered the flying red horse in the rain the morning I arrived at Wollomombi; but the red telephone booth also came to mind because of its Clark Kent and Superman associations. Symbols of flying. Flying away.

You wish, I said to myself, as I steered the car downhill, towards the Kempsey Road turn-off.

*

Carrie returned from cleaning the school not long after I came home. She knocked on my door. I'd taken off my shoes and was trying to have a nap, stressed, more than tired, after the experience of the school inspector's visit.

Yer not feeling good?

I'm good, I replied, coming out of my room. Mr Harris the school inspector dropped in unexpectedly and I guess the visit surprised me. He said I was doing okay, but who knows what he was really thinking?

He's a tough one, that Mr Harry Harris, I'm told. Never gives away much. A strict man, they say. A man o' God. That's what Ron says. An' he's not usually wrong about such things. You'll be fine, don't worry. I'm sure he thinks yer doin' a good job. Did he smile much?

No. Except when I offered him some of my mother's cake.

See. I bet the cake won 'im over.

I bet it didn't. Nor was it meant to...By the way, I'm going to the manse for dinner tomorrow night.

That's ok.

Scots' Corner

The events of the previous day's afternoon heralded the kind of routine that I would follow from now on, more or less: often driving into Wollomombi after I had afternoon tea with Carrie, visiting Bill Higgins or the Clarks, going to the general store and then returning to Jeogla.

Sometimes I would travel further than Wollomombi, a short distance to the Falls, and spend time by myself, going beyond the rails of the lookout and walking down the track as far as I thought was safe before stopping at the edge of the precipice; it was a sight that drew me back many times. The amount of water pouring into the chasm varied, depending on the rainfall; but whether it was the water, or the chasm or the total experience of getting off the main road and into the forest, it always seemed a new experience. Just to be there.

More than once I saw Wally Edgar and we'd wave to each other. At first, I'd slow down, thinking he might want to talk, but he'd just keep walking, dog at heels, busying himself with sheep or fixing barbed-wire fences. At the last exit, from his paddocks, one had to open another large gate, and then close it. There was a cattle grid on either side of this gate, both precautions against his sheep wandering off the property.

Rarely were there other people at the Falls during these times. Late in the afternoons was not a good time for sight-seeing; travellers would be leaving, resuming their journeys, back to town or towards the coast. This was a good time to come here. Just to listen to the wind and birds, the silence. I'd never experienced these moments of solitude in the city. Being here was like being on the bridge over the Oaky River… Birds. Trees. Water.

Prior to this, the very next afternoon after the school inspector's visit, I decided to visit the Falls before going to the Clarks for dinner. As I was walking down the track, to stand at the edge of the precipice, lying across my way, was a black snake. Wet, inky black. It turned its head towards me, partly raising its body, slowly, deliberately, its tongue flicking incessantly. I could see its red underbelly. The glassy-black points of its eyes. I was frozen. Worse of all, what should I do? Neither of us moved. Then as if deciding for us, it lowered its body, flat against the earth, turned its back on me, formed a number of s–shapes before straightening out and slithering off, into the undergrowth, down towards the Falls.

I became intensely aware of my breathing and backed off, step by step, knowing now that there was nothing to fear, knowing that the moment of encounter was over. Had the snake sensed my fear and left me alone?

When I arrived at the manse and told the Clarks they laughed, especially Alex, who said I was lucky to have met it out in the open. They'll strike if you corner them and they feel threatened. If it happens again, wherever you are, just back off, slowly. Leave them alone. You've intruded into its domain, not the other way around.

I felt scared stiff, if you must know.

Hey, that's nothing to be ashamed of – it's all part of the country experience, of settling in, as you might say. Now, I've got a surprise for you. There's time before dinner, so I thought I'd run you out to Kilcoy – to the oldest Presbyterian church and cemetery in the district

Ok, but why would you want to do that?

Show you a bit of history, mate This place is called "Scots' Corner".

How far?

Not far. We can be there and back before dinner …Jill knows we're going.

I accepted Alex's offer happily; this was a chance to see more of New England.

When we arrived, the small church reminded me of St John's at Wollomombi, set under trees, surrounded by paddocks and hills, and a forest further back.

Special, isn't it? I said.

Mate, you have no idea of the history of this *kirk*. He stressed the word and fell silent. Whenever I come out here for a funeral or a christening, I know I've arrived at a very special place. All the original settlers are buried not far from here.

We walked around the church.

This piece of land was given by Roderick McLennan and dedicated in the late 1870s, but the church itself was built and opened a few years later.When I come out here I understand why I became a minister.... No Uniting Church for these elders. They voted to remain true to the Presbyterian faith. I'm part of a tradition. I'm continuing a legacy. No Papists here, he said, and laughed.

No, I bet there's not.

At first it helped to understand where I was posted to... Then I understood that these people are my parishioners. I'm now a part of their lives and they're a part of my life. Come on, let's drive over to the cemetery. It's about a mile away.

A Presbyterian cemetery?

Mostly Presbyterians; there are a few other denominations buried there, but not many.

It was like arriving at a farm. The entrance to the cemetery was through a gate with the word KILCOY painted on a sign. I could see headstones directly before us.

This cemetery came about the same time as the church but wasn't dedicated until the late 1890s, Alex said.

I read some of the inscriptions and the names which were all of Scottish origin: Cameron, McLennan, McPherson. Nearly every second one was a McCrae. Many of the graves were unmarked.

They remained together to the very end, I said. The named and unnamed.

Many worshipped here and chose to be buried here, the

dour old Scots. Bit of a mess – all this rusted wrought-iron and wooden plaques – even the crosses are turning into dust – but there are plans to have the cemetery restored one day. They even talk about creating a memorial garden. This place is holy, mate… For me, it's like going to Iona.

Iona?

An island off the west coast of Scotland; it's where St Columba landed and brought God's Word.

Mostly dead flowers decorated the plots, although flowering shrubs struggled through the weeds.

I tried to absorb it all in one full sweep before we left. Granite, marble, obelisks, angels and urns. The late-afternoon sky. Surrounding hills. Trees. Then it occurred to me, how the small church a mile away, while resembling St John's, was not unlike my school at Jeogla.

We better get going back, Alex said, lighting up a cigarette.

*

The school year turned into March and Easter was due at the end of the month. I mentioned to the Clarks how much I was looking forward to going home.

It's a pity so much of the weekend has to be spent driving, I said. A total of sixteen hours. Or near enough.

Why don't you fly home? Alex suggested. Leave your car at the airport or I can drive you out. My parents and Jill's are coming up for Easter, but it won't be any trouble. If there's no one to pick you up at the other end, catch a taxi. Save your car and save some time. You can be home on Thursday night and return the day before school goes back.

Fly home? What a clever idea! I'd never have thought of that myself – nor would my parents. To fly implied spending money and I had absolutely no idea what an airplane ticket cost.

How much will it cost? I asked.

Not sure, mate, Alex said.

Jill spoke, It's not as much as you think, Peter. I fly to Sydney for my checkups. It's easy to book through a travel agent in town.

They both saw me blink and look at her when she said the word *checkups*.

She spoke again. I have only one lung and have to go to Sydney for regular checkups. The cold climate is not good for me. When I was a baby I developed whooping cough; this led to me having bronchiectasis...I lost a year of high school when I was fifteen and had part of a lung removed. Years later, the rest of the lung was removed.

So why are you living up here?

Because of Alex's work. That's more important than my health. Besides, it's not that bad. When winter comes I stay indoors and keep warm.

That's doing it for God in a big way, I said.

I don't mind, Jill said, although I must admit a posting to a warmer part of the state would have been preferable. What did you think of Kilcoy? she asked.

Peaceful... Beautiful... Lonely. The sort of place one could wander around for days and probably not be found. Stay away from the main road. Sleep in the church. Look up at the stars – and maybe see God. Like the souls buried in the cemetery. I bet they see God. Time means nothing to them anymore. Maybe ghosts wander around up there at night?

Ghosts?

Spirits, if you prefer. I liked it very much; but it's like all the silences around here. They haunt you. They might even drive you mad after a while. Don't get me wrong, I do like it, but I don't think too much isolation is good for anyone. Surely we were meant to talk to other people. That's what I find when I go into Armidale. It's good hearing people's voices. Talking to the shop assistants, hearing them reply to my questions. Becoming a part of the life in the streets.

That's quite poetical, mate, but we're all supposed to see God when we're dead. Kilcoy or elsewhere. That's what it's all about. Finding God.

Are you sorry you were sent here?

No. I regard it as a privilege. If I was back in Sydney, life would be too comfy. Out here it's a challenge. Surely, you can see that in your school?

Yes and no; but it's not something I was fully trained for – nor was I prepared for it. You know the story of the father teaching his son to swim? He just threw him into the deep end of the pool. Well, I regard my appointment to Jeogla as something similar.

So, what do you think of the idea of flying home? Alex asked.

I think it's a good idea. I might even book a flight next Saturday when I go into town. Thank you both for dinner and letting me have a shower.

We talked a while longer and then I said goodnight. I left them on the front garden of the manse, in the same spot where I first met them in the rain. I remembered how Jill hurried in out of the rain and, now, it was the same farewell. A hurried goodbye and she returned indoors.

Does her health get bad? I asked Alex.

No, not often, but that's because she manages it well; but you can never be sure. A cough or cold brought on by a sudden change in temperature can effect her breathing. She's a wonderful wife, and I'm lucky to have met her....Well, mate, have a safe drive back to Jeogla. Keep your eyes on the road ahead, not the stars.

Accident at Oaky River Hydro Dam

Sunday, 12/3/67

Dear Mum & Dad,
How are you both feeling? I'm very well and even though the weather is getting a little bit colder, I'm think I'm getting more used to it.

Before I forget. Mr Sloggett will be in Sydney this week. He said that if he gets time and the chance to come out and see you, he will. He will only be in Sydney for three or four days. If he has the opportunity he will try and come out to Regents Park.

Mum, thank you for wanting to buy me some warmer clothes. Yes, I will need woollen underwear for winter. Everyone tells me how cold it gets here. It's like Europe and nothing like Sydney. I am buying some new slippers when I go into Armidale next weekend.

I have also decided to fly to Sydney for Easter and will send you the flight details when I get them.

Last time I spoke with P she told me that she is going to Queensland with her family for Easter so I will not be seeing her.

We have had some very bad news recently that I must tell you about. Two men working at the Oaky River Power Station were welding near an empty petrol tank when it exploded. One man, Des Wunsch had a damaged hand, and the other man had extensive injuries and died. His name was Kelvin Faint. His daughter, Donna, has been taken away from the school by her mother and the two Wunsch girls will also be leaving. Our school numbers will be down to thirteen.

Last week I had dinner with the Clarks in Wollomombi. I also visited a very old church and cemetery in the district at a place called Kilcoy.

I am starting to like the country more and more. You have to live here to learn to like it. I read your letters much faster now because my reading of Polish is getting better.

Last Sunday we had Mass in the local hall. A priest came out from Armidale. His name was Father Kevin Nolan. There were six or seven people. I didn't expect that many because most of the people here in the district are Presbyterians.

Lots of love to you both,
Your loving son,
Peter

Wyatts Creek

On my next trip into Armidale I visited a travel agent and made a booking to fly to Sydney on the Thursday night, 23rd March, after school broke up. I would leave my car with the Clarks at Wollomombi and Alex would drive me to the airport. I was flying for the first time in my life! With East-West airlines. On a Fokker Friendship. The plane would leave at 8.30p.m., fly via Tamworth and arrive in Sydney at 10p.m. I would catch a taxi home. That would give me four full days at home and I'd return on Tuesday, 28th March, leaving Sydney at 3 p.m. When they were finalised, the arrangements seemed all too easy. The unknown factor was the reception I'd receive in Sydney from my parents, especially my mother whom I thought might regard an airfare as being excessive spending.

Before sending the flight details, I rang and informed my parents. When I used the word "flying" there was a long silence at the other end.

Why are you flying when you can drive? she asked.

I explained the time factor involved and how much extra time I'd have in Sydney.

Is that all? she asked.

Isn't that enough, Mum? I'm homesick. I want to see you and Dad, the house, the garden, the chooks, the dog…

Just take care of yourself…Come home safely.

I love you Mum, goodbye.

I hung up and went to Central Park where I wrote a letter home and included my arrival and departure times for Easter. If I posted the letter today, a Saturday, it wouldn't have to wait until Monday to be picked up, as it would from Jeogla This way, the letter would be in Regents Park by Tuesday, or maybe even Monday.

There was a sense of relief in posting that letter that I never expected to experience. I'd made a decision based on what someone else had suggested and I carried through with that decision. Flying to Sydney! Not a big deal for many people, but a first for me. Even the name of the company, East-West Airlines, had an exotic, adventurous ring to it.

Next morning, not long after I woke up, and had my breakfast, Ron's truck drove into the Sloggets' yard. It was already a warm day and, even though autumn had started, I could already tell from the temperature in the rooms and around the house, it was going to get hotter.

Blackie and Brownie barked at the visitors and Suzie, barked back, although she was no match for the two kelpies chained to their wire run. Back and forth the noise continued until Ron yelled at his dog and it retreated beside him, and Elmo spoke to his dogs, waving his arms as he did. Both sat obediently, never taking their eyes off Suzie.

The teacher in? Ron asked.

Here he is, Elmo replied. I'd come walking from around the front of the house. Ron had his back to me. From the smoke that rose in the air above his head I could tell he'd lit up another cigarette. Suzie turned and watched me, but stayed close to Ron.

Good morning, Ron, I said.

I knew Granma and Carrie were in the house, as was Gerald. Maybe he was still asleep. I could see his ute in the carport.

Peter, said Ron, school holidays are coming up – and I know you'll be going home, but you can't go home even for the holidays without first having been out to Wyatts Creek.

Why not? I intend coming back.

Of course you are. I've got to go up to "Overdene" and do a couple of hours work for Mum and Dad…How about I pick you up on the way back and we go out to the Creek? There're new litters of pigs to be seen. The Creek's running full after the rains we had and there's still a fresh smell of autumn in the air; then it'll be winter and it's colder than cold out there.

You'll freeze...We can do another trip in spring, when the lambs are born. What do you think?

He made it sound like we were going to the end of the earth on this beautiful Sunday morning. In Sydney, I'd be getting ready to go to church, alone or with my parents. Was the weather like this in Sydney?

I'll be ready. See you.

Come on, Suzie...See you, Mo. Tell Carrie I'll drop around later. By golly it's good to be alive, Suzie...We're going out to the Creek, Suzie, the Creek. Where you can chase all those bunnies.

The truck started up and he was gone, uphill and away, the man of few words.

What's all that about? Carrie came out from inside the house.

Ron dropped in, said Elmo. Him and Peter are going out to the Creek later. To look at piglets before Peter goes home for the holidays.

Oh, my...Carrie said nonchalantly. The Creek'll be there when Peter comes back. You will come back, won't you? She laughed and walked back into the house.

Why not? I replied. Ron says this is the nicest place in the world.

Well, he'd know, wouldn't he? Elmo said and went back to working in the tool shed.

I was left there, standing alone. For a moment I wondered what had actually been said. Did I really agree to go out to Wyatts Creek with Ron Diamond when I'd planned to go up to the school? Everything happened so quickly.

Blackie and Brownie were lying on the ground, their tails wagging. I went over and patted them. I thought of Bobby, our dog back in Sydney, and thought how he'd like it up here – being able to chase rabbits and bark as much as he wanted to.

I spent the remaining part of the morning reading poetry, especially Judith Wright's poetry in the Penguin anthology.

"Bullocky" and "South of my Days" resonated with me, with its character of a man drawn from local history and the story of the poet's life, captured in the image of a circle of blood and these mountains that I was living among. How strange to have ended up living in the country that inspired a poet. Where exactly did Judith Wright live? Was the bullocky a real man or a created character?

Maybe I dozed, or thought I'd dozed, but a voice from outside my room, Come on, Peter, let's hit the road and dirt track. It was Ron Diamond. Suzie's barking followed, as if to hurry me along.

As I stumbled out of my room, Carrie appeared and handed me a hat. Here, take this, it's gonna be real hot. We don't want yer comin' back lookin' like a piece of watermelon, do we?

I took it without looking, but once in the truck I remembered a conversation I'd had with her about wearing a man's or a woman's hat. Holding it in my hands now, I decided it could have been either. Made of thick straw, with a wide brim, and a cord and toggle that went under the chin. But she was right, it would keep the sun off my face.

Suzie sat between us, eyes dead set on the road ahead. I asked, doesn't this dog ever ride in the back of the truck?

Never. She's my mate and I wouldn't put a mate in the back where the lambs and calves go. Would you?

I suppose not. I wonder where Gerald was this morning? I asked, remembering his ute out the back of the house but no sign of him.

Probably sleeping it off. He likes to go out drinking with mates from Wollomombi or Hillgrove on a Saturday night, especially if there's a dance going. He's been lucky to make it back in one piece so far– or he sleeps in the ute and comes home next morning.... So, what's new? he asked.

I've booked a flight to Sydney for Easter.

That's exciting.

First time flying for me. How far do we have to go?

Oh, a few miles past the school, then we turn off and go through a forest where it's dark and gloomy. Trees are so tall not much light gets through. Then we come to Wyatts Creek and you'll see some of the best Herefords on the Tablelands, even if I say so myself. So, what did you do this morning?

I read poetry. What do you know about Judith Wright and her poetry?

Oh, I haven't read that much.

I've been reading one called "Bullocky".

Oh, that'd be about Ted Chalker. He worked for the Wrights hauling timber and supplies – you know, flour, sugar, tea and so on to "Jeogla" and "Wallamumbi" stations. He also carried horse feed…Nice bloke. Very quiet. Now, there was a bloke that deserved to have a poem written about him.

What about "South of My Days "?

Can't say I know that one?

Where was she born?

On "Wallamumbi" station. Philip Arundel Wright is her father, Chancellor of the university in town and the family's had Wright College named after them. Judith's mother died and PA remarried.

And you've met her?

Strewth, Peter, of course I have…I know them all. Grew up with them.

Does she still live here?

No, she lives in Queensland. At a place called Tamborine Mountain. Now, enough of that book talk. Let's enjoy the scenery.

Don't you ever get tired of it?

Never! No two days are the same – whatever the season. I'll say it only once, but you have to open up your senses – don't have preconceived notions of country people or the land. We're humans, too, and as good as you people from the city.

The school inspector, Harry Harris, said much the same thing to me.

And I hope you listened. There's a bloke that's hard as nails but couldn't be fairer. When he comes to inspect the school and you –just be yourself. Don't try and pull the wool over his eyes. If he sees a fault he'll show you how to correct it. Listen….Are you listening to me?

Yes.

What did I say?

To be myself. Don't pretend to be someone I'm not.

That's right…Now are you ready?

For what?

For the turn-off to Wyatts Creek.

When?

Right now.

The truck swung to the left and lurched over a couple of bumps before settling into a track that had been worn into a series of ruts, long and deep; they would level out and begin again.

Ron saw me looking at a number of high red-dirt mounds, looking as if they'd been pushed up out of the ground by hands.

Ants, he said.

That high? They must be five or six feet each.

That'd be right.

We passed the skeletons of some cattle, lying bleached in the grass.

What happened?

They died in the drought we had. Some I had to shoot. They were past saving.

The trees were the most awesome, tall and spotted; they created the gloom that we were driving through.

Gumtrees, Ron said. And stringy-barks. This forest is one of nature's greatest creations – this forest and others like it. They run right down to the Styx River and beyond.

How do I find the river?

Don't turn off here. Just keep driving. There's a sign on the bridge. Blind Freddy couldn't miss it. If you go alone, be careful. It's spooky down there.

By now I was becoming accustomed to Ron's cigarette smoke, the little dog that sat between us, and the way the conversation had changed from poetry to teaching to an appreciation of the scenery.

Here we are, he said. Come on, you can close the gate.

He stopped the truck and we got out.

Once we put the gate and track behind us, we came out of the forest and into open country, a tract of land that had been cleared right up the horizon. It was flooded with light. We were above it, looking down on what must have been the remains of a house, a number of sheds, including what looked like a woolshed and several pens around the buildings. Sheep and cattle grazed, ignoring us as we drove down into the lower end.

As we walked over, noises were coming from one of the sheds – snuffling, grunting, snorting sounds that I knew were pigs. The smell was strong, blowing into our faces.

Ron called out in a high-pitched voice that got higher and higher, Here, piggy, piggy, piggy…

Suzie got excited, started growling and dancing around us, running towards the pens. She started barking.

Quiet, Suzie! Ron yelled. Do you want to scare them to death. Can't have that, can we?

Piglets appeared in each of the pens, crashing through mud and filth stalks of corn and green refuse, falling over each other, pushing their snouts against the timbers, squealing, squeaking, shaking in the expectation of being fed.

Where are their mothers?

Oh, each one's in her pen, probably lying down, happy to have them off her teats.

How many piglets are there?

About thirty.

That's good.

Not really...See how they're spotted.

So?

That means some bastard wild boar got in and did the damage...And that means I won't get the price I want at market.

Can't you make the pens "wild boar proof"?

I can – and I do, and sometimes it works and sometimes it doesn't. Only way to keep them out is to shoot them – and that's easier said than done...Come on, let's mix some corn and mash.

From a forty-four gallon drum in one of the sheds Ron scooped out several measures of mash, the sort I'd seen my parents give our chooks and ducks at home, and pour them into a huge metal bowl that resembled a baby's bassinette; he then brought in water in a steel bucket from a tank outside and, using a wooden ladle, mixed the lot until it resembled a loose-running porridge. From another drum he scooped out equal amounts of dry corn and added it to the mash. He poured it all into a trough in one of the pens and lifted a door separating the piglets from their food. Again they bolted and fell over each other, squealing with delight, snorting with joy as they shoved their snouts into the food, feasting with delight.

Where's their mother? I asked.

Oh, probably still sleeping it off. She'll come out when she knows they've had enough. Now, we've got to do it all over again twice. Watch, okay, because when we come to the last one – you're going to do it.

Me?

Who else's here? he asked laughingly. His cigarette had burnt down to a stub and he threw it into the mud of the pen. Suzie watched us from outside the rails, obviously used to this part of the routine which meant she could only be an observer.

When it came to my turn I did everything I'd seen Ron do.

Very good, he said, except next time you have to stir with a bit more energy. Work it in more, spread the water and corn evenly.

Next time?

Of course, he laughed. There'll be a next time. You'll be wanting to come out again to Wyatts Creek, wait and see. This is the start of a new education for you. Poetry! Poetry's got its place – but wait and see what this does for your poetry. If feeding the pigs doesn't inspire you, nothing will…Let's go, I think it's time we checked out these sows, they've had plenty of time to come out.

Inside all three sheds, to which the pens were attached, a massive sow lay on her side, caked with mud, half asleep, making crude grunting noises, sounds that seemed to be coming from the earth itself, up through the concrete floor where they lay on beds of smelly straw. Pink teats in a row, like small fingers, stuck out from their bellies. Their eyes were half-open, as if they'd been drugged. The noises coming from the bowels of the earth continued, and they continued to ignore us. Each lifted its head, and each dropped it again. They could have been huge stones. The presence of flies was overwhelming.

Leave them, Ron said emphatically. They'll come out when they're good and ready.

I'm thirsty, I said. I'll just go and have a drink from the tank.

No, you won't…That's stagnant water in there…You never drink stagnant water.

We'll have a drink from the creek, as we go. Ready?

Go where? I asked.

For a walk over Wyatts Creek. I'll bring a rifle in case we run into those boars. And a waterbottle…Got your hat on, I see.

The sun had climbed higher during the time we'd been in the pens and pig sheds, passing from east to west and stopping overhead, pinpointing our presence deliberately, aiming its fire onto Wyatts Creeks.

Boy, I said, wiping my face, that's hot.

The spaces between Ron's truck and the buildings had lengthened, as had the length between us and the buildings, the further we went into the lower paddocks, keeping to left as we did, close to the forest but still out in the open. Suzie chased rabbits but caught nothing, not even a dragonfly. Ron walked with his rifle slung over his arm, pointing to the ground.

Now you can have that drink of water you wanted, then we'll head out into the open, cross the horizon and return in a circle. That'll be a good day's exercise and help to keep you healthy. You've put on weight since you came here, have you noticed?

Yes, I know. It must be Carrie's cooking.

Don't complain.

I'm not.

Here, over here...This way.

We were into the secluded part of the forest again, but not very far in, when I heard the sound of running water. Before us ran a creek. Granite boulders that I hadn't paid any attention to screened the entrance, on a slope, as if erupting from the earth and getting caught in the process centuries ago – firmly set, waiting to be washed away or another eruption.

Drink away, Ron said, like this...

I watched as he walked to a particular spot, clearing a passage as he went, stooped down and, with both hands, cleared a patch of watercress, then, scooping up the water he brought it up to his mouth. He repeated the process several times, stood up, wiped his mouth and said, *Aahh*, that's so good...Couldn't be sweeter. He wiped his mouth with the back of his hand, took off his hat and ran his hand over his head. Now, it's your turn.

I did as he'd done, pretending I'd been doing it all my life. You're right, I said, it does have a sweetness to it.

It's all the rain we've had. Keeps the water running and keeps it fresh. Mind you, it tastes even better when there's been a dead cow or two through it – further up in the hills.

Are you serious? I asked.

Course I am, Peter, you should know me that much by now.

Suzie was lapping water and running through the creek.

Birds twittered around us, invisible but present, their songs a delight to hear.

Ron filled the water-bottle. And you ask if I ever regretted living here, Ron said. I sometimes think I should rename this place Paradise Creek. Let's get on with it, hey. We've got a way to go yet.

Out in the open we veered left, back downhill and out into the open.

Crows flew overhead.

An eagle circled, becoming smaller, then larger, as it climbed and descended in circles, up and down: like a kite being drawn on an invisible string.

Ron asked me about my family, as Carrie had done. I told him my family's story in much the same detail.

Oh yes, war's a terrible thing, he said. Waste, waste and more waste. By the way. How do you feel about taking an Anzac Day service.

I don't know the first thing about it.

Leave that to me, he said. A local school teacher has to be there with the children. You got any problems with that?

No.

Good.

Why?

You'll learn by and by, as they say.

Oh, before I forget, the permission came through for your Dingo Destruction Association to be able to hold its meeting in the school.

Knew it would.

How much further?

A bit.

We'd walked for what seemed like an hour. The sun had turned behind us, in the west, so that it's heat was now on our necks and backs. Suzie walked with her tongue hanging out, panting but still running ahead, trotting when she fell behind. She'd lost interest in chasing rabbits that now were fewer and fewer.

We've had fires through here more than once...They leave everything charred; but it grows back. Livestock has to be saved first.

He sounded like he was talking to himself.

We crossed gullies and skirted more granite boulders, shapes that resembled skulls and arched backs, huge shoulders, massive rumps, the kind of prehistoric outlines associated with mythology or archaeology. A step back into time, or even further, whatever that phrase meant out here, if at all it had a meaning. The air was hot, motionless, but still a leaf would drift out of the forest, across our view and fall at our feet. I watched how Ron would take off his hat, wipe his face and neck but not break his stride; there was a purposefulness in the way this wiry man walked, as if he was in his own kingdom, and knew its every stone and blade of grass. I adjusted the hat I was wearing, but without taking it off. Unlike Ron's hat, it seemed too large, but still it kept the sun off my face. I remembered what Carrie said about returning and not looking like a watermelon.

At first, cattle and sheep grazed around us, but as the heat grew they stood in pairs or groups under trees. The house and sheds were dots in the distance.

Reaching the end of the horizon, he said, Not a bloody boar in sight. I think we should think turn back. Here, let's stretch out and have a drink.

We sat behind a boulder and rested in its shade, our

backs to the sun. Neither of us spoke. The silence was broken only by the sounds we made when we drank. Ron called Suzie over and poured some water for her into his cupped hand. Poor girl, he said. Didn't catch any bunnies. Never mind. Here, have a drink from daddy.

You talk to her like you would to a child.

She is a child, in a way…Just not a human child.

Ron was thoughtful. Several times I thought he'd speak but each time, he stopped himself.

He was attempting to say something but couldn't find the words.

I thought I'd say something, instead, but without quite knowing what the words would be….This place, I said…Your place…

Ron spoke, reflectively, gazing into the distance. You should see this place when the wattles are in bloom, Peter, it's like standing at the door of heaven. After a pause, he said, Let's head back. It'll be slower now we'll have the sun in our faces.

He was right. I walked without looking up, my head lowered, hoping that the hat with its wide brim would shield my face from the sun, looking sideways and talking to Ron when I had to. Even our conversation, little by little, ebbed to a trickle of words until it stopped altogether, and all we could hear was our breathing, at first slow, long and deep and then barely audible, as if our bodies had dispensed with something that was necessary. Ron smoked his last cigarette back at the boulders and that, also, became something that belonged to the past. We were no longer two human beings walking across the New England plateau. The longer we walked, we seemed to be vaporising, becoming two spirits returning from a horizon we hadn't reached. Motion became automatic, effortless. Thought was non-existent, The sun burnt down on my head like a giant magnifying glass, intensifying the sky's glassy blue, piercing every singular strand of my straw hat. I wiped sweat from my eyes but it continued to blur my vision. So I gave up, and walked through a watery haze that ran down my cheeks and into my mouth, moistening my lips and giving me salt to taste. I savoured it, licking my lips each time another drop trickled down my chin and onto my lips. If they were tears, afterwards I would understand, but I neither cared for what I forgot or what I believed had happened. I felt affiliated to those granite boulders that gave me rest, to the water from the creek that quenched my thirst and the man whom I walked beside but stopped talking to. Thin and wiry, smoking a cigarette and wearing an old Akubra hat, he looked like my father. I matched him, stride for stride, as the farm house became more than just a speck in the distance, as water tanks and pig pens materialised, and a small dog ran ahead, barking, because she, too, was coming into familiar territory. Crows were cawing from the sky and from the branches of fallen trees. Magpies sang in the forest. Parrots flashed crimson, green and blue over the old homestead. I was about to ask about this old farmhouse.

As if he'd read my thoughts, Ron said, I had a family living here once. They let the place go to ruin. When they left, I didn't fix a thing. That kept more tenants from moving in.

A string of short words, and the spell was broken.

Our journey across Wyatts Creek was over.

The presence of pigs was overpowering, the smell, snorting and squealing in the mud, the filth, pressing against the pens. Sows and piglets together. Rubbing their bulks against the timber frames that contained them, eyeing two men and a small dog as if they would trample them, devour them.

Want to have another rest? Ron asked.

Yes, I said breathlessly, and pushed the hat off my head. The walk, slow at first and then brisk, had left my legs with the wobbles.

Here, he said, and threw me the water bottle. Pour that over you...Drink it slowly.

I did as I was instructed and returned the bottle. With what remained of the water, Ron drank. He also cupped some into his hands and let Suzie drink. Wagging her tail, she drank and looked thankfully into her master's eyes.

This time I eased myself down against the stand of a water tank, and sat in its shade. The ground was damp because water had dripped from the tap. Ron sat on a broken veranda, opposite me, rolling another cigarette. He asked, You ever smoked?

No, I said. I tried one when I was nineteen and it made me so sick I never tried another one.

Ah, you mustn't've inhaled properly.

My friend Michael Politi showed me, behind my parents' garage, but my eyes watered, my nose ran and I spewed. I reckon he did me a favour.

Could be, could be, Ron mused. He was looking at the sky in the same absorbed way he did back at the boulders. By now, blue tobacco smoke was rising into the air. He took off his hat and flapped his shirt that had opened up, in an effort to cool himself. Ever think you'd be here? Hundreds of miles from Sydney, watching and smelling pigs, admiring the sky, teacher-in-charge of your own small school, being your own boss, the world at your fingertips, reading poetry in Carrie and Elmo's home?

No, but remember I was sent here to teach children, that's the first priority. All those philosophical possibilities weren't considered by the Powers-To-Be when they sent me here. I'm a serial number like my predecessor, and his predecessor, and his, and so on…

Ah, I think you're being a bit hard on yourself…I saw things in the war I'd rather forget, but they helped to mould me, make me who I became and am…I wouldn't want another war, but I don't regret going and fighting for what I believed in. Golly, Peter, that's what it's all about, not just doing what you want but what's wanted of you for the greater good. You got sent here because they obviously thought you were the best one for the job. Do you think they send slackers out to places like Jeogla…Blokes whose spirit will crumble at the first problem? Think about it. Use your brain. You've got one, you know – not like those poor little squealers who are being fattened up for the market. If I thought they were useless I'd take this rifle and put a bullet into each one of them. Like you, they've got a purpose….Now, I'm just about finished with this cigarette, and when I am, we'll head back to civilisation. The pigs'll miss us, you know, they're pretty clever, the old pigs. Just watch them when we're leaving. Listen to their cries. It's like they're human and they think we're abandoning them.

Sure enough, when we got up, heading back to the truck, the squealing began at a level unlike before – with a panic in their cries that bordered on the insane. They were trampling over each other, sticking their snouts through the fence railings, each of them an individual that desperately needed to be touched, assured they weren't being left behind for good.

Makes you proud to be a farmer, Ron said, as he turned the truck back up the track, towards the main road.

Ron dropped me back to the Sloggetts' home and drove off without saying hello or goodbye to anyone.

I almost staggered from the cabin of the truck into the house where I found all of them except Gerald, sitting around the table, drinking tea.

Mind if I plop down here? I asked, taking off my hat

G'day, stranger, said Carrie laughingly. Been out ter see the world, I see?

The hat served its purpose? Yer face almost looks normal.

Here, drink up, said Elmo. Looks like you could do with a bit of refreshment. He poured me a cup of tea, two sugars and milk. Just like the way you like it.

I didn't take a watch, I said. How long was I gone?

Long enough, said Carrie.

Seriously, though, I said.

Few hours, Elmo said.

Granma nodded and smiled, ate more of the scone she was buttering, and stirred her tea.

So, come on, don't keep us in suspense, said Carrie. What did yer learn?

We fed some pigs, walked from one end of Wyatts Creek to the other and back – got worn out in the heat. We rested among some granite boulders...

But what did yer learn? Carrie was eyeing me, trying to elicit an answer out of the ordinary. But what was it? What had I actually learnt?

I don't know what I learnt. If seeing pigs and piglets up close, snorting and squealing like they did – trampling over each other in their own mud and slops, then that's what I learnt. I helped Ron mix their food and poured it out into troughs...What do you mean, What did I learn?

About the land?

That it's not an easy life on the land, the work's hard, there are wild boars out there and we didn't find one. I learnt that water in the creek tastes better when a dead cow's lying up stream in it...

Hee, hee, Elmo, Carrie laughed, Ron's still tellin' that one to everyone he takes out there.

Hee, hee, Granma echoed. Hee, hee. She was smiling from ear to ear.

Carrie persisted with her question. But did yer like what you saw, them hills and paddocks? Aren't they somethin' else? Yer know Ron's got some of the best land aroun' these parts. He's a good farmer. Always has been. Buys good stock...an' knows when ter sell. Bit of a legend, our Ron.

Like yourself, I thought.

Why don't you go an' freshen up, Elmo suggested. Cool off; have a snooze. We don't want you lookin' worn out when you go home for Easter.

Easter? Granma asked. Is it Easter? Her eyes lit up.

Soon, Mum, soon it'll be Easter. Then, turning to me, she explained. Granma likes to dress up fer Easter. Her best clothes, yer know...Likes ter look flash. We go into Wollomombi fer the church service. She likes the hymns an' ter see her friends, or what's left of 'em. What'll you be doin' in Sydney?

It'll be church on Good Friday, probably by myself and then on Sunday it'll be to a Polish Mass with my parents. We usually go to Bankstown – a few miles away. There's a Polish community in that area. Or we might go to Cabramatta. There's a Polish Mass there also...Knowing my parents, I'd say it'll be Bankstown. That's where most of their friends live. They all stand around and talk for ages after the service. Or, if they've made arrangements we might go to somebody's place for lunch..

Betcha can't wait?

Yes, I'm keen to see my parents. Also, I hope to catch up with a couple of friends – one in particular. His name's Kevin...We became friends in high school...We failed the same exams and passed the same exams. Don't ask me how or why, but I think it's Fate. Meant to be, I suppose...Sure, Elmo, I'll go and freshen up and have a snooze, as you say... By the way, thanks for the hat. It made a big difference.

Told yer it would, Carrie said triumphantly. Jest leave it on the front landing and take it whenever yer need it.

I cleaned myself up, got into some fresh clothes, and lay on the bed.

The words were on the tip of my tongue, ready to be written down; the images still fresh, vivid. The sounds. I could hear the pigs and birds, the sound our shoes made as Ron and I walked across the paddocks of Wyatts Creek. I felt the burning sun. Saw the blackberry clumps, the boulders. I heard the water running in the forest; and I heard, above all else, the crunching sounds underfoot as Ron knelt down to drink. Teaching by example, pointing for me to do the same, as I watched him wipe his mouth with the back of his hand.

I started to write, but the words didn't make sense. I tried again. And again, I stumbled. The emotions I felt were powerful.

Again I tried and again I couldn't get past the first few words. In frustration I tore the page from the pad and crumpled it up.

There'd be no poem about Wyatts Creek.

A Surprise I'd Never Get Over

In Monday's mail came a letter from Harry Harris informing me that he would be coming to the school for an inspection on the 3rd August. I had four months to get prepared, do everything that a first-year probationary had to do to get a satisfactory report.

Also in the mail came a year's subscription to *Poetry Magazine*, taken out for me from the Poetry Society by Frank Davidson, as a gift and incentive to keep writing poetry, and maybe try publication. There were no other personal letters.

I read through the School Gazette and checked which forms had to be filled in before the Easter break. The only date of note that applied to my school was the return of Requisition and Stock record for the basic skills testing programme.

*

No, of course they can't sack you, said Bill, laughing, while we stood on the veranda of his school. I've never heard of that happening. Harry Harris will give you advice – pointers – on how you can improve your performance, but he can't sack you. Simple as that… If you want to get transferred to a staff school then you apply. Stop worrying…Remember there's a small schools inservice course right after Easter and we'll go to that….and you'll meet others like you, in the same boat, or those that faced the problems you think you're facing.

Thanks, Bill. I feel better already.

When are you going home for Easter?

Thursday night. Alex will drive me out to the airport and pick me up when I return on Tuesday.

Can you smell the change in the air? Bill asked. How it's slowly changing? The weather, I mean. Becoming just that bit sharper, crisper, with it being autumn and all that... Watch the trees, especially when you're in town ...All those browns and clarets, the reds – the maples – around Central Park, everything gearing up for a full-blast autumn and then winter. New England can be really beautiful. When you get a chance drive out to Gostwyck – down towards Uralla; have a look at the chapel there...all covered in vines. Walk down the avenue of elms. There's a property down there called "Salisbury Waters". Have a look at that. Then go up to the university and check out Elm Avenue. When we go into town for the shopping we make an effort to go and have a look at the university.

All this coming from Bill Higgins! I thought, surprised. He was starting to sound poetical.

So what's new?

Apart from the date of my inspection, nothing. I thought I'd go and see Alex and Jill. Double check about Thursday.

You know what's happening to you, don't you?

What?

You're getting impatient to get home. Perfectly normal.

Is that right?

He was right. I said goodbye. If I don't see you before I leave, I'll see you when I return. What about you? Going away?

Thought we'd go over to Newcastle...See some friends. Maybe stay at Merewether Beach.

We said goodbye again and promised to catch up as soon as the Easter holidays were over.

Maybe we can go to that small schools inservice course together? Bill asked.

Sure.

There's also the New State Movement elections as soon as we get back. You haven't forgotten, have you?

I did forget, actually.

It'll all be waiting here when you get back. Try not to

think about it.

I'll try.

Bill was right about the weather, I thought, as I got into my car. The air was crisper. You could feel it on your skin. There was a change in the smell of the vegetation, also, if you breathed deeply.

*

The Clarks asked me to stay for dinner but I declined. I hadn't told Carrie that I wouldn't be back for dinner, and I thought that I should eat at home for the rest of the week. I felt surprised in deciding that, never expecting that I might say no to a meal at the manse.

I repeated the departure and arrival times of my trip home with East-West Airlines.

Be here by six-thirty – earlier if you like – Alex said. I'll have you at the airport by seven thirty or a quarter to eight. You have to be there half an hour before departure.

We talked about Jill's trips to Sydney, to visit her parents, sister and the visits to her specialist, the man who continues to "save my life".

Sitting in that kitchen, having tea and biscuits with them I felt a stranger and, yet, not totally. These were the people I first encountered some eight weeks ago and who'd become part of my life. I mentioned to them that I'd stopped in to visit Bill Higgins before coming here.

There'll be the New State Movement elections after you return, Alex said, but before that there'll be Anzac Day celebrations. Any views on that?

No, I have no views but I don't have a problem with it. Why? Ron Diamond mentioned it also.

It's a sensitive issue here because Bill won't participate in the Anzac Day service we hold in Wollomombi.

Why?

Why? Why? Who knows, mate. A lot of people think

Anzac Day is all about glorifying war. That kind of thing... If you get my drift. The Education Department has to be represented and we need a teacher. The teacher from Jeogla comes across and looks after the kids from both schools.

And how does that go down here? Bill not participating, I mean?

Like a lead balloon.

I don't have a problem with taking a role in this service. My mother named me after her brother who died in the Second World War in Europe. I think it's about remembering and honouring the sacrifices that men and women made and make.

Okay, that's good. The local Anzac Day marshal is Ron Diamond and he organises the service.

Naturally, I said and smiled.

Mate, you have no idea about the influence that man wields.

Why?

He's like your landlady. Born and bred here...They know the countryside like the backs of their hands. Are passionate about it without bragging. They don't just live and work in New England. They are New England.

Ok, I said. I'm heading off. See you about six or earlier on Thursday night.

By now the return drive to Jeogla had become routine. As I turned right at the Chandler I eased off the accelerator and let the car idle over the dusty twists and bumps outside "Chandler", Jimmy and Doug Browning's property. This was where Gerald often came in the evenings, to have a drink with them or the three mates would go off shooting rabbits or kangaroos. Alex was right about Ron and Carrie, but these young men, also, typified what New England stood for, the hardiness of survival, the loneliness of living so far from a major centre, raising sheep and cattle through droughts and floods. Seasons of loss and gain. Like the animals and birds in the forest, it was a game of survival. I looked down the paddocks at the homestead and thought of the number of times in the last two months that I'd driven past here, and how lonely the homestead looked, with two or three windows with a light inside, sometimes one, and sometimes none. Dogs would bark at approaching motor vehicles; then both dogs and motor engines would fade into the night, into the kingdom of frogs and crickets, nights-sounds, the flowing river, the sleeping trees and damp earth, under the cold New England stars.

By the time I returned Carrie had already come home from cleaning the school. Her next duty would be to go and milk Peggy in the paddock across the road, and then return. She would set about preparing dinner. I would retire to my room, read, listen to music or write letters. Sometimes I walked down to the dam. By now the geese had become accustomed to having me around. They, too, would retire to their nests in the grasses around the dam and hills, doing whatever geese did as evening approached. I enjoyed watching them waddle off, their long necks waving above the tops of the grass, their sense of duty achieved.

Tonight, I went out to the kitchen when she returned and we carried on in idle talk, neither settling on one topic or the other; but in between our sentences the silences grew longer, deeper. Carrie continued preparing dinner. I could hear Granma shuffling about in her room. She came out and settled down in front of the TV set in the lounge room. Carrie went in and turned on the set for her as she did every evening. It was a bit early to put on the fire so Carrie wrapped a blanket around Granma's legs and left the light on for her.

An episode of Loony Tunes was showing. Elmer Fudd was shooting at Bugs Bunny and missing him.

Granma was already laughing

She likes being there like that, in her chair, near the fire, but it's a bit early for the fire, don't yer think, Peter.

I suppose so.

She like ter watch the cartoons, then the news and whatever show's goin'....So, are yer lookin' forward ter getting' on that plane?

I sure am.

Suppose you'll ferget all about us as soon as it takes off?

No. Why would I do that?

Home...It's all about comin' and then goin' home.

Sure, but I'll be back in a few days.

Won't be the same, will it?

What do you mean?

You'll have changed – when you return, I mean. It'll be like startin' all over again at Jeogla.

No, it won't. It won't because I've got to know you, Elmo – your family...Ron, Bill, Alex and Jill...

Jest don't ferget us.

So that was her problem! Thinking that I'll forget them when I'm away. That was the reason for the long, deep silences.

Mrs Slogget – Carrie, I mean – I won't forget any of you or this place. I already know that I probably won't stop talking about you – and how Jeogla inspires me to write poetry.

Poetry? She asked. My, my. She raised her eyebrows and pulled a face. Never had a poet before. Did'ja learn poetry from all them books in yer room?

I read a lot of it...yes, but that's only part of the answer. It's more than that...

Hmmm, Sounds all a lot too clever fer me. Imagine, that, a poet under me roof. Well, I never!

She walked around the corner from the kitchen into the TV room. Mum, teacher 'ere's a poet, she said laughingly.

I followed her around to see what was happening. Daffy Duck was flying into a tree, getting knocked out. Stars and planets were spinning on the screen. Granma was laughing her head off, oblivious to anything Carrie was saying.

Never mind, she said.

That's right, I echoed imitating her. Never mind.

Don't go getting' all upset.. Touchy, aren't we?

Just call out when dinner's ready, I said. I'll be in my room.

But, still, I sensed, something else was bothering her. Something she wanted to articulate but wouldn't or couldn't.

The portable record player I'd brought with me sat on the dressing table; using an extension cord I was able to plug it into the only power point in the room. When I played my records up at the school I played them loudly, but here, under the Sloggets' roof I played them softly, even when they were rock 'n' roll and deserved to be played loudly. I played a lot of the Righteous Brothers, The Mamas and the Papas, Roy Orbison, Everly Brothers, Rolling Stones, Beatles. Or, I read poetry and wrote.Sometimes I fell asleep while waiting for dinner. Classical music I only played at the school where it sounded better on a larger record player.

My books were still in the cartons, stacked on top of each other.

I'd learnt to identify the locals, coming and going, by the sound of their motor cars, especially when they slowed down or sped up after the cattle grid opposite the house. Being driven slowly or quickly, no two cars sounded the same. Gerald drove very quickly if he was returning from finishing the mail run, up from the Big Hill. He'd gun the car over the grid and then hit the brakes hard, often skidding, and immediately do a hard left before turning into the home yard. Then he'd stride into the house, throw his hat onto a table or chair, as if to assert himself: a working man returning home, ready to be waited on, his dinner on the table. Gotter have a wash, he'd say. Others, like Wally Frizell drove slowly, barely raising the dust on the road, as if there was all the time in the world to go the few miles beyond the school to his property, and even, then, wondering perhaps if he shouldn't keep driving on. George Gray drove slowly; so did Ron. Tourists travelling between Armidale and Kempsey, especially if they were towing a caravan, drove even more slowly. I'd been told that the road became more and more narrow, as one approached Five Day Creek, and in places it was no wider than a "goat track". Two cars could not pass each other, one having to reverse, to allow the other to pass. Gerald had asked me to accompany him on his mail run if I ever had a chance, and he'd show me what fun it was, taking the turns around blind corners. When I asked, how did he know if there was any oncoming traffic or not, he'd reply, I just know.

We ate in silence mostly. Carrie talked about the coming Easter holidays and the relatives that'd be coming to visit from Armidale and Coffs Harbour.

Oh, we have lots of relatives comin' then – mostly from town. Why the place will be crawlin' with Sloggets an' Williamses.

She was starting to distract me from my thinking. In three nights I'll be home in Sydney. After that, in less than a week after that I'll be back in Jeogla. Time coalesced into a single speck of awareness.

I helped with washing the dishes and drove up to the school. Here I had freedom to listen to music softly or loudly, make a cup of black tea and have a biscuit. I kept all these in airtight tins I'd bought in Armidale.

As always, before unlocking the school, I stood on the veranda rails to reach up to the fuse box and turn on the outside light. This time I stopped, sat on the bench that ran along the school wall, and did nothing.

The same sounds that surrounded me at the Sloggett home were here in an overwhelming abundance: frogs, crickets, the living breath of a forest that I couldn't comprehend but felt its touch on my face and on the timbers of the school, on paddocks, the whispering pine trees in the yard. In the moonlight I could make out the moving shapes of cattle, the Diamond's house through the pine trees where there were lights in the windows and Bob Frizell's property to my right, a spectre, without lights.

What was happening? I wanted to cry and laugh at the same time. The longer I sat the more uneasy I became, restless. Under my breath, I started cursing my appointment to Jeogla Public School, regretting I'd taken up the offer of the teachers' college scholarship after the failure at Sydney University. I should have asked my parents to pay off the bond, and afterwards I could have repaid them. Why didn't we do it? Why? Then I wouldn't be here, sitting in the dark, somewhere inside a forest on the New England Tablelands, shivering, breathing cold air and looking up at the moon and stars, the labyrinthine spaces between them.

Before thinking about what I was doing, I rushed inside the school, turned on the light. Getting paper and a pen from my desk, I wrote urgently, in a flood of words, as if my life depended on it. When it was finished, I added a dedication:

Wyatts Creek

- for Ron Diamond

Relics overgrown with moss and briars –
these granite hills that rise like humps
or arched backs of ancient stone-made gods:
remnants of unknown worlds existing
in dreams or at split moments of waking
when crows and dingo depart and leave tracks upon
the ashes of sleep: reminders of some terrible instinct
by which we might easily confront death itself.

Gullies of charred thorns and evergreen frost –
bare acres of ploughed or unturned soil
which neither proud nor humble can journey over
by words or gestures that span nothing
but a face: nothing but the empty hollow
of a man who must live with snow and drought,
or poverty and death, in order to be Solomon
and yet ignorant of the text across whose pages
he treks with livestock and family,
being neither Abraham nor Ishmael – but captive
of the land out of which his years will grow and wither
in the silence and solitude of bordering forests.

Only, here, no legends will be written about him;
he will die as leaves and his own fears die,
not upon, but within the eternal season –
the season of crumbling mountains and bleeding trees,
the season of crows with burning wings
and dingoes with eyes burnt out by frost.

His was the hand that turned water around
a valley, snapped a branch as you would a friendship.
By firelight he disclosed gorges and horizons
of sleep and how to avoid marshes of nightmare
calmness and frenzy –
as well as his love in those acres
of evening shadows and morning stars,
watching entire landscapes held in the ascension
of silence that rises from the ground like a mist;
and then the crush of pebbles underfoot as a man
stoops down
to drink from a creek, solitary as Christ in Gethsemane.
The wine need not have come from Cana in order to be
sweet.

When I finished writing I felt the coldness inside the school had clamped itself around my head, shoulders and back, as if to claim me – payment for those minutes when I was left totally uninterrupted and was able to write my poem, the poem that I thought would never be written, left behind, lost among the acres of Ron's property, washed away by the waters of Wyatts Creek.

I made a cup of tea. While I drank, I looked down at the poem on the desk. I hadn't touched it since I stopped writing. No deletions, crossing out or rewriting. A straight write, non-stop. The paper could have been water, running purely among the pebbles of words written on its surface. I was reluctant to touch it. The poem ran over two pages and all I did was move the two sheets alongside one another so I might read it as a continuum, without losing the train of ideas. There was a strangeness to this poem that I hadn't felt about any other I'd written. It was like it was saying, *Don't touch me. Hands off.* Why would a poem say that, make me feel that way? It made sense and it didn't. For me, that was always a good sign. Understanding a poem but at the same time not understanding it. If it worked at a subliminal level, I was happy with that, but if it failed at an intellectual level, I didn't mind that, either. "Intellectual" could come later. I had the poem, and that was all that mattered. Without knowing why, I knew this poem was special.

I dipped a biscuit into the tea and let it dissolve in my mouth. I sipped the tea slowly and felt it warm my insides. There were no blinds on the windows.Beyond the brightness of the room there was pitch-black. Did anyone ever look into the windows when I was working here at night? Probably not. But how could I ever be sure? What did possums and owls make of these window squares and rectangles of light in their domain, shining in the night? Or the animals in the paddocks?

The poem stared at me. I stared back. I sipped the tea.

A conversation sprung up between us. Well, weren't you a

surprise? I asked.

I am a surprise. A surprise you'll never get over.

Why not?

There are more like me waiting in the paddocks and gullies, in the creeks and rivers, on the main road and dirt tracks, behind very single tussock of grass you drive past. In the flight of every bird. In the room of the house you're living in. The lives of these country people too. We're all waiting.

For what?

Figure it out, it's not hard. Once you get over your feelings about where you belong or don't belong.

You mean…?

Yes, that's what I mean.

How long will you…?

The rest of your life.

Why?

What you're doing will make sense one day, in the meantime it will give you more satisfaction than anything else you could have chosen.

I didn't chose you.

No. Did you ever think that it chose you?

Then…?

That's how it happens. Enjoy it. The lives of the children you teach will be enriched by it…And the lives of all the others you haven't met. The school inspector will tell you that when he comes back.

I stopped talking. This was becoming delusional. A conversation between myself and a poem. What would my parents say? *Get a good night's sleep*, that's what they'd say.

Without thinking twice, I folded the poem and put it into my inside coat pocket. Turning off the light in the school I locked the back door and made my way back to my car, parked beside the yellow gate. I didn't care what time it was or wasn't.

Somewhere in the distance a bull was bellowing.

The chill air scratched my throat as I took deep gulps.

I was conversing with myself. That wasn't reality. Taking these steps. Touching my car. That was reality.

I thought, *A poem can't talk. No more than a tree.*

As I got behind the steering wheel, I could hear the folded paper in my coat creasing, as if replying to my thoughts.

I drove off, the headlights from my car creating a ghostly illumination through the trees, then down the yellow-dust road and into the night.

When I got back, the Sloggetts had gone to bed.

First Flight

At breakfast, Carrie said, I didn't hear you come in last night. Was it late?

I don't know

You should rest more, goin' up to the school late at night like you do, can't be good fer yer eyes an' brain…An' readin' all them books.

She was starting to sound like my mother. I'll have a nice break soon enough, I said. Promise I won't open a single book.

As if, she laughed. Be like askin' a bird not ter fly.

I liked her allusions to the natural world, something else she had in common with my mother. I reckoned if the two of them met they'd get on splendidly. Proverbial peas in a pod. No nonsense women who saw through people's motives. Life itself had been their teacher. Experience had chiselled and honed them.

Feelin' excited? she asked.

A bit, I replied. A series of lessons dealing with number, spelling, reading, language studies, writing and written expression flashed through my mind; there'd also be singing, a scripture class later today and social studies, natural studies. Poetry appreciation, also, from one of the school magazines in the blue cupboard. All necessary.

'Bye, Carrie said, coming outside to see me off, waving as I drove out the gate. She hadn't done that lately.

The sun was rising above the tree-line as I approached the school turn-off, its light already reflecting off the school and making it appear white, streaming through the tops of trees. A glorious morning. Heraldic. I thought, Easter can't be far off.

As I opened the yellow gate and walked down the footpath, it occurred to me that the gate, as much as the car, represented security. If I could make out the gate in the dark

I would always know that the car was within arm's reach. The weird conversation I had with the poem remained in my head. I couldn't remember that kind of experience before. It could "speak" in its own voice, as a poem, but to actually address me, as that poem had done, was strange.

After assembly, Christine Frizell said, Dad said he saw you up here last night, sir, it was real late.

Did he? I asked. You should tell him next time to come in and have a cup of tea. It'd be nice to have company.

He reckons you work up here a lot at night.

Yes, sir, said Jennifer Cundy. You do. We seen you lots of time.

After the accident at the Oaky River dam and the three girls had moved into town with their families, we were down to an enrolment of thirteen pupils, however, a new girl, Jennifer Cundy had been enrolled in the Infants. She lived along the main road, down towards the Styx. She was bright, chirpy, as the saying goes and never hesitated to add her contribution. This time, she added, Bogey man might get you!

Everyone laughed.

My Dad sees you, too, said Darryl Williams.

And our dad, chimed in the three Moult brothers.

Well, please tell your fathers and mothers there's an open invitation for anyone to drop in whenever they want to. If the lights are on, it means I'm working up there.

Yes, sir, they said in unison.

*

We knew that at any moment we'd be hearing a car pull up and the Reverend Clark would knock on the door and enter, Bible in hand, carrying pictures and activity sheets for them to complete after the day's lesson.

When he did enter everyone stood up and addressed him respectfully. He looked like he'd just washed and shaved, combed his hair and put on a clean collar above his light-blue shirt front. Jesus himself could not have made a more welcome appearance.

Sit school…Thank you, he said. Can anyone tell me what season we are in?

Easter! Fourteen voices spoke as one.

Very good. What does that mean?

Holidays! Michael Burleigh answered. He made everyone laugh, including Alex and myself.

Yes, yes, the Reverend Clark finally responded. Surely it's about something else, isn't it?

Going to Sydney for the Easter Show – which no from up here does, said Christine Frizell glumly.

Why do you say that, Christine? I said. It was not my place to stay in the schoolroom while Scripture was being taken. Usually I stayed outside, marking books on the veranda or, depending on the weather, I'd take it out to the shelter shed. I was about to go outside when Christine's answer made me stop.

Our parents've promising since we were little to go to Sydney for the Easter but we've never been.

We could see the Harbour Bridge if we went, said Bruce Frizell.

Most of the others stared at them, surprised and interested, as I was, to see the direction our scripture lesson was taking.

What about Jesus Christ? the Reverend Clark asked. Do you think he's been to the Easter Show or to see the Harbour Bridge?

He doesn't have to go, sir, said Michael Burleigh. He's God and he knows everything about everywhere.

I was starting to think that maybe I'd stay, sit in at the back but not say a word. As if he'd read my mind, Alex said, Stay if you like, Mr Skrzynecki.

I'll sit up the back. Won't say a word, I promise.

I watched and listened how Reverend Clark skilfully turned the conversation back on to the theme of the Resurrection. He used the word ”promise” over and over, equating the promises that humans make to the promise that Jesus made about returning from the dead. He would die on Good Friday but would return on Sunday. That was a promise.

Alex told them he'd been working on a ship when he felt God calling him to be a minister. He promised God that he would. The children sat, open-mouthed, arm folded on their desks, taking in every word, their eyes riveted on him.

And I did that, he proclaimed in his strongest Scottish accent. I kept my promise to God....So when Jesus said he would rise on Easter Sunday, he did. He threw off the shackles of Satan by conquering Death. He gave us new life. He gave us the promise of the Resurrection.

We could have been listening to a sermon in a church, any Christian church, that Alex wore a Presbyterian minister's garb made no difference to the message he was preaching. He said he had Easter "activities" for them to do on worksheets. At that point I felt I should go outside and let him finish the lesson by himself. I could hear the children talking as they competed their work and Alex praising them for their efforts. He concluded by saying The Lord's Prayer with them and wishing them all a happy Easter.

*

Carrie had gone up to the school to do her cleaning and Alex and I were sitting in the kitchen, drinking tea and eating homemade cake.

She looks after you, mate, like a mother.

You reckon it's that bad?

It's not bad. It's pride, possessiveness. You're her responsibility as long as you board here. Be grateful.

Apart from Bill and Ron, Alex was a person I was

learning to associate with more and more ideologically. The disagreements over religious affiliation were not a major problem; but I sensed a sense of alienation in his situation that was similar to mine. Both of us were from Europe, from two small countries that had been oppressed politically. Both countries had histories of survival. Australia was our home now, but he spoke about Scotland with a twinge of homesickness in his voice – in the same way I often heard my mother speak of the Ukraine. When he spoke like that, I think I understood him better than at any other time. The real difference between us was in the nature of our postings to New England : he was doing his job for God, I was doing mine for the Education Department. I liked him and felt comfortable in his presence. I equally liked Jill, who had a feeling of friendliness about her that seemed to rub off naturally on anyone as soon as they met her. *Nice lady, that Mrs Clark,* Carrie had said at the outset. *Real nice.* Others spoke about her in a similar fashion.

I better go, mate, Alex said. I've got a funeral to prepare for.

Kilcoy?.

No, this one's in town. St Paul's.

I watched him drive off, waving as he reached the road and turned left.

Granma was in her room, Gerald hadn't returned from where he was working and Carrie was still at the school. I changed my clothes and went for a walk down to the very bottom of the Sloggett property where a creek ran across it. Directly opposite was Lex McCrae's property, "Bixton Park", where the horses ran in the afternoon sun.

So I walked across the road to get a closer look.

Even, now, without a sunset, they looked magnificent, grazing in the paddocks, occasionally throwing up their heads and shaking their manes, – or one would gallop towards me, perhaps expecting food, then gallop off.

Another would follow, then retreat.

A man appeared from the homestead and waved to me. It was Lex, smoking his pipe. He beckoned for me to come closer. I walked uphill and he walked downhill. We met halfway. Fencing wire seemed a good divider because it contained the horses and allowed an old timer like Lex to remain in his kingdom. I was the outsider, the intruder, the young teacher whom I knew he tolerated, but looked down on.

G'day, Mr Teacher. How'd yer be?

Pretty good, thanks Mr McCrae.

Haven't forgotten what's on after Easter?

You mean the Anzac Day service?

No, I mean the election for the New State we're goin' ter have.

Are we?

Yer can bet yer last pound on that, sonny.

He was facing west, peering through squinted eyes into my face, puffing on his pipe, trying to fathom me. What was he making of me? If he could have said it, I'm sure he would have said, *Crikeys, who has the Education Department sent us?*

A horse cantered over to him, stood by his side, tossing its head, allowing him to stroke its head and nuzzle him.

This one thinks I've got some sugar or an apple in my pocket, Lex said. Spoilt them all, that's what I've done. Like ridin' horses?

Nope, I said firmly. They actually scare me, if you must know.

How come?

Years ago I was thrown by a horse. I was only four or five.

They should've put yer straight back on.

They did.

What happened?

I hung on for dear life, but I screamed so much they took

me right off.

Yer makin' this up.

No, I'm not. Someone took a photo. I still have it. The horse was called Pig because it was fat.

Well, if you change yer mind let me know. Come over and I'll pick out a quiet one for yer....Carrie not home yet?

No, but soon.

You'd be goin' home for Easter?

Yes, flying home on Thursday night. Can't wait to see my parents.

Okay, I might see yer at the Anzac Day service if I don't go into town...But I'll certainly see yer on votin' day.

He turned around and the horse followed him, slowly at first as if in sympathy with the slow progress he was making.

I waited to see if he'd turn around, but he didn't. He gave the horse a gentle nudge with his elbow and it pricked up its ears, shook its mane, snorted and galloped off, joining the others.

Before setting off downhill, back towards the creek and the Sloggett home, I stood and took in the scene. I'd never seen Jeogla from this point. Almost an aerial view. Looking down on the place where I was living, seeing it laid out, seeing the road, tracks and trees, buildings, clothesline, chooks and geese, dogs. Beyond the rise where Carrie kept her cow Peggy a line of trees cut across the sky. That was where the sun set before it set fire to the paddocks where Lex's horses ran. I opened and closed my eyes, repeatedly, trying to imprint the image in my brain.

Suddenly the moment was broken. Dust on the road to my right meant a car was travelling towards the cattle grid. Through the trees along the side of the road I could see it was Carrie, returning from the school.

On Thursday afternoon, Susie Frizell put up her hand and

asked a question that silenced everyone in the room. Sir, are you really going to come back after Easter?

She was a quiet girl, one who was shy and content to let others lead the way. She only spoke when spoken to and was often reluctant to answer. Her question surprised me, but I also detected a tone of sadness in her voice. That puzzled me. Even as she spoke she seemed to draw back physically in her desk, put her hand up to her mouth and freeze in the act of speaking, as if she was apologising for asking the question.

Of course I am, Susie.

She shook her head and lowered her eyes, but didn't say anything more. A momentary silence fell over the school, until I said, Okay, let's pack our bags.

Once more, the normal routines of a day's end started. I looked up and saw Susie in that same position, sitting almost apprehensively. She saw me watching and started doing what the others were doing, packing her school bag.

They all set off, on foot and in the motor vehicles that came to collect them, towards the Styx or towards the Oaky River dam, waving to each other, their *Byes* and *Happy Easters* touching like swallows in the air, before becoming lost in the surrounding hills and forest.

Most of my packing had been completed the day before. I hated long goodbyes and sensed an urgency in doing what I still had to do. I decided to go to the Clarks before the hour I originally said I would. Urgency and impatience had conquered me.

I couldn't wait to get away from Jeogla.

Yer mind yerself, now, Carrie said, an' tell yer mother an' father we've been lookin' after yer – an' we will when yer come back.

I said yes to everything she said. Elmo hadn't returned from Nowendoc. Granma sat in the corner of the room, smiling at me and occasionally waving goodbye. Gerald came storming in, angry for some reason he didn't explain.

He muttered, See yer later, Mr Teacher, as he slammed the door of his room behind him. I heard him as he threw himself onto his bed.

Ignore 'im, said Carrie. He might've forgotten to take 'is tablets. I'll see 'im before I go up ter do the cleanin' of the school.

Goodbye, Carrie. I can't put what I feel into words.

'Cause yer can't, that's 'cause yer all choked up.

I gave Granma a hug, Carrie also.

At the door of the car, I said. See you all on Tuesday evening.

I'll have dinner waitin' fer yer, Carrie said.

I got into the car, waving as I drove off.

Blackie and Brownie were barking madly.

The geese had waddled in single file, up from the dam, their heads waving above the grasses, standing there, watching me.

*

Alex and Jill were surprised to see me. Hey, you're early, mate. Anything wrong?

Come in, said Jill. I'll fix us all a nice cup of tea. It's the anticipation, she said. I was like that the first time I flew down to Sydney. Nerves get the better of you, and all your good resolutions fall away. You want to run away, and you don't want people to see you in that state.

Hey, Cassie, Alex called out. Stop that barking, will you! You know Peter by now.

Cassie continued barking, bounding around the yard as she did. You could hear her from inside the manse. Alex went out and threw her a tennis ball. That'll keep her quiet for a while. Chasing rabbits, possums and tennis balls. Any one of those will keep our Cassie happy!

Raindrops fell against the window, hard, like small stones. They quickly came in sheets, whipped up by a wind that was nonexistent ten minutes ago. The corrugated iron roof echoed with the rain.

Where'd they come from? asked Jill.

From the sky, dear. Looks like we're in for a spot of wet weather, Alex replied.

But just as quickly as the rain started, it stopped, carried away by the wind that continued sweeping over the manse. Cassie started barking again, scratching at the back door, until Alex got up and let her indoors.

Now, lie there, in the corridor, he said. The big dog flopped down, her tail wagging, head on paws, happy to be inside.

By the time we had to leave for the airport the wind had sprung up again. Spatters of rain were falling.

You might have a storm, Alex said.

What happens? I asked, trying not to show my nervousness.

Oh, nothing. The pilot flies above the rain. It's a different world above the clouds.

We said goodbye to Jill. I'd parked my car under the trees outside the church. Jill saw me looking at it.

It'll be safe there, I promise. Right as rain, so to speak. Have a safe trip home – and we'll see you in a few days' time.

Just a sec, mate, Alex said, as he stopped and rolled a cigarette. Best way to go, mate, rolling your own.

By the time we'd reached Commissioners Waters the gusts of wind had strengthened and the rain was more frequent. The straight road into Armidale was a welcome sign. The airport lay on the other side of the city.

The rain might blow itself out by the time the plane takes off, I said.

It's not the rain that matters, mate, Alex replied. It's the wind.

I wasn't sure if he meant that reply as a joke, but I didn't look at him and thought he was serious. This was my first flight. Rain and strong winds!

*

I checked in and we stood at the plate-glass window, staring into the oncoming darkness, at the Fokker Friendship already on the tarmac, it's white colours and twin propellers standing out from the background of New England paddocks. I thought it was the most handsome aeroplane I had ever seen, although I thought the tail was too large and the end of the fuselage could have been more slim-lined.

Alex was smoking another cigarette he'd rolled himself and seemed indifferent to our surroundings. People walked around, back and forth, others sat on lounge chairs, talking, others were reading papers. This was a universe I was not accustomed to.

You can go, I said, if you like. I'll be right from here on.

No, mate. I'll wait till the plane takes off. I can see you're a bit nervous because of the weather. Don't worry about Tuesday...I'll be here at four-thirty when your plane comes in...And you'll be back at Jeogla by six o'clock to have tea with the Sloggetts....It'll be just like you'd never been away. He laughed, and looked me in the eyes. Relax. Nothing's going to happen to you or the plane. That's why there's a pilot and co-pilot. They're the experts.

The flight was called and we said goodbye, shook hands and I followed the line of passengers out onto the tarmac, along a yellow line to where a flight steward stood and welcomed the passengers. I could see baggage being loaded towards the front of the plane. We, the human cargo, were loaded from the rear. Far in the distance, beyond the immediate paddocks, I saw lightning flash.

I'd asked for a window seat and received one that was four from the front, on the left side, under the wing, behind the propeller A woman sat next to me. My seat had became part of the fear and curiosity that had engaged me from the moment I realised we might be flying into a storm. I realised I could be crushed beneath an aeroplane's wing – or shredded to smithereens by a propeller! The image was too gross to contemplate and I shrugged it off as best I could. We weren't even airborne and I was already dead! How could one's imagination discard reality so easily? Become locked into a virtual chamber of horror?

I stared at the lights of Armidale airport and the people silhouetted inside the departure lounge.

Rain was starting to fall.

The captain's voice came over the intercom and advised the flight crew to prepare the cabin for take-off.

The left propeller came to life as a flight steward's voice advised us to observe the safety features of the aircraft and the procedures to follow in case of an emergency.

The right propeller started up and the pitch of the engines rose higher.

I was so lost in looking out the window I failed to notice that the buildings of the airport were receding. We were reversing, straightening out, and taxiing to the far end of the airstrip. The plane seemed to bounce more than run forward as it progressed.

Finally it stopped, did a semi-circle, and faced the opposite direction. The revving of engines grew higher and higher, cut back, paused, and lurched forward suddenly, the way a motor vehicle does after it's been revved up and the handbrake is let go.

I looked down, as far as I could, but only saw a series of lights go whizzing past, becoming a blue, as the Fokker Friendship gathered speed. The bumps became more severe. Everyone in the cabin seemed to be shaking, heads and shoulders all at once. We were in semi-darkness. Earthlings blasted into outer space. To be lost forever, among the planets and stars, over New England. Consigned to a Circle of Hell never imagined.

My insides came up into my mouth; my breath pushed

out of my lungs. The lights on the ground were now tiny pinpricks. I realised we were airborne. On our way to Sydney via Tamworth.

The plane rose steeply, but not in a straight line, more at an angle. Winds were pushing it backwards, but it still rose, trying to climb above the wind gusts. Armidale had slipped from sight. I couldn't see any lights on the ground. I realised we were flying through clouds. The woman next to me had put her hand up to her mouth and I thought she'd be sick; then she reached for the brown paper bag in the pocket of the seat in front, and she was.

What was happening? It was as if the captain was doing a loop-the loop. Was he allowed to do that? What if the aircraft flipped and didn't straighten out?

His voice came in over the intercom and he assured the passengers that everything was under control. Everyone should have their seat belts fastened. We were experiencing some turbulence and would soon be levelling out. The flight into Tamworth might be bumpy, but it was safe. While he spoke, the roller coaster ride continued. Do not leave your seats, he emphasised. Everything is under control. He added, Rain is falling in Tamworth, but we expect a much smoother flight into Sydney.

I kept peering down, trying to see what I could possibly see, through a window that didn't permit much of a view. Black. Black. An occasional light and the window splashed with rain, but soon we were landing in Tamworth and told to remain in our seats. A bumpy flight and a bumpy landing. At least we were on the ground. Cabin lights came on. Flight stewards collected bags from all passengers who had been sick, and we were told that more passengers would be joining the flight to Sydney. The flight was full. People were laughing, talking among themselves, expressing delight in *having made it*. The woman next to me smiled feebly and hid her face in a handkerchief. She barely looked up. I thought she was going to be sick again.

The discernible feeling among passengers was one of relief. Someone called out *Three cheers for the pilot...Hip, hip, hooray.* Applause followed. I wondered if the pilot or co-pilot heard any of it.

We sat on the tarmac for at least twenty minutes. Passengers boarded and luggage was loaded. Rain started. Stopped.

The pilot's voice came through the intercom. Flight crew, prepare cabin for take-off.

Again, we went through the protocol of having the aircraft's safety features demonstrated and procedures to follow in case of an emergency. Passengers were told to leave their seatbelts on and cabin lights would be dimmed.

Not long after we took off from Tamworth the stormy weather lessened. The plane was travelling more smoothly, although it still dipped and rose, but with less frequency; it levelled out and passengers were told not to move around the aircraft unless it was absolutely necessary. Refreshments would be served. A tail wind was assisting. The flight would take another hour. You could feel the aircraft veering to the left. Our flight path would take us over the towns of the Upper Hunter Valley, and then follow the coast to Sydney. Lights were switched on. Many passengers also turned on their reading lights.

There was an informality in the cabin now, a calm, a less stressful atmosphere than before. People were talking softly among themselves, laughing, drinking tea and coffee and eating snacks that had been brought around. Had the danger passed? Had we ridden out the storm?

I craned my neck to look out the window. Clouds. Darkness. Tiny points of light. Were they farmhouses? The ocean lay beyond the darkness and the points of light, to the east, where I thought I saw lights out at sea. What light there was, intermittently, through the cloud cover, only revealed patches of shadows, formations that I supposed were hills, forests, ridges of mountains. The aircraft was flying smoothly. I imagined the incoming waves breaking into surf, onto beaches and rocky coastlines. We seemed suspended by an invisible cord, barely moving through space. At one point, the captain informed us that we were passing over Muswellbrook and the lights ahead were Singleton. You could see the grids of streetlights. Once we turned and passed over Newcastle the lights became numerous and there were coal ships waiting off the coast, strung out like toys, dotted with lights. We were told to enjoy the remainder of our trip and once over the Central Coast our descent to Sydney would start.

Now I could see the ocean, stretching to an horizon that lay in the black distance, beyond the curvature of the earth – and I knew that was a destination we would never reach, no matter what the time, how long or far we flew. The darkness had become darker, except that now lights punctuated it like ideas appearing in a poem, illuminating the moment of inspiration, flooding it with light until it became a completed poem, free of the darkness. A star.

Gradually they began to appear, the outer suburbs of Sydney and their magical lights, in all the colours of the rainbow, like jewels scattered onto a black satin rug, on display in the night sky.

After we passed the Central Coast the Fokker Friendship dropped in altitude and began its descent into Sydney, coming in from the north, over the harbour and the city, bumpy at first, as it came in lower and lower above the rooftops of suburbia. I had no idea which suburbs we were passing over, but I immediately recognised the Harbour Bridge lit up in orange and yellow lights, like something I might have made many years ago with my Meccano set. Cars were moving along it, in both directions. I could make out boats moving over the shining water of the harbour.

Were there any ferries? Those emblematic yellow and green watercraft that I associated with my first memories of travelling to Manly and Taronga Park Zoo.

As the aircraft dipped from left to right, right to left, passengers turned their heads to get a better view of the city below. We levelled out and came down, landing almost straight away, hitting the airstrip with an audible thud, at the same time the brakes were applied. We taxied to the terminal and were told to stay in our seats until the engines were turned off. The captain would alight first.

It was a protocol that was completely new to me, just as it was when we boarded the plane in Armidale. At least the rain had stopped, although a strong wind blew across the tarmac. I held my briefcase against me as I entered the arrival lounge, and made my way to the designated carousel to collect the suitcase I'd brought with me. The arrival lounge was packed with people – a much larger crowd than the one in Armidale, everyone on the watch for the appearance of their baggage and people who were looking for people also.

Once in a cab, I settled down to the last stage of my trip home. The plane was to have arrived at eight-thirty but now it was nine o'clock.

Sydenham, St Peters and those suburbs closest to Mascot were foreign to me, however, once we were in the Canterbury-Bankstown area I recognised where I was and knew that Regents Park was not far away.

What would I say to my parents? What would they say to me? It was nearly ten p.m.

I started to think of Jeogla and what I'd left behind. In my mind's eye I tried to imagine the road in the darkness, long and unbroken, between Jeogla and Regents Park and found that I couldn't.

I thought of the Sloggetts asleep in their weatherboard home, the hills and forest surrounding my small school and saw the stars shining above it. I remembered the screeching cockatoos and squabbling soldier-birds. I thought of the Styx River and the trip I was planning to take by myself. I thought of Lex McCrae's horses and Ron Diamond's pigs, how the geese watched me when I was leaving.

Home

Here we go, mate, 10 Mary Street.

The cabby's voice woke me from my reverie. I looked around into the darkness and recognised immediately where I was. My home. The veranda light was on, as were the lights in the lounge-dining room.

Thanking the driver, I paid him and collected my baggage from the boot. The taxi drove off and I walked into the front garden hearing the familiar rusty squeak of the front gate as it opened and closed. I could smell the roses that grew down the length of the footpath, even though they weren't in bloom.

Before I could ring the bell the door opened and my parents stood in the light, wordless, welcoming, their arms held out. My mother was crying. My father seemed choked with emotions, tears in his eyes. We kissed and hugged one another, shook hands, still without a word being said. The dog was running around in circles, woofing, jumping up on me and pawing with happiness. Finally, my father spoke, Come in, come in, let's close the door. It's so good to see you again.

Have you eaten? my mother asked. There's food in the oven, being kept warm. I made one your favourites. Rissoles, mushroom sauce, browned potatoes, carrots and peas. You must be starved. Come in and eat, we can talk later.

See, Mum, I made it.

Why wouldn't you?

You were very worried.

Ah, you're being silly.

How was your flight? my father asked.

Very good, I replied. Not a single thing to worry about.

Suddenly, it struck me. I was speaking Polish! For the first time since leaving home I was speaking Polish face to face with my parents – and not just over the telephone from Armidale. I don't know why that was an important realisation, but it was.

I've got so much to tell you, I said….It's such a different world at Jeogla…Mum, Dad, it's been such a big change.

I'm sure it has, said my mother, but you eat first and then have a bath and we can talk. What we don't say tonight we can say tomorrow and the next day…Your room's ready. I've laid out fresh underwear and pyjamas. Now, no more talking. Eat!

I knew they would sit and watch me eat; it was just like being with the Sloggetts. Carrie never took her eyes off me, and neither did my mother.

*

We talked until after midnight, or at least most of the talking was done by me. My father listened intently, my mother asked questions relating to the Slogett family, their house, their animals, what kind of vegetables or fruit they grew. I had to explain that it was only a small block of land, a holding, not a farm like Ron Diamond's property, both at Jeogla and at Wyatts Creek. My parents were interested in these facts, as unimportant as they might have sounded to me. My father was impressed that Elmo was a foreman with the Forestry Commission and was surprised at the distances he had to travel to work on Monday morning and then return on Friday afternoon. He must be an excellent foreman, my father said.

We went to bed and I felt a sense of relief at having arrived home safely, after the storm between Armidale and Tamworth. Satisfaction, too, because I'd made the decision to fly instead of drive and carried it through. There was something deeper, however, that slowly rose through my consciousness as I drifted into sleep: I knew I'd survived the first two months of my appointment to Jeogla Public School.

The last thing I remember was the beacon light at the end

of the wing on the Fokker Friendship, flashing in the dark, as we took off into the darkness, rain spattering the window, and the first gust of headwind slamming into the aircraft.

Sleeping In

I awoke and knew immediately that I was in my own bed at Regents Park. I waited to hear the rooster crow, but no rooster crowed. Trains travelled beyond the end of Mary Street, beyond Clapham Road and Carlingford Road, on the south-western line to Liverpool, and I heard these several times. Growing louder meant they were travelling from Sefton to Regents Park, growing fainter meant they were going to Sefton. These were the "red rattlers", so-called because of the noises they made when in motion. Light was coming into my bedroom, even though the Venetian blinds were still closed and the curtains drawn. I reached over to my bed table to and read the time by my wristwatch. It was nearly noon. Noon! No wonder the rooster wasn't crowing! I'd slept in, nearly twelve hours. Why hadn't my parents woken me?

I dressed and went out to the kitchen. There was no one there; then I saw my mother coming in from the laundry.

Where's Dad?

At work. Half day only because it's Good Friday...My, but you've slept well. All that air travel must have tired you out. Would you like something to eat?

Too late for breakfast, isn't it?

Doesn't matter what you call it. It's never too late to eat. Come, sit down, tell me all about "Jee-og-ola".

It's pronounced differently from how it's spelt. It's pronounced "Jogla" – without the "e" being sounded.

Do you expect me to understand all that? So, what is it like? How many people live in this town?

It's not a town. I don't know exactly how many people live there... It's a place in a farming district. Cattle and sheep. The nearest shop is at Wollomombi – and that's six or seven miles away. The city of Armidale is thirty-three miles away and that's where the shops are...Saturday is the big day when we go into Armidale to do shopping, get our hair cut, meet friends and family...

But you don't have friends or family there?

No, I don't, but I am getting to know the place more and more and I like going into the shops and meeting people. There's a teachers' college in Armidale and the University of New England. I think that maybe next year I'll start my studies again at the university as an external student. I'm sure I can carry over the pass in English that I got at Sydney University.

Yes, yes, all very good, but will that make you happy, do you think?

Why not? Why shouldn't it? Besides, having a degree will be important as part of my professional development as a teacher.

If you say so.

Anything wrong, Mum?

No, why?

I feel like I'm getting a strange reaction from you, about Jeogla and this study I might undertake.

It's strange having you home after two months, not knowing where you're living or how things have been for you. That's all.

Things have been good. Do I get homesick? Yes, I get homesick. Sometimes I think of home non-stop for hours; then something comes up. I go somewhere, or meet someone – or I see an eagle in the sky or horses grazing on a hillside and my mind goes off into another direction. I have all the time in the world to read poetry, listen to music, try and write poetry. Or just watch the grass grow?

Are you still writing poetry?

Trying to?

Write, write...What will it ever get you or where will it take you? Will it put food on the table or pay your bills?

No, it won't; but that's not the point. We've had this kind of discussion before, Mum. Nothing's changed. I do it because I have to do it – and, in the end, I enjoy it. It's not for money or anything else like that...It is poetry. That's the best I can explain to you.

Well, this is your breakfast. Enjoy it. Even poets have to eat, don't they? Your father and I don't want you to starve because of poetry.

She placed a plate of fried eggs and bacon in front of me – as well as buttered toast, jam, milk and a pot of tea.

Thank you. This is better than any meal I could get in a restaurant.

What are you going to do today?

I'll go up to the church for the three o'clock Good Friday ceremonies. After that, I don't know. I don't really want to go anywhere. Does that sound strange?

Not at all. I don't blame you for wanting to stay at home... How are things going with you and P?

As far as I know, all good. She's gone to the Gold Coast with her parents – but I don't have a phone number for her. Maybe she'll call?

Does she still plan to travel overseas next year?

I think so. She hasn't said that she won't...You know it's always been her plan. She has a sister in Dublin. Why do you ask?

No reason. If she wants to travel, she'll travel. What about you and her? What's the future?

Don't know, Mum. Well just have to work out something when I come home for the May school holidays. Won't be long. About six weeks.

What do you intend doing now?

I thought I'd give Kevin a ring. After that, I thought I'd walk around the block and continue up to the church.

That's a good boy. Don't forget we're going to Mass together on Sunday.

Which Mass? Australian or Polish?

Polish, of course. We can't let that tradition die out.

Even before I asked the question I knew what she'd say.

Chrysalis

The weather was warm. Blue sky. No clouds. Autumn but without a chill.

I walked down the back garden and stood on a bench under the back fence. Looking over the bushland that grew behind our house, I saw Duck Creek with its tall bulrushes, Jensen Oval and the swings and playground that had been my childhood Garden of Eden. Further off, lay Sefton and then Chester Hill – and Virgil Avenue – a suburb I believed, as a child, I could reach out and touch. Instead of the fibro and brick cottages of suburban western Sydney, I saw the paddocks and hills of Jeogla, the scene that lay directly behind the school and formed part of Ron Diamond's property. Were my eyes playing tricks on me? The longer I stood peering into the distance, I heard pewits nearby, Willy-wagtails along the creek and sparrows behind me, in our garden. At the same time I heard crows, rosellas, soldier-birds. I thought I even saw a flock of black cockatoos flying out of nowhere. I blinked, rubbed my eyes and stepped off the bench.

Time to go and ring Kevin. Unfortunately, he wasn't at home but I left a message with his father to say I'd call back later. I wanted to ask him about his school in the inner city and talk about my experiences at Jeogla. I said goodbye to my mother and said I'd return after the service at church.

Instead of taking the shortest route I turned left out of our yard and headed towards the row of factories that had been built in Bellona Avenue, beyond Mary Street and ran parallel to "the pipeline", three huge pipes that carried water from Prospect, in Sydney's far west, to Potts Hill reservoir at Yagoona.

Even though most of the land had been built on, there were still several vacant blocks where paperbarks, eucalypts and prickly scrub grew. These areas were part of the childhood neighbourhood where I grew up with my friends: Johnny, Roger, Christine, Lynette, Kasimir, Charley and Teddy McPhee, the last being the only boy from our group who wasn't a child of "New Australians" – as the Baltic, Slavic and Mediterranean immigrants to Australia after World War II were called.

The only factory that interested me was the one where I worked while I was in my last three years at high school. Greaseproof paper was manufactured at Lion Brand products. Huge rolls of aluminium foil were brought, they were cut to size and packaged. So too was waxed bread wrapping paper. Wrappers were made for Johnson & Johnson Band-aids. At one point, I remember a demonstration been given by a representative from a company promoting glad-wrap. No, said someone from the office, it'll never take off.

The row of pink oleander bushes that screened the factory from the road still existed, growing more densely that when I last saw it. As a boy I discovered that Monarch butterflies spun their cocoons on the underside of the leaves and became what I learnt was a chrysalis. Going on a search to find one was always an adventure, and finding one was like finding a jewel. They hung frail and delicate in the breeze and shone like polished silver or bronze or gold, depending on their maturity and the angle at which the sun's ray hit them. There was always a multitude of colours in them, and it wasn't until I knew what an opal was that I could relate the colours of one with the colours of the other. Bringing one home was inviting disaster. They never survived. Once the leaf was picked and died, so too did the chrysalis.

Walking west into Chisholm Road was like walking through a tip. Both sides of the road were covered in rubbish which people had dumped; weeds had grown up through much of this and no effort had been made by the council to clear it. A pair of strays appeared from out of the bushes, barking and snarling at each other; they ran into one of these piles, scavenged and ran across the road to another pile. They disappeared down the embankment of Duck Creek, itself littered with rubbish. I thought of Wyatts Creek, where I'd drunk water because the day was hot.

Consummatum Est

Along Clapham Road, into Helen Street and over the railway bridge brought me onto the other side of Sefton and there, up the hill, stood the parish church of the Immaculate Heart of Mary: a church and a primary school.

I entered before three o'clock and found the church nearly filled. The service would be long and devout. Lots of prayers and hymns. An elderly couple watched me looking for a place and moved along in the pew.

Thank you, I whispered and knelt down to pray.

You're very welcome, young man, the lady whispered back.

I'd brought my missal and read that the service was called "The Solemn Liturgical Afternoon Service of Our Lord's Passion and Death". Counting ahead, I also found it was twenty-two pages long. From past experiences I remembered some of the ritual that lay ahead, but the part I always liked the best was the reading of the Passion of Our Lord by St John. Long, tiring, but also spiritually moving, it stirred feelings in me like nothing else in the New Testament story. Or maybe it was because I'd heard and read that of all the evangelists St John was the most poetical. There was nothing sadistic in the description of Christ's suffering and death. A narrative that contained the full story from Christ's betrayal by Judas to the burial of Jesus. Succinct. To the point.

Readings from the Psalms and Old Testament occupied the first part of the service. The congregation stood, sat, knelt, prayed, responded. So did the celebrant and altar servers.

Everybody stood for the reading of the Lord's Passion. Here was the centrepiece of the day's worship.

There were words and phrases that always appealed to me... *torrent of Cedron...lanterns and torches and weapons...*

scabbard... ...praetorium...Caesar...place called the Skull... "it is consummated"...The congregation knelt and paused at this point.

As the Gospel continued I thought is was like listening to a fable, a mixture of folklore and mythology, except I knew from my schooling that this story was unique, like no other in the history of the world. I knew that Jesus would die on a cross but would rise from the dead in three days. How could that be? In our Bible history classes we learnt that Jesus was both High Priest and Victim; he allowed all this offering to happen for the salvation of the world.

There was poetry in this story, powerful images, symbols, a text to be written, sacred and untouchable.

The second part of the service was "The Prayer of the Faithful". We prayed for the Church, the Supreme Pontiff, the Needs of the Faithful, Unity of the Church, Civil Authorities, All Orders and Degrees of the Faithful.

The Adoration of the Cross followed. Singing, kneeling, adoring, as piece by piece a covered crucifix was uncovered. At each step the priest would say, "Ecce lignum crucis"... Behold the wood of the cross.

Finally, when the crucified Christ was revealed, it was taken to the altar rails and the congregation, one by one, would approach the altar, genuflect and kiss it.

After more hymn singing, including the "Pange lingua".... Sing O my tongue... Holy Communion was distributed. Many of the congregation went up to the altar, many didn't. I hadn't been to Confession, but decided I was in the state of grace, and I went up. As I did I thought of Jeogla and Wollomombi, and the halls at which Mass was celebrated at a small table, with a handful of people attending. I wondered if this service was being held there, now, or would the Catholics in the district have travelled into Armidale?

I was lost in thought when the last prayers were said. The congregation was standing and responded with "Amen" after each prayer.

The priest and altar boys returned to the sacristy. I knew that the ciborium which held the remaining hosts from Communion would be taken to a designated place. The altar would be stripped. The sanctuary lamp lit.

The service was over; it had taken two hours.

Long Way Home

I felt worn out. All that praying, singing, kneeling, standing. The church service had proved more tiresome than I'd remembered. The last words of Jesus rang in my ears. I could not shake them. *"Consummatum Est"*....

The churchyard was packed with parishioners, standing around and talking, laughing, talking about cups of tea being available in the school hall. Men were smoking and children ran around their parents. Considering Jesus had just died, the atmosphere was anything but devout; if anything, it was celebratory. The direction home was downhill and that made walking easy. Instead of heading back over Sefton station I turned right, towards Birrong. From there, I turned towards Regent Park, over the railway line and pipeline next to the public school.

The intention was the same as when I set out for church, a desire to see as much of the area that I'd left behind two months ago. I gave no thought to specific streets or people that I knew lived in some of the streets and I had an hour at least before dinner would be served. My father would be home by now and probably having his bath. There was satisfaction in knowing that my parents weren't worrying about me – and I had no cause for worry either.

My circuit around the suburbs reminded me of the first walk I took around Armidale and how that affected me; but that was a new city, the streets and people – everything – were a new experience. This was the area where I'd grown up. I saw the train lines and heard the trains even before they appeared. I smelt the food from shops that were closed and the beer from the Regents Park Hotel as I passed along Amy Street, even though it was Good Friday and the hotel was also closed. *Jeogla*, I whispered to myself. *Jeogla*.

Fred Sams, the barber, had his shop almost directly opposite the hotel. Wearing glasses and smoking, he coughed while he cut my hair. In his white barber's coat he looked as much a doctor as a barber. He had three daughters and a beautiful wife, tall, statuesque. I loved listening to Fred talking about his days in Coonabarabran and how hard the fettlers worked to earn a living during the Depression.

A Commonwealth Bank had been opened up on the corner of Amy and Regents Street – on a block of land that was otherwise overgrown with blackberries. Standing on the corner, you got the best view of Amy Street in either direction.

What had changed, I asked myself, in the two months I'd been away? Nothing, that I could see.

Turning around, I walked up Regent Street to my primary school, St Peter Chanel's, on top of the hill. Here, I'd received my first education in Sydney at the hands of the Sisters of St Joseph. For a while, my mother worked for the nuns, as a cleaning, washing and ironing lady. Most of the nuns were Irish immigrants, and they were uncompromising educators, good at instilling the 3 Rs but also quick with corporal punishment, the cane or the ruler and even knuckles into shoulders and back. The parish priest was Father Cornelius Donovan, also from Ireland, a big man with red hair and an aquiline nose, who was respected by one and all. Good at religious, social and financial organizations within the parish, he became a legend in his own time.

I don't go into the schoolyard but stand at the gates like someone who is lost. What good would walking through the yard do? Buildings have been added since I left in 1955 and the only two I recognise are the convent and the main building which also served as a church. Wooden and glass partitions would be folded back on a Friday afternoon and the classrooms became a church.

Looking over the suburb, towards Berala, it's not Berala that I see but myself on the Sloggett property, looking east to Lex McCrae's farm. There must be something wrong with my eyes. I've travelled from New England to Sydney, but my eyes still see something I wanted to have a rest from seeing. The Sloggett family's faces appear like apparitions in the darkening light. They are watching me. A shivery feeling passes through me and I pause a moment to stay with them, welcoming them, as it were, to my part of the world. I want to say, *See, here's my old school.* Instead, I hear myself blurting out, What are you all doing here? As I do, they vanish.

You okay, pal?

A man is standing behind me, watching me.

I'm fine, I say, and start to move off.

Thought you might be havin' a spell or some such thing. You look like you've seen a ghost.

I have, I say laughingly and walk away.

Fruitcake, I hear him say.

Turning around, and right into Kent Street brings me up to the track that runs along the railway line, a popular shortcut to avoid going across Guilfoyle Park and the shopping centre. A footbridge over the line takes me to Park Road, opposite Babcock & Wilcox, an engineering firm. The road has become increasingly popular as more and more of the vacant land is being bought up and slowly turned into an industrial estate. Clydesdales once belonging to Smeaton & Campbell, bakers, grazed in a vacant allotment that still belongs to the Railways and where bunkers from World War II exist under mounds of earth, overgrown with weeds, creating a pastoralist scene. Steam trains used to stop here and fill up with water from a tower that stands like a relic, empty and useless.

The chill of late-afternoon wrap itself around my head and I start to hurry, past a row of ten shops on our side of Regents Park. The corner shop is a fish-and-chips and the smell of hot chips makes me hungry. After all, it is Good Friday, and a piece of fish would be nice. Again, images of Jeogla come into my head.

Nick, the Greek owner, greets me. Ah-ha, you come for fish today? How come I not see you for long time?

Yes, a piece of fish, please, I say, and watch him drop it, already battered, into the bubbling dripping. It hisses as he pushes it under. No chips? he asks.

No, thanks. Just the fish. I explain that I've been away, teaching in the country.

Why in country? Plenty schools in Sydney. Hey, you come back. We like you here.

He barely speaks two sentences to me whenever I've come in before. He walks around, head lowered, deep in thought or pain. He always reminds me of Atlas, the weight of the world on his shoulders. Now he's become a friend, concerned about my absence.

Well, yes, maybe, soon. I can't stand having to explain what I don't want to explain about signing bonds for the Education Department and three years' obligatory service to where I've been sent.

Okay, fish ready, he says. I watch him pull out my meal with a pair of tongs and place it on a draining grill above the bubbling fat, then, before wrapping it on a sheet of butcher-shop paper and a few sheets of newspaper, he asks, Salt? Okay? And I give you piece of lemon. Nice food for Good Friday. Jesus will die on Cross.

It's past three o'clock. Jesus is already dead. I pay him and say, Goodbye, Nick. See you next time.

I pray for you, he says.

When?

When I go to church.

Not today?

No – me Orthodox.

I'm cold now, walking home over the pipeline bridge, eating my piece of hot fish, licking my fingers and thinking how good it tastes. Chips would have been good, but if I eat too much now I won't eat my mother's dinner.

*

As soon as I enter the house my mother asks, What have you been eating?

A piece of fish I bought at Nick's. The dog is standing beside me and licking my fingers. I've thrown the paper into the bin.

Where's Dad? I ask.

Having a bath. He worked in the garden after returning from work. Now he needs to rest. Where did you go? she asks.

After church I walked around the suburbs...You know, up to the shops, my old school...

And what did you find?

Nothing.

Did that upset you?

No....I didn't expect to find anything.

So why did you go?

Just wanted to.

Are you missing Jeogla?

Sort of...It's hard to explain...

Don't bother. As long as you're happy.

I am happy, Mum, but I...I keep seeing pictures of Jeogla in my mind and I think I can reach out and touch a tree – like the one growing outside my window where I sleep. At night, Willy-wagtails sing in it. They're drawn by the light from my window or if it's a full moon.

You can't learn that in Sydney?

Yes, I can – but I haven't. That's the point.

Ah, here's your father. Go and wash up. Dinner won't be long. Oh yes, before I forget to tell you, Kevin rang. He's coming around tomorrow.

Swapping Stories.

After dinner I sit with my parents and watch the ABC News. They never miss it and swear by James Dibble. He reads the news, so it must be true. My parents think he's a gentleman. I should grow up and be like him. I avoid going down this path of argument with my mother. Her mind's made up. I doubt if even God could persuade her to think otherwise.

I never asked you, she says, How was church?

A very holy service, but that ceremony is too long. The church should shorten it.

You must learn to put up with little problems like that, she says. Do it for God. Christ is now lying in the tomb. Remember that and be respectful.

Tell us more about the place you live, Peter, my father asks.

So I tell them what I've already told them in my letters home, trying, as I do, to be as enthusiastic as I can be. Geographical location, farms, animals, weather, people. I recount the afternoon of going to Wyatts Creeks with Ron Diamond and feeding the pigs, Lex McCrae's horses, the cemetery at Kilcoy, Alex and Jill...even Cassie their dog. By now the names are rolling off my tongue...Wollomombi, Armidale, Oaky River, places that I intend visiting, Uralla, Point Lookout...Styx River...

I sense that my father is impressed when I talk about farming, horses, sheep, cattle, although he still refers to them all as "cows". They are both impressed when I describe Mrs Sloggett's cow, Peggy, and how much milk she gives every day. Mrs Sloggett's up with the first rays of the sun to do the milking, and returned before I'm out of bed. A few times I've heard her walking past my bedroom to go to where Peggy is kept, then the return trip, not long afterwards. Mrs Sloggett wears gumboots, I can tell from the sound of her footsteps. My boarding place is not really a farm, I repeatedly tell them, but a small holding surrounded by big properties. It's too cold to grow grain and crops of any sort, but the whole of New England is rich in cattle, sheep, timber and mining, a new industry that will become even bigger. So I tell them, that's what the locals tell me.

We talk a while longer and then I tell them about the plane flight and how exciting it was, but I don't mention the storm and how people became sick on board. I describe how the city looked laid out at night, the lights shining like jewels. I say I can't wait for the return flight, hoping it won't be a bumpy ride.

My father tells me he has started work at a new Water Board site in the Warwick Farm area, not far from Liverpool and Green Valley where he's been for the last couple of years. He's still a pipe-layer, officially, as the terminology goes, but his kind of employment is referred to commonly as a pick-and-shovel man; it's hard, manual labour, but he never complains. It's work, it brings in money, and the money pays the bills and has helped to pay off the mortgage on the house. My mother's work as a cleaning lady and "domestic" for various families in the Strathfield area has also contributed.

*

Time has slipped away from us. The evening is colder. The volume on the television set was turned down so we could talk. We are yawning and say goodnight. The dog is let outside and he'll sleep in the laundry where he has a bed.

The lights are all switched off in the house and I lie in the darkness, noticing how differently I felt last night, as the effects of the travel quickly put me to sleep. Tonight, it's not so easy, although I yawn, and feel sleep tugging at my eyelids, trying to close them; but it's inside my head that the problem lies, not in my eyes.

I'm back at Wyatts Creek with Ron and we're feeding the pigs. We finish the task, but the animals keep squealing and pushing their bodies against the rails of the pens that contain them, sows and piglets alike. They have been fed but that is not enough. Each of the sows is massive and, unexpectedly, the rails start to crack. More shoving, lurching and grunting and the sows have succeeded in freeing themselves and their litters. Before we know it, Ron and I are pushed onto our backs, fearing for our lives, trying to fend off the oncoming attack. The muck in the pens is putrid, a nauseating smell that makes me retch. Ron is trying to turn away, to reach for something that he can use to defend us. Before we know it the sows have trampled us.They stand over us and begin to tear into our flesh, bodies, arms, faces legs. Blood is running from our bodies, all over the floor and into their mouths. Chunks of flesh are torn out and gobbled. The pigs are enjoying themselves while we are dying. Their squealing is that of joy, delight, happiness because they have triumphed over the humans. I swear that I can hear words. *Ha-Ha. How does that feel? The shoe's on the other foot. Take that, you murderers!*

My parents rush into my bedroom. The light's switched on. Wake up, they cry. You're having a nightmare!

It takes me several minutes to compose myself and tell them I thought I was getting eaten alive by pigs!

Goodness me, says my mother. I've never heard of that nightmare before…Here, have a drink of water, It'll help clear your head. Whatever were you thinking to bring that on?

I was trying to get to sleep, but I must have already fallen asleep. Those pigs were awful, tearing me and Ron Diamond to pieces like we were cabbages – and they were enjoying themselves. They could speak, do you believe that? They could speak!

There, there, says my father. We'll turn off the light. Just settle down and don't push yourself trying to get back to sleep. Let it come naturally.

It's your imagination, my mother says. All that

poetry writing and reading books you do. It's not good – overworking your brain like you do.

*

Kevin and I sit on the back steps, swapping stories, talking about our respective first postings, and what we thought of them.

I said I was still surprised, totally unprepared to be sent to a one-teacher school in the bush. Honestly, they could have sent me to the moon and I couldn't have been more shocked.

Kevin laughed and lot and this brought on a real uproar. What about me? A school that's been declared a disaster area by one of the churches? I'm doing charity work by turning up each day.

You're doing God's own work, I said.

I told him about the encounter with the black snake and how I thought the plane would crash on take-off from Armidale.

I bet your mum was shocked, he said.

I never told her, I replied. Did anyone else from our section get a small school posting?

No, as far as I know you were the only one.

Huh! I wonder why?

Because they thought you're handsome and would sweep all the farmers' daughters off their feet.

There are no farmers daughter at Jeogla, Kev – only those that go to school and those that are married.

So, what's there?

Much as I've told you. Nothing; but there's the sky and forests, and hills and paddocks and gorges and waterfalls, bird life like you wouldn't believe, there're horses and cattle and sheep. The night sky is a palette of jewelled colours, icy and frozen, on an icy black canvas…You get the feeling you could reach up and touch the Milky Way... The silences are deafening…And there's rain, lots of it…

So what's it all do to you?

Don't know…I suppose it takes me into myself and out again? Creates a state of mind – or soul – or whatever you want to call it. It takes emotions from one end of the spectrum to the other.

Gee, that sounds special.

Is it? It's like trying to explain God. In the end, you can't, but you live with it and it repays you. A stiletto that pierces your heart but allows you to live…Anyway, how're things with you and Kerry?

Really good; we go out and we're very happy.

I say that P and I are still serious but she's gone to Queensland with her parents and didn't even leave a phone number. Don't know more than that Kev.

Why don't you invite her up to Jeogla? She could stay at Mrs Sloggett's.

And what? Cause a scandal that'll get me sent back to Sydney or – worse still –

Tibooburra.

Why do you always think of the worst possible outcome?

Hey, that's not you doing penance for your sins up in New England. You're in Sydney, remember, having the time of your life – while I'm counting sheep that leap gullies and cattle stopping at a grid.

Are you staying for lunch, Kevin? My mother has come out and stands in front of us, hands on hips, smiling benevolently at her son and his friend whom she 's always regarded as a distant son – and who she thought, was destined for greater things than her own son. After all, Kevin's father is a bank manager, a much respected man of the community, and Kevin, no doubt, has the right breeding to climb to the pinnacle of professional success.

Oh, said Kevin, blinking like a calf that's had a bunch of daisies passed before its eyes. What are we having?

Fish, my mother replied. Redfish. I caught the bus to Auburn and went to that excellent fish ship – you know the one, Peter, don't you, opposite the railways station, in the main road – the one that sells fresh fish? And I chose the pieces myself. I'm doing them in batter.

Yes, please, said Kevin. What else are we having?

Potatoes and beans. We grew them ourselves.

Yummy, said Kevin, rubbing his stomach with his hand. Can't wait, Mrs Skrzynecki. Thank you.

What a nice boy, my mother said, as she returned to the kitchen.

A short time afterwards my father came in from the garage where he'd been sharpening his knives and axes.

We all sit around the table in the kitchen and eat redfish and vegetables. Kevin asks for seconds, as I knew he would, and tells my parents all about his posting to a school where the children are poor, where there are many single parents and alcoholic fathers. He says the only time they get presents in their lives is when Santa Claus brings them.

My mother proceeded to tell me that maybe, after all, my school at Jeogla wasn't so bad. At least all have parents and they go home to a good meal. Don't they?

Yes, they do, I said.

My father asked, So Peter's posting was decided by Fate?

I don't know, Kevin said, but someone has to accept these appointments. Children have to be schooled and teachers must be sent to schools.

We talk about children and families, about the blessings of Easter and how lucky we were to have come to Australia. I still reckoned I would have preferred to have stayed in Sydney, but at the same time I kept thinking about the Oaky River and the view I had whenever I stopped my car on the bridge. I remembered the first time I heard black cockatoos flying over the river and how disturbing the sound had been – as if an invisible door had been opened up somewhere, in a foreign landscape, and my flesh had been torn in that moment.

Gee, your cooking's great, Mum, I said, turning my mind away from water and black cockatoos.

*

After lunch Kevin and I decided that before I flew back to New England we'd go to the pictures; the trouble was that I didn't have a car and he said he'd come over and fetch me. Or, I could catch a train to Bankstown and we could go to the pictures there. Bankstown has three picture theatres and there was sure to be something showing that we'd enjoy.

Okay, call me on Monday morning and we'll make it definite. I don't care where we go, Bankstown or Auburn.

I saw him off, and returned to my room. There were poems that I wanted to read over, especially the last few from Jeogla. I hadn't written anything new since my poem about Wyatts Creek, and hoped that Ron or his family would like it someday if it was published. As I watched my father moving around the house and yard, doing jobs in the garden or the chook shed, I thought how he resembled Ron and Ron resembled him. Both were thin, wiry men, and both smoked. One had been a prisoner of the Germans in Europe, the other had fought in World War II in the Middle East and in New Guinea.

Both were men of the land. Each, in his own way, is a survivor.

Alleluia

The word that I've always associated with Easter is "Alleluia" and everything it stands for. Easter bunny. Easter eggs. School holidays. Going to church. Easter. The Risen Lord. One of the most significant events in the Catholic Church's liturgical calendar, the other being Christmas. Alleluia! Praise God!

We attended Mass at St Felix's Catholic Church in Bankstown, on Chapel Road, opposite the Three Swallows Hotel. A midday Mass. Celebrated in Polish.

The church was packed with young and old, children, parents, grandparents, families who had known each other most of their lives, a congregation that extolled the virtues of their faith in prayers, responses and hymn-singing. Worship of the very finest, liturgically and communally. This band of brothers and sisters and their offspring had survived World War II, migrated to Australia and continued to pray for the return of the Motherland from the rule of Communism. They prayed to God through the intercession of the Supreme Pontiff and, especially, through Our Lady of Czestochowa, the Black Madonna, Patroness of Poland. Just as the Risen Lord triumphed over Satan, so too, the Catholic Church would be victorious over Communism.

After Mass, the congregation milled inside the grounds of the church just as they did in our parish church of the Immaculate Heart of Mary. Men lit up, smoked, talked of work and how good it was to be having a holiday. Theirs was a different camaraderie to that of the women folk. Women showed off their finest Sunday clothes, furs included, gloves and hats, watches and bracelets, summoned children to their sides so their compatriots could see how were blossoming as they grew up in Australia. I was presented more than once, told to be patient whenever I wanted to work myself through the groups, while my mother proudly told her friends that I had become a teacher and had a school entrusted to my care in my very first year of teaching.

In the country, too, my mother added. Among farmers of great prosperity. In an area of New South Wales called New England.

You must be so proud? a lady asked my mother.

Yes, I am, said my mother.

You must be very competent? a man asked me.

I shrugged my shoulders, smiled, and walked away.

Arrangements had been made for us to go to a home in Edwin Street, off Chapel Road, at the southern end, for lunch. five or six families, all Polish, or a mixture of Polish/Ukrainian and Russian. This would be like old time's sake, when I was growing up, being taken to a gathering that would go on until evening; men would get drunk, they'd sing and argue; women would concern themselves with cooking and feeding the children, except, now, the children had grown up and become young adults themselves.

I wished that I was back in Jeogla, but said nothing

The Grabowskis are going to give us a lift to Edwin Street, my father said. As he spoke, a white Valiant came speeding into the church yard, screeching to a halt. I knew the driver would be Chester, son of the Grabowskis, also an only child. He'd skipped Mass, but returned to drive his parents.

Pile in, folks, Chester urged. It's not far to go. Six of us squeezed in.

Chester drove as if he was being pursued by devils. Fast. Slamming on brakes. Screeching to a stop. Around corners. Accelerating so fast we were pushed back into our seats.

His parents said nothing.

We arrived at our destination. See, he laughed. That didn't take long.

Are you coming in, son? Mr Grabowski asked.

Nah, sorry. I've got a date. He winked at me and said, You know what it's like. Can't keep a young lady waiting.

I smiled and nodded, feeling queasy.

We made our way into the home we were visiting, as the sound of Chester's car accelerated towards the district hospital, disappearing around a corner.

Why is he in such a hurry? my mother asked.

He's not in a hurry, Chester's mother replied. He's always drives like an idiot.

One by one the other families arrived, couples and those with younger children. There was no one my age. I sat with the men while they drank and then we all filed indoors, to a sumptuous meal, prepared with love and care: European food, that included beetroot soup, cabbage rolls, dumplings, roast beef, sliced *kielbasa* on plates, various hams, potatoes, peas, red cabbage. The mixture of smells came from the kitchen long before food was brought out. They made my mouth water. I was ravenous. Grace was said most solemnly by the head of the family in whose house we were guests. Then we sat down to eat, drink, talk, laugh, reminisce and cry.

By six o'clock the afternoon's feast was finishing, the group breaking up, returning home. Speech was slurred, high-pitched, teary. Men were drunk or on the point of being drunk. Women laughed shrilly. The house was full of cigarette smoke. A man was playing a piano accordion on the back veranda. His songs were melancholy. His voice baritone. One day he would return and free the Homeland. Over and over, the same song. Soldiers were marching off to war. Bombs were falling. Above the celebrations, in our hearts and minds, the White Eagle – emblem of Poland – soared in triumph above the Communist Hammer and Sickle. More than once during the afternoon I thought of my small school standing like an isolate on the Kempsey Road. What was the weather like in Jeogla? How many relatives had come out from Armidale or over from the North Coast, and were enjoying Carrie's cooking?

The Grabowskis offered to give us a lift with Chester who

was coming to collect them, some time before midnight.

No thank you, my mother replied, almost spitting out the words. We will end up on top of an electricity pole, not in our warm beds.

I walked back with my parents to Bankstown railway station, uphill, and we sat for an hour on the semi-dark platform before catching the train to Regents Park. My father was not drunk but neither was he fully sober. He was happy, giggling a lot. My mother was teary but joyful, glad she and my father had reconnected with people they'd met on the boat coming out from Europe. As we travelled in the train, I tried to see my parents objectively, as an outsider might, but couldn't.

We returned after nine o'clock, to be greeted by the dog, barking with delight and wagging his tail madly.

As we stepped into the house, I said, Alleluia.

*

On Monday, Kevin and I went to the pictures at Auburn to see a rerun of "Thunderball" and on Tuesday morning I booked a taxi for noon; it would take an hour to get to the airport and my flight was leaving at 3 o'clock.

An uneasy morning, with my parents showing their regret at my having to leave, the dog sensing something was going to change from the routines of the past few days.

I couldn't sit still for five minutes, telling myself that I was returning to another kind of "home", a different "family" – and the freedom of having time on my hands for writing and reading.

I'll be back in May, I kept repeating to my parents.

Have you packed? my mother asked.

Ages ago, Mum. It's all done except for my bag sitting at the front door.

Please continue to show common sense in everything, Peter, my father said. Drive carefully at all times.

Not like Chester.

No, especially not like Chester.

When you're returning in May, make sure you get plenty of rest the night before. That won't be an hour trip in an aeroplane.

Yes, Dad. I hear what you and Mum are saying.

So, before you go, my mother said, pack these sandwiches I made for you.

I'll carrying them in my hand luggage. I can eat them at the airport or on the plane, I said with a big smile on my face. I'll also phone you from Armidale as soon as I arrive.

And don't forget to pray – and go to Mass whenever you are able. Don't forget God or the religion you were baptised into.

The taxi arrived. We hugged and kissed, said our goodbyes. My mother was crying and my father held back his emotions. The dog kept looking up at me, wagging his tail, waiting for an explanation. I bent down and hugged him. Be good, I said.

I'll make another cake and send it for your birthday, my mother said through her tears.

Another departure.

⁕

I walk to the taxi without looking back. The scent of flowers makes me think of a perfume shop.

I stop trying to recognise suburbs I don't know. We drive in silence. The taxi driver strikes up a conversation, but I answer only with a "yes" or a "no". He quickly realises I don't want to have a conversation, and stops talking to me.

The taxi smells of cigarette smoke.

The day is bright.

IV

Awesome

Flying back to Armidale via Tamworth was an awesome experience. What I failed to see at night on the way down to Sydney, I saw in detail, on the return flight. Once again I was on the left side of the plane and saw the inland New South Wales.

I saw the curvature of the earth.

The different shades of green, the browns, the khakis, townships, villages farms, paddocks laid out in patchwork colours, forests, rivers, creeks, dams, cattle, sheep. From the window seat again I tried to retain as much of the scenery as I could; it was like committing a series of photographs to memory. The imagery became more stunning when the aircraft levelled out above the clouds, passing into a silver-blue sky; it was like were flying into a different world, into a different time zone, heading for an invisible horizon.

Too easy to say the view below resembled an endless field of cotton, lit up by the sun, only just starting to descend, its colour more silver than gold. I had never seen such a view in my life. Paddocks, oceans, mountains stretching into the distance, yes, but nothing like this view. Pity we would have to descend, leave it behind and return to something ordinary, even though the distances below were anything but ordinary on the climb through the clouds once we left the Sydney Basin.

Only a handful of passengers left the flight at Tamworth but more boarded and the plane was full. Once we were airborne, the light outside darkened. We were travelling below dark clouds. Rain started. With the sun behind us, the brilliance of the sky dissolved into a grey pall, and the mountains below resembled spectres, rushing, looming up to meet us, then disappearing into the formations of a landscape to which they already belonged.

⁕

I couldn't see Alex in Arrivals. After collecting my baggage I waited outside the terminal, unsure of what to do next. I didn't have the telephone number of the manse in Wollomombi, and a taxi out to Jeogla would cost the earth plus more. Darkness had started to settle over New England. A light rain was falling.

I was standing alone, and I began to speak to the sky, under my breath, unable to contain both my joy and resentment. I'm so happy to be back– but you can't help yourself, can you? You send me another rainy welcome.

A voice in my head answered, It's a state of mind. Try to live in it – and even if you don't want to, you will.

I realised this was a similar conversation that I had with the Wyatts Creek poem the night I wrote it.

Was New England controlling my thoughts?

Before I could reply, I heard a voice coming from the car park. It was Alex, Hey, mate, sorry I'm late.

He came running up, out of the rain, stepping under cover to where I was standing.

How was your flight? he asked, shaking hands with me.

Awesome, I replied.

A Lifetime into Less than an Hour

I was as interested in what'd happened at Jeogla, while I was away, as Alex was keen to hear what I'd done Sydney, so that, when either of us spoke, it was as if we were trying to cram a lifetime of experiences into less than an hour, the time it would take before we arrived at Wollomombi.

He smoked in the car and it made my eyes water.

I'll put it out, mate, he'd say. Just one more puff.

No, I'm fine.

Okay, just this last one. Promise.

Many of the locals whom I knew at Jeogla had come to Alex's Easter service at Wollomombi, he told me. A beautiful service, earnest in its prayers and deliverance of hymns. My parents and Jill's came up from Sydney. They will all be going back tomorrow, then it'll be just me and Jill and dear old Cassie.

The rain fell straight at the windscreen and then would fall away, as if it, too, wanted to hear our conversation. The slap-slapping of windscreen wipers reminded me of a pair of eavesdroppers who wanted to add their own contribution to our conversation. The weather was much the same as when Alex drove me to the airport. Rain. On. Off.

I wanted to tell him about the restlessness I felt when I first arrived home, about the need to walk around my suburb and the dream I had about Ron and me getting eaten by pigs. What would a man of God make of that dream? That was too hard to go into, too full of emotions I felt were highly personal. The grossness of the imagery, the pain and the tears it produced. None of it eligible criteria for a warm welcome home. In a car that had become suffocatingly hot, and being pummelled by rain that offered a cool relief outside.

Would Alex stop the car, I thought, if I asked him to? So I could wind down the window and get some fresh air. We could park off the road in any number of places, in rest areas, under trees; but I said nothing because it wasn't my car, and he might feel offended.

You've got to learn to relax more, mate, Alex said. Try not to let things get to you.

Have you seen Ron?

I have. He came with his family to the service. Didn't say much, but that's his style. We talked about the Anzac service coming up soon. It's held at Wollomombi. At the flagpole outside the church. You'll come with the Jeogla school kids – and you'll have the kids from Wollomombi. Nothing fancy. You represent the Education Department.

I remembered the earlier conversation we'd had about Anzac Day. I said nothing but thought of my mother's brother and the coloured portrait she kept at home: my mother and her mother, on either side of a shy-looking young man, his hair combed back, wearing an embroidered shirt, the kind I had never seen men wearing in Australia. My mother carried the portrait with her when she left the Ukraine for Germany before the outbreak of World War Two. When we migrated to Australia she bought it with her.

Ah, come on, snap out of it. Whatever you're thinking about, remember where you are and why you're here.

Was it Alex speaking?I could have sworn it was that other voice, the voice of New England that now seemed to be living in my head.

As we neared our destination I thought how much territory our conversation had covered. Past, present, future, eclipsed into the time it took to drive in the rain from Armidale airport to a small village further to the east.

At the manse in Wollomombi I met Jill's parents, Alf and Joy, and Alex's parents, Margaret and Alex. All from Sydney.

Alex's parents talked about their migration from Kilmarnock in Scotland to Australia, and their pride in having a son who accepted a calling to the Ministry of God.

Jill's parents spoke less but listened more, while Alex lit up another cigarette and told us that, as a young man, he was only interested in running with the boys and having a good time.

Now, you're running for God, son, Alex senior replied. Carrying God's banner.

With our daughter by his side, Alf added, laughed softly, modestly, and fell into silence.

And a lovely girl she is, said Joy. Always has been. Wouldn't harm a fly. Would you, love?

Aye, said Margaret. She is a bonny lass.

Jill sipped her tea, said nothing, and looked into the cup's depths.

I finished my tea and said I must go. Carrie would no doubt be waiting with dinner.

I'll see you out, Peter, said Alex. Come on, Cassie.

I said goodbye to the visitors from Sydney and hoped we might meet again.

Once outside, Cassie bounded out of sight, into a paddock, her black head visible above the grasses, woofing with delight.

My car started. I thanked Alex for all the trouble he'd gone to.

Ah, mate, I understand a bit of what you're about. You'd do the same for me, wouldn't you?

Of course.

Okay. See you.

I waved goodbye, reversed my car and drove uphill, towards the main road, into a light rain. My baggage safe in the boot, my car running smoothly, I felt at ease, knowing that a meal was waiting for me, plus a conversation with the Sloggetts, and a warm bed.

If the feeling of flying above the clouds was awesome, so was the feeling of stopping on the bridge over the Oaky River.

I had arrived at one of my favourite places at Jeogla.

There was comfort knowing that a river flowed beneath me.

I waited for night sounds, birds, crickets, frogs to filter into the car, but I only heard the sound of rain falling onto my car. I was surrounded by a feeling of familiarity, warmth. Sitting in my car, like this, waiting for the arrival of a voice. Not feeling disappointed, however, when it did not eventuate.

Bookcase

The Sloggets had eaten by the time I arrived, and it was dark. I parked my car at the side gate and knocked on the front door.

I'm home, I said, as I heard someone coming to the front door and opening it.

Carrie stood there, a grin from ear to ear. Thought you'd got lost. Have yer had dinner?

No, just a cup of tea at the manse.

Come in. Get warm.

Granma was in her usual place, watching TV. I smiled and nodded to her. She did the same.

Elmo and Gerald were washing up in the kitchen; they stuck their heads around the corner and said hello.

Why don't you go an' freshen up first,Carrie said.

Good idea, I said.

As soon as I turned on the light in my room, I was surprised by the sight of a bookcase in the far left corner. The Sloggets had put a bookcase in while I was away.

I came straight back into the kitchen and said, Thank you, thank you. What a great surprise.

Do you like it? Carrie asked. It was Elmo's idea. You can take yer books out of them boxes and even put yer little record player on the top.

Thanks, Elmo.

You are welcome, he replied.

Wow! I said again, trying to express my gratitude. Just go and have a quick freshen up. Okay? Only be a minute.

I returned and sat in my usual place while Carrie took out a plate of food from the oven. Been keepin' this warm for you. I knew you'd be hungry. So, how was Easter?

Pretty good, I said, and felt good about saying it. Not much happened. What about here? I asked. Did you have many guests?

Enough. We had relatives from town and from the coast, didn't we, Elmo? Place was full on Sunday fer lunch. I did a leg o' lamb, a potato bake, vegies, custard an' ice cream for the kiddies. We had a feast. What about you?

My parents and I went to Mass and then to a friend's place for lunch. Got home late because we didn't have the car. Travelled by train to get home. Yesterday I went to the pictures with mate called Kevin. He's a teacher too – but he got an appointment in the city. You could call him lucky.

Elmo said, I reckon you're pretty lucky also. He gave me a stare to emphasise the point, continuing to wipe a saucepan.

Are yer changin' yer mind about likin' to live here?

No, of course not. Why would you ask that?

Me an' Elmo thought that before you went to Sydney, well, we thought you was startin' to like Jeogla a bit more.

Yes, I was, and nothing's changed the way I feel.

Kids'll be happy ter have yer back.

How come, I asked?

I was talkin' ter some of the mothers at church – and they all reckon what a great teacher you've been to them kiddies. They reckon they couldn't've asked fer a better teacher.

That's kind of them, I said.

They said all those other subjects you do – like poetry an' art an' handicraft makes their kiddies really happy.

I suppose that's something.

I ate in silence and they watched, even Elmo and Gerald when they finished washing up and wiping. Carrie handed them my plate and cutlery and they washed and wiped those also.

Grandma came through to the kitchen, nodded and said softly "Goodnight", then she went off to the bathroom, preparing, as she always did, to go to bed.

We talked for a short while longer and, one by one, took our leave from the kitchen.

After returning from the bathroom and having a wash

I thanked Elmo and Carrie for the bookcase again. Gerald had gone to his room, with his customary "hoo- roo" to everyone as he closed the door behind him on the landing.

In my room I unpacked my bags from the trip and got ready for bed. A series of images ran through my head, right from the plane's take-off and that silver brilliance that came from flying above the clouds. I remembered my parents and our goodbye. I remembered going with Kevin to the pictures, as well as the blue of the Bahamas in "Thunderball". What was it about colour? How dull the world would be without it. I remembered sitting in the car on the Oaky Bridge, reassured that a river was flowing under it. The river that was black at night; but in the morning would be green or grey or blue.

As tired as I was, and trying to sleep, the knowledge that the bookcase was in the room prevented me from sleeping. I turned on the light and, as quietly as I could, started unpacking my books and records, hoping I wouldn't wake the Sloggets. Two or three times I dropped a book, its thud like the sound of a toe stubbing. Sorry, I whispered to no one.

But it didn't take long to unpack the boxes that now sat in an adjacent corner emptied of books and their words and pictures, and vinyl discs, 7" singles and EPs, as well as 12" LPs, their music waiting to be released by the small turntable that needed an extension cord and double adaptor before I could plug it into the single power point I had in the room.

Two Big Events

Ron was waiting for me when I drove up to the school in the morning.

How was Sydney? he asked. He stood in the same paddock where I had my confrontation with Ullum, leaning on the top strand of fencing wire, hat back on his head, drawing on a cigarette.

Sydney or the little I saw of it was fine. My parents are in good health. Alex tells me it was a fine Easter service in Wollomombi.

He had something on his mind, I could tell and, as if he'd read my mind, he came straight out with it. Anzac Day, have you forgotten what we talked about?

No.

That's good. Make sure you don't. It falls on a Tuesday and it's a public holiday. That's the first thing to remind you about.

And the second?

Four days later we'll be having the referendum on the New State. That's really a big issue around these parts.

And?

You and Lex will be running the show here at the school. How do you feel about working with him?

I don't think he thinks much of me, to tell you the truth.

He's like that…He's an old bloke and very much set in his ways. You leave him to me. I'll have a talk to him if necessary. Ah, don't worry about a thing, she'll be apples…

Suzie, whom I'd been pretending didn't exist up that point ran under the bottom strand of the fence and ran to play among the school children, most of whom had arrived by that stage.

I'd better be going, Ron, I said, I've got to put up some work on the blackboard. At this rate nothing will get done.

You're the best public relations person the Education

Department could've sent us, you know, don't you?

No. Why?

You work too hard – and you worry too much. If you were working in a factory or in a shop some people might say you were trying to show them up.

That's why I'm here. That's what I'm being paid to do. Work hard. Besides, I like my job, crazy as that sometimes sounds. If I hadn't been appointed to Jeogla I would be crawling to work in my car in Sydney traffic, and I would never have seen what I saw above the clouds yesterday.

And what was that?

I saw myself in a place that I'd never been in before. Looking at clouds that were like snow. The light was golden as…

Wattles?

Sort of...

Never can tell, can you? He was staring above the roof of the school, to where I knew the uneven line of the tops of trees was visible. A truck roared past, going to the mill somewhere deep in the heart of the forest, where I'd been told there was a forestry camp, and men doing the same kind of work that Elmo did at Nowendoc.

Before I could answer a group of children came running up, followed by Suzie, yapping her little head off.

Come on, Suzie, teacher here has work to do.

The little dog squeezed under the fence and was gone, ahead of Ron, leaping happily into the air as she did, like she'd been let off a chain.

Oh Suzie, you silly sausage, Ron laughed. Just who are you trying to impress?

Miss Enid Isaacs

By now the whole school had arrived and lined up, even before I had unlocked the door. Assembly had become a formality, and after a short welcome-back-to school speech the children filed in.

We talked about the Easter holidays, where some families went, and whom they visited. Some travelled to Tenterfield, Khancoban and Coffs Harbour; others stayed at home. There was a willingness to talk and share ideas that contrasted with my arrival on the first day of school. The eyeing with suspicion of the newcomer into the district was not there. "Sir" had become part of the Jeogla "family" and was approached in a casual but not-too familiar manner.

Sir, Roslyn Turner asked, we were wondering, at home. what your name means? My parents said I could ask you.

A surprise question. I told her it was Polish and was a carpentry term; it referred to someone who worked in timber or wood, like a cabinet maker or a crate maker.

While were talking a car pulled up and a lady walked down the footpath to the door. She was carrying a large rectangular box. The children started looking around in expectation and whispering. They knew who she was..

She knocked on the door and I went out to greet her.

I'm so sorry I hadn't come out earlier. My name is Enid Isaacs and I'm the librarian at the city library in town… Welcome to Jeogla…I hope your appointment is a happy one. She was still holding the wooden box. Do you mind if I put this down?

I introduced myself. Here, let me take it from you? Please, come in.

A shortish woman with greying hair, she wore glasses and had a beautiful smile. As we walked past the blue cupboard, she said, I hear you're a lover of poetry.

Another surprise! I am.

And you teach it to the children?

I do.

Excellent. They need more of that sort of thing. I'm so glad to have met you. I love poetry. And I also like the works of Jane Austen. Do you like her writing?

No.

Oh?

As we entered the schoolroom, the children stood up, showing signs of recognition, smiling, a little nervous, as if an absent aunt had appeared out of the past and was standing in front of them.

I put down the box, and introduced Miss Isaacs.

Good morning, Miss Isaacs, they replied.

She laughed, Good morning, children. Do you remember me?

Yes, Miss Isaacs, most said.

Please, sit down. Now, seeing that you have a new teacher, should we tell him why I'm here?

To bring new books for us to read, Christine Frizell replied.

That's right. Every term I'll bring a new box and take away the old ones…And of course, you're all welcome to come to the library when you're in town – and you can borrow more books. Those who haven't joined yet, remember, it's never too late. Has anyone joined the library recently?

Not a hand went up.

Well, never mind, Miss Isaacs said stoically. You can anytime, alright? Any questions?

Nobody replied.

Miss Isaacs looked at me, and sighed. I must be off.

Can't I offer you a cup of tea? I asked.

No thanks…Two other schools must be visited by lunch time and then back to the office.

Two other schools? I asked.

Jeogla is the furthest on my itinerary this morning. On the way back I'll visit Chandler and then Hillgrove. Goodbye, children.

At the door, I shook hands.

Why don't you like Jane Austen? she asked.

I had to study *Emma* at university, I said.

So?

I found it a boring book.

So, if I may ask, what is your favourite novel?

In the moderns, I said, *A Portrait of the Artist as a Young Man* and probably *Sons and Lovers.*

And in the Classics? she asked.

Treasure Island and *A Tale of Two Cities.*

That's a strange combination.

The first is the best adventure story ever written, I said confidently. The second is about sacrifice

Excellent! Excellent! Inspire the children, Mr Skrzynecki, inspire them. She pronounced my name remarkably close to the correct Polish pronunciation. Next time we meet we must discuss poetry.

How did you know I was teaching poetry to the children?

Here in the country, Mr Skrzynecki – may I call you Peter? – people talk like nowhere else. Be careful what you say and where you say it. Gossip spreads like a bushfire…You know, a little word dropped here, another word dropped there…People talk because there's often not much else to do. Are you Anglican, by any chance?

No. Catholic. Why do you ask?

I am Anglican. I am also involved in the life of the church in Armidale. I thought perhaps you might like to come to one of our services…Never mind.

Sorry.

Come around to the library and have a cup of tea. You know that Judith Wright grew up in this area.

I do.

Do you know her poetry?

Somewhat.

We can talk about her poetry, if you like.

The children are getting restless, Miss Isaacs, I'd better get back to teaching them. They must think they're still on holidays, I said, as a series of hooting noises came from the schoolroom, followed by squeals of laughter and clapping.

I hurried back and there, in the back row, Michael Burleigh and Darryl Williams were making hooting noises, like owls, while the rest of the school laughed and clapped.

Why? I asked, when the noise died down.

No reason, sir, Michael said with his mischievous grin. Alan said they saw an owl at their house, and I pretended I was that owl.

Me too, sir, said Darryl.

Alright, settle down. I wonder what Miss Isaacs would say if she were here?

Everyone looked at me, their expressions revealing nothing, saying, That's all it'd been, a piece of harmless fun.

Actually, I said, I thought your owl imitations were very good.

Everyone laughed.

At that moment, Susan Frizell's words returned, asking if I was coming back after the Easter holidays.

Art Under the Trees

To my surprise, among the general school mail, there was a postcard inside an envelope from P that she'd posted from Surfers Paradise. I opened it, full of excitement. The weather was beautiful up there, she and her parents were having a wonderful holiday, and she was looking forward to seeing me in the May school holidays. Even though they were staying at Surfers Paradise, the scene on the card showed lorikeets at Currumbin Sanctuary feeding from a dish of food held out by a disembodied hand. The birds fascinated me, and I spent a long time looking at their colours – more than I did reading what P had written.

The rest of the day passed uneventfully. I remembered Alex saying that when I returned it would be like I'd never been away. He was right. The day was hot and the air motionless, midges flew around the veranda, soldier- birds sang in a raucous chorus every time someone came outside. Their peace had been invaded. The school and its grounds no longer belonged to them. None of the children seemed interested in any of the lessons set for the afternoon.

With the whole afternoon ahead I suggested we go outside and do Art under the pine trees where it was cool in the shade. Let's concentrate on forms, I said, choosing basic shapes and joining them into a picture.

Sitting outside, I told the children to take in the view. Before us lay the school yard, running at a slope, empty of buildings except the two toilets and the incinerator at the far end; to our immediate right was the shelter shed. At the far end of the school yard, in the paddock that also belonged to the school and where the sheep grazed, a small creek ran among the trees, barely visible. Behind us stood the pine trees, huge, green, dark, offering shade, the sound of a wind in their branches, even though no wind blew.

Piece by piece we broke the view into shapes, triangles,

semi-circles, rectangles, squares until it resembled an abstract picture.

Connect the shapes with lines, I said, and don't just draw what you see in front of you. Draw what your mind thinks it can see – not what it actually sees. Then put in the colours – and it doesn't matter what colours you choose. Trees don't have to be green and the sky doesn't have to be blue. Forget the rules. Paint your pictures in the colours you'd like your picture to be.

I heard words and phrases like *okay, let's go, wow-ee, this is fun!*

While they worked I remembered the Art classes at teachers' college, how we were taught basic elements of Art and shown prints of works by traditional and modern artists, European and Australian. One French artist, Henri Rousseau, the *Dounanier*, fascinated me. The simplicity in his paintings was unique; every one of them was almost a dream in concept – a combination of childhood fantasy and storytelling. Lush jungle scenes, children, animals, flowers, all in a style that could have been called "child-like". I thought that one painting especially, *The Sleeping Gypsy*, was a masterpiece, and the artist who painted it a genius.

The children finished their paintings. The shapes, as we examined them, were all present. Circles for sky and squares for paddocks, triangles for pine trees and blue lines for an imaginary creek running through trees.

We sat in silence, listening to the birds, saying nothing.

Okay everyone, inside, pack up and wait for your transport. There'll be no homework tonight but make sure you know your tables and check the last Spelling list you had to learn before the Easter break.

They all left. One by one. In two's and three's...On foot, by motor vehicles, to their homes along the Jeogla Road, down to the Styx River and the Oaky River Hydro Dam.

As always, an immediate sense of emptiness came over

me, a feeling that neither music nor books could fill. I was missing human contact, not hearing voices and being able to speak back to them. The echoes of the children's voices trailed in the air, on the veranda and in the empty schoolroom; but slowly, the walls absorbed them, and they floated out into the air, in the forest and along the same road that their owners had gone.

I cleaned up and headed back to the Sloggett home.

New Enrolments, A Birthday Cake, Others Like Me

The next day there were three new enrolments at the school. The first was Jennifer Cundy, cousin of Wayne Williams. Her family had moved into a house down on the Styx River, near the old saw mill, where her father, Alan, worked as a trucker for a logging company. Her mother's name was Jeanette.

The other two new enrolments were a sister and brother, Jennifer and Andrew Stace. The family had come from the north and their father was working as a farmhand on one of the properties. Jennifer had long blonde hair which she wore in plaits. Andrew was also blonde-haired, a boy who was wiry and strong. We learnt quickly that there wasn't a birdcall in the forest that he couldn't identify. When I asked how he'd learn them all, he replied, Dad taught me.

We welcomed them to the school, and they quickly made friends with the other children; although Jennifer often skipped by herself, her mind seemingly on matters other than what the children were doing and Andrew, very often, could be seen at the far end of the playground, walking around by himself and listening to the sky, at those corners of the yard that were nearest to the forest. Many times I'd see him cupping his ear, listening for a sound that may have been a birdcall or an echo of a birdcall. In his check shirt and blue jeans he gave me the impression of being a junior logger or farmhand who had stopped by the school on a detour, waiting for his time to leave.

In term of the school's longevity, the enrolment of the three new children was a godsend. After the accident at the Oaky River Hydro Dam, our numbers had dropped by three. Now they were back to fourteen, and the future of the school staying open looked good.

In the middle of the following week there was a small cake from my mother for my birthday and a card from P. I was expecting the cake but the card was a surprise. That afternoon, I decided to break protocol, and ring her from Jeogla which, for privacy reasons, was something I'd never done before; but no sooner had I rung the post office, I was told the line was busy. I'd forgotten it was a party line and that meant waiting. After sharing a piece of cake with Carrie, she wished me a happy birthday, we drank our tea and I drove to Wollomombi. The red telephone booth was empty and I'd brought plenty of coins.

I knew my father wouldn't be home from work yet but my mother might be. She did the shopping after leaving work in Strathfield and was probably home not long now, unpacking and getting ready to start making dinner. My father, returning from a suburb on the Liverpool railway line would be home shortly. Deciding against ringing them first, I rang P and, as before, her mother answered the telephone.

Hello, dear. Hello. Happy birthday greetings are in order, I believe.

Thank you.

Do you feel any older? She asked.

No, I don't, I said. I feel on top of the world – and that's probably a good sign. Tell P her card arrived. It's lovely to get letters from home.

Did I ever tell you I taught in a one-teacher school in Western Australia?

Did you? I asked, surprised to hear this piece of news. When?

Oh, before I was married. It wasn't unusual for young female teachers to be sent to the country, as we say. Shortage of men teachers during the war.

Oh?

You have my sympathies – or support – I should say. Do you get lonely, dear?

Do I get lonely? My girlfriend's mother asking me if I get lonely? Four hundred miles away from her daughter?

Yes, I do.

Well, you're young still. Learn to pray, if you can't do that, then read, occupy yourself with reading and maybe writing. That will keep your mind active.

I do that, anyway. I'm here to teach children – and it's something I enjoy doing.

You're a bright young man, very ardent and intense. They are good qualities to have, believe me, I know. You will do well in the teaching profession.

Why was she talking to me like this? The topic of conversation had begun so pleasantly but was becoming irrelevant to what I wanted to ask. Was P at home?

No, she's not, dear. Don't be too despondent.

Tell her I rang, will you? And say that I'll try on the weekend when I go into Armidale.

Of course, dear. Happy birthday, once again.

I hung up the phone and looked outside. There was Frank Robson, standing in the doorway of his store, grinning at me, as if he'd guessed what I'd been talking about. He waved to me.

G'day, Peter. Happy Birthday.

Thanks, Frank. Who told you?

Never mind who? This is a small place. Everybody knows everybody's business. I hear you've settled in real well. Getting to know the locals. The school kids think the world of you – what with all that culture you've brought from Sydney.

Are you trying to be clever, Frank?

He just laughed and toddled off.

With Frank gone, I felt free and returned to the telephone booth. I rang home and my mother answered, What a lovely surprise! she cried out. Happy birthday, darling.

Mum, thanks so much for the cake. Mrs Sloggett and I had some for afternoon tea.

Is wasn't too dry, was it?

No. Your cakes are never too dry. The cake was perfect.

I can still taste it in my mouth.

I'm so pleased. And did it arrive in one piece? It didn't get broken, did it? It's a long way to send a cake. At the post office they always ask me, Where is this place called Jeogla?

Everything about the cake is fine. I'm ringing to say thank you and because I'd like to say hello to you both. Is Dad home?

He is, as a matter of fact. You're very lucky. He didn't catch the train home today. Someone from work was driving through Regents Park and gave him a lift…Here he is…

Hello, Peter, my father said. Happy birthday…Have you had a good day?

Yes, Dad. We've had some new enrolments at the school so the numbers will be good for this year and next year. It's great to hear your voice and Mum's.

We talked for a few minutes and the pips kept reminding me to feed more money. Finally, I said goodbye to both parents and promised to call soon. Thanks, again, for the cake. It was special, Mum.

I remembered that tomorrow I had to send a note to parents advising them the school would be closed one day next week. I was attending an in-service course for teachers in small school and was going in with Bill Higgins. Parents had to be advised beforehand.

Returning to the school I wrote a note in longhand on a master sheet and printed it off on the school's Fordigraph hand stencilling machine, a stainless-steel, cylindrically-shaped machine that had to be kept filled Fordigraph fluid, and which smelt strongly of methylated spirits. The fluid had to be ordered from Sydney and arrived in tins that reminded me of flour or biscuit tins, fawn and vanilla coloured, with red printing. I ran off the necessary number and returned to the Sloggett home.

Carrie asked, Why did yer return to the school?

I explained about the in-service course and having to

hand out notices to parents.

Darryl did that also, she said, although I can't remember any of the others doin' it...but maybe they did.

Well, I replied, it must be done.

Where's the course been held?

At Armidale Public School. I'm going in with Bill.

Anzac Day's comin' up. Maybe you'll git 'im to change 'is mind about takin' the Chandler kiddies to the service. Be good if yer could.

I know. Others have mentioned it to me. It's his business, really. I can't tell him what to do about like Anzac Day.

Well, have a good day. Will yer be needin' lunch to take in?

No thanks, morning tea and lunch are being provided. I'll be home for dinner

*

Next week, as we drove towards Armidale, Bill asked me, Do you know the names of the other small schools in our area?

No, I don't think I do...I know your school and I know there's one out at Hillgrove.

There's six in our inspectorate altogether...The others are Rockvale, Thalgarrah and Wongwibinda. We'll be having the annual athletics carnival against each other. That'll be held at Chandler where we've got the biggest oval.

I parked in Faulkner Street. This is very impressive, isn't it? The buildings and grounds. They must have everything.

They do. This is also the local demonstration school for the teachers' college – up there, on the hill..

From my various trips into town I'd seen the teachers' college from a distance, admired its hilltop location and its neoclassical columns. The garden was spectacular with a large circular fishpond in the centre.

I've driven around it, I said. Special.

Special? Bill repeated. It used to be a goal and they hanged them up there. The college has one of the best art collections in the state. Out the back they've recreated an educational museum. You should go up. It's like stepping back into last century. All mid-Victorian stuff. Blackboards on easels, maps of the British empire, globes, original writing slates and the old desks.

I've got most of those at Jeogla.

Mate, Jeogla is the modern world compared to what's up there. Come on, let's go.

We were handed the day's program at the entrance of the school and steered towards the hall. In the distance, I could see the school inspector, Mr Harry Harris, cup of tea in hand, talking to a group of men and women.

Who are they? I asked.

Probably some of the lecturers from the teachers' college. They'll most likely be presenting the sessions, telling us what we already know.

They must be experts?

Maybe they are, maybe they're not, said Bill. You'll learn soon enough there's nothing like working at the coalface. That's where the real experts teach.

Just then a group of men came towards us and Bill introduced me to them…Theo, Geoff, John…This here's Peter, he's the new teacher at Jeogla. We all shook hands.

These were the other teachers from the rest of the small schools in the cluster that Jeogla belonged to.

Is that all, I asked, six teachers?

Crikeys, no…said Bill. Wait another fifteen or twenty minutes and this place will be swarming with teachers. They're coming from all over the place….from up Guyra down to Uralla and out to Yarrowyck…Two-teacher schools, as well, you'll see. We're going to meet the inspectors too. I believe there's a group of them coming from Tamworth.

While Bill was speaking I watched as Mr Harry Harris slowly made his way through a group of people towards us, at the back of the hall, smiling and shaking hands as he did. He waved, but I wasn't sure who he was waving to and I didn't return the gesture. Again, he waved, nodding as he did, as if to say, Yes, you.

I waved back and before I knew it he was in standing before our group, shaking hands and smiling. Good morning, gentlemen, he said enthusiastically. Are we all ready for a day's learning?

I stared at him as if I'd landed on Mars. Like the others I nodded, meaning Yes I am ready, and smiled, feeling overwhelmed in the presence of the man who I remembered suddenly would decide my future as a teacher in a few months. I said nothing more, stepped back from the group and fingered nervously the programme I'd been given.

Ah, Mr Skrzynecki, Mr Harris said, I believe you met Miss Enid Isaacs recently? He edged himself away from the others until he stood facing me, on the periphery of a circle that was breaking up.

The back of the hall had become full of people, as Bill said it would, and many were standing shoulder. Many were taking their places in the seats.

Yes, she came out to the school with a box of books Lovely lady, I added. Charming and Old-worldish, if you know what I mean. She treasures books and promotes the classics, I think…She cherishes reading.

And what better gift to leave children? he asked.

The best, I replied. Take away reading and you take away the world.

Exactly my feelings, Mr Skrzynecki. Coupled with a sense of the divine, traditional Christian values that we were raised on. Did you know she was a church elder of her parish?

No, but that doesn't surprise me.

We must protect our values, Mr Skrzynecki, our beliefs, whether they be the reverence for Christmas Day or the respect we hold for Anzac Day. Any thoughts on the latter?

Here was the reference to Anzac Day again. What's wrong with these people? Alex Clark, Bill Higgins, Ron Diamond, Harry Harris. By now they all knew what I stood for. Was this some kind of test?

I'm all for Anzac Day, Mr Harris. I'll be there with my school – and, I believe, I'll be combining the children from Chandler with our group.

Excellent, Mr Skrzynecki. Wonderful. I look forward to hearing all about it at a later date.

He smiled benevolently and moved off, towards the front of the hall where other dignitaries were assembling, as a microphone was being tapped in readiness for the program to begin. I made my way over to the other teachers from our cluster group of small schools in the centre of the rows of seats.

Just after nine-thirty the course started. We were first welcomed by a spokesperson for the Area Director of the North-West region who unfortunately had to attend a conference in Sydney. The principal of the school then welcomed us and said what an honour it was to be hosting such an important event at his school. The third welcome was from Mr Harry Harris who, as local District Inspector of Schools, said what a pleasure it was to see all the teachers from his inspectorate here, on time, despite some having to travel long distances. He talked about sacrifices having to be made and, eventually, it will be the children who benefit from these sacrifices.

By morning tea we sat through two sessions, Why Is the Small School Still Relevant in Today's Society? and How To Organise Your Timetable Effectively.

I took notes and it made me remember taking notes at teachers' college, although none of those notes related to teaching in remote areas of New South Wales.

Another two sessions plus question time followed before lunch, by which time I was ready for a sleep. Bill nudged me two or three times when he saw I was starting to nod off.

Lunch was provided. We were asked not to go into town for a pub or club lunch as the last two sessions would begin on the dot and more much had to be shared between teachers, especially those who were new to the "small school" environment. This'll be your chance, Peter, Bill said, to say what you think.

We sat outside in the sun, each holding a small plate of sandwiches and cup of coffee or tea. The food seemed more refreshing than the ideas put forward by some of the speakers.

It's about planning and co-ordination, I said, knowing your subject matter but most importantly having a passion for teaching. I'd say if you don't like it, you should get out.

Theo, one of the other teachers heard me speaking and said you didn't have to be a genius to know that.

I said that I wasn't pretending to be a genius. I was simply stating what I'd learnt in my short time at Jeogla.

Theo, who lived in town with his mother, was the teacher at Thalgarrah, said he was happy in his job. He did the best he could and was staying put – even though there was talk in the district that some of the schools might be closed in the near future.

Not if you keep your enrolment numbers up, everyone agreed. They can't force you out. But apparently they could. It's not present enrolments that counted, but future enrolments. Projected figures could run into the next five years. The Education Department could make you do that. Everyone had a view on that, pleasant or otherwise, and in the half hour we had for lunch,the views revolved around the future of small schools as an educational investment. Luxury teaching, one inspector had said to a teacher. That was the in-phrase. *Luxury teaching.* And couldn't be justified on economic grounds.

By three o'clock it was the final round-up time for questions and Bill Higgins stood up, pointed to me and asked me to tell the assembly what I thought of being posted to Jeogla and what the appointment meant to me. I was the only one in the group who was "first year out".

Every head in the hall turned to me and looked at for a statement, listened for something profound I might have to say.

I stuttered and said two things, both of which contained contradictions.

Firstly, I said I disliked being sent to New England, but then I said that I was loving it.

Secondly, I said we weren't prepared enough at teachers' college for this kind of appointment but that didn't matter. I could teach myself.

I sat down, surprising myself at how quickly everything had been said. Two sentences, and it was over in a flash.

The hall broke into applause.

The true spirit of the small school teacher, someone called out to me. Hear. Hear.

Well spoken, young man. Welcome to our club. A hand reached out and shook mine.

You'll make a great teacher, another voice said.

Another hand shook mine.

Let's get out of here, Bill, I said. I want a drink of lemonade.

I need to light up, he replied, taking his pipe out of his pocket.

Let's go to the pub, voices were saying all around me. Let's go to the pub.

Mr Harry Harris came up and shook my hand. I look forward to our future conversations.

It was around five o'clock when our group left the New England; others had gone off to the Imperial.

Gee, mate, Bill said, Back there at the school. Are you trying to get into the school inspector's good books?

What are you talking about? I asked. I don't even remember what I said.

The drive back to Jeogla was slow. I didn't drink but Bill had had a few beers. Want to talk politics or Anzac Day? he asked.

No, I replied emphatically. Let's talk about the world – this world – this slice of Nature around us, that we're driving into, enjoying, breathing its air. Let's forget what we learnt and look ahead to what we've still got to learn.

You sound like a bloody philosopher, mate… Well, excuse me for breathing. Mind if I smoke?

I don't care.

Yes, but it's your car.

Whatever you like, Bill, I'm glad the small school conference is over and we can get back to our other lives.

What do you mean?

I mean to where we can start being teachers again – but also pupils.

You're nuts, you know.

Probably.

I was feeling on such an inner high, riding such a plateau of exhilaration that nothing could have knocked me off it, even a granite boulder hurtling through the sky.

Anzac Day

Anzac Day fell on a Tuesday and it was a public holiday. A bright day, with a breeze blowing that promised good weather from early light.

Such a special day, Carrie sighed, an' the Lord has given us nice weather. She was packing the cakes and sandwiches she'd made for the meal in the community hall after the Anzac Day service that was being held in Wollomombi. Always a special day, she repeated, as if daydreaming. Reminds me how the men went off to war, proud in their uniforms...Marchin' through Armidale, to the railway station, an' off to a war many'd never come back from... Most did, however, an' are alive today...Men like Elmo an' Ron an' Bruce Wright...Makes me proud to be an Australian. What time are yer goin' into Wollomombi.

Ten o'clock start, Ron told me. I'll be there before that. Muster the children from both schools around the flag pole and let the ceremony take care of itself. Everyone seems to know what to do.

Ron'll have a bugler out from town, a soldier from the local unit. Ron always arranges that, even when he's marchin' in town; but these last few years he's been out here, lookin' after things closer to home. Best Anzac Day marshal New England ever had. Been a councillor on the shire too, an' involved in Rotary an' Fire and Rescue Protection. You name it, Ron's been there...an' he never asks a penny for himself....

What about Gerald?

He an' I will bring Granma.

How does Elmo feel about not being here?

Elmo's fine about that. He'll go into Nowendoc for the service. Can't be helped if he can't be 'ere. Some years he can, other years he can't...Did yer see the wreath I made?

No, where is it?

Out the back.

I'll go and have a look right now.

Blackie and Brownie had learnt not to bark at me by now; they strained at the collars and wires that held them, wagging their tails, standing on hind legs, pawing the air.

Under the clothes lines, beneath a tree that grew alongside the chicken run, stood a wreath made of eucalyptus leaves and bush flowers.

You like it?

I sure do. Where did those orchids come from?

Secret place down at the Styx.

It's beautiful… Talented, aren't you?

She blushed and turned away, like a school girl, hands up to her face. Go on with yer, don't be smart.

*

When I arrived at Wollomombi I was surprised by the large number of people gathered outside St John's church, in the area in front of the flag pole where a flag hung at half mast. I could see Alex in his minister's vestments, surrounded by many of his parishioners. Among the faces I was surprised to see Lex McRae. Someone must have given him a lift. Ron and his wife were there. So were Frank and Mrs Robson. Wally Frizell and his wife. George Gray was there and the people from the Jeogla post office. Children from my school and from Chandler were mixing, all dressed in their best clothes. Some of the girls wore Red Cross nurses uniforms. Most of the boys wore white shirts and ties. Some wreaths had already been laid at the foot of the flagpole. Carrie, Granma and Gerald arrived not long after I did, with Carrie carrying her wreath. I shook hands with all the parents I knew and some from Chandler, all expressing their thanks for being here with the children. I remembered what Ron had said about the ceremony taking care of itself. One of the Wollomombi locals said to me, Thank you for being here.

More people arrived. Standing on the incline from the Jeogla approach, looking down on the village, the numbers seemed to have doubled in the ten minutes since I arrived. I walked down and stood beside the children. Under Ron's direction, they'd been rounded up by their parents and minders and placed to the right of the flagpole, slightly behind it. They looked bored. They knew what was expected of them. No playing up. Maybe it didn't matter to them that a teacher was here, but it did matter that their parents were.

A bell rang from somewhere and people gathered around the flag. Alex, dressed in his cleric's clothes, appeared from inside the church and addressed the assembly from a microphone placed at the entrance of the church.

Everyone fell silent immediately, barely a cough or whisper could be heard. From where I stood beside the children, I could see the whole gathering. Many of the elderly sat in chairs.

My fellow parishioners, citizens, visitors and Australians all alike, we are here to celebrate the Anzac tradition, he commenced – and those ideals of courage and mateship that never die but endure. They were established on 25 April, 1915 when the Australian and New Zealand Army Corps landed on the Gallipoli Peninsula. Anzac Day is the day when Australians remember those who have made the supreme sacrifice for ideals that we hold dear and cherish in our lives. Even for someone like myself, a new arrival in Australia, it is heart-warming to see such large numbers attending memorial services across the country, in cities, suburbs, towns and villages like Wollomombi. Now, before I call on our guest speaker, let us bow our heads and say the Lord's Prayer.

Young, old and in-between prayed, some with bowed heads and other staring at the sky, into the trees and into the sun. Magpies sang their morning songs loudly and triumphantly, as if they also knew this was a special day.

Alex continued, Our dignitary this morning is Professor John Challis from the Classics department at the University of New England. Professor Challis is a former infantryman who fought in France and Belgium during World War II. He rose to the rank of captain and when he returned from service he recommenced his studies in the field of Classic Literature. He is a highly respected scholar in his field and we are extremely fortunate to have him come out from Armidale to deliver this Anzac Day address. Please welcome Professor Challis.

The assembly applauded.

Thank you, Reverend Clark. The professor stood tall and straight, the wind blowing his white hair, his chest covered in medals and coloured bars. I thought they looked magnificent shining in the sun. He cleared his throat and spoke. My dear friends, Australians old and young, it gives me great pleasure to have accepted this invitation to address you on Anzac Day. For the young people today it might seem difficult to understand why we should have gratitude in our hearts for what earlier generations of men and women have sacrificed for us. We live in peace. In a country that that attracts people from all over the world. Australia is a good country to live in. Men and women gave their lives so that this freedom we enjoy might remain ours. I could recount to you battles from Ancient History, from the times of Homer and Virgil, from Julius Caesar and Hannibal. Wars that were fought for wealth and power, fame and glory, personal aggrandisements. Today, battles are fought so that peace may be achieved and maintained. Risks are taken and everything is in the stakes. Australia has never experienced war as it has been experienced in Europe or the Middle East. The men and women of our armed forces fought to make sure that we were safe. Today, a new generation of our soldiers, airmen and sailors is serving in troubled parts of the world, including Vietnam, and while we pause to remember the Anzac heroes of the past we must also remember these new heroes who are risking their lives in the defence of their nation and community.

He continued to speak of the Australian character, of mateship, of Australians banding together in times of adversity. He reminded us that happiness must be paid for. He reminded us that freedom and courage go hand in hand. Our soldiers have preserved our nation and kept it safe through their sacrifice.

We are here to celebrate, he concluded. To keep alive the memory of those who have died so that we may live in peace.

He stepped back from the microphone and applause broke out. Slowly and in a subdued manner at first but then it grew into a more vigorous response from young and old ; it died down and organ music could be heard from inside the church. It occurred to me that it must be Jill, whom I knew played the organ. Once again, a microphone placed inside the church carried out the notes vibrantly and clearly, and Alex said, We will now sing "O God, Our Help in Ages Past."

It was not a hymn that I knew from my childhood or schooldays, but I could relate to its sentiments and hopes for the future expressed in its elemental words and references to the "rising sun", the "endless years", the "thousand ages" and "eternal home". All that made sense.

We have said the Lord's Prayer, but we shall also have two further reading from the Bible, the Reverend Clark said, the first being from John 15:10-13.

You could sense the crowd shifting in thought, from hymn to Gospel reading, like a car going down in gears, adjusting to the pace of speed. Alex read, directly into the face of the rising sun, and into the faces and hearts of the assembly:

> "If ye keep my commandments, ye shall abide in my love; even as I have kept my Father's commandments, and abide in his love".

> "These things I have spoken unto you, that my joy might remain in you, and that your joy might be full."

> "This is my commandment, That ye love one another, as I have loved you."

> "Greater love hath no man than this, that a man lay down his life for his friends."

When he finished reading, the assembly murmured, "Amen."

The second reading is Psalm 23. I will read it slowly, and those of you who know it by heart may recite it. In this prayer we affirm our faith in God. When darkness falls, and our faith is at its lowest, let us turn to God, who will never turn away from us.

> "The Lord is my shepherd; I shall not want.
> He maketh me to lie down in green pastures;
> he leadeth me beside still waters.
> He restoreth my soul: he leadeth me in the
> paths of righteousness for his name's sake.
> Yea, though I walk through the valley
> of the shadow of death, I will fear no evil: for
> thou art with me; thy rod and thy staff they
> comfort me.
> Thou preparest a table before me in the
> presence of mine enemies: thou anointest my
> head with oil; my cup runneth over.
> Surely goodness and mercy shall follow me all
> the days of my life:
> and I will dwell in the house of the Lord for
> ever."

A solemn hush fell over the assembly; it seemed that even birds stopped singing. Only the wind could be heard in the pines, singing a different psalm.

Alex spoke. I would now like you ask the new teacher from Jeogla Public School, Mr Peter Skrzynecki, to come forward and read the poem that has been chosen by our Anzac Day marshal, Mr Ron Diamond, for the occasion. It is "In Flanders Field" by John McCrae.

No one had told me about this. I was dumbstruck, as I made my way through the crowd to the microphone. I whispered to Alex, Why didn't you tell me?

Surprise mate, he whispered back. Here, take this.

He handed me a sheet of paper. Typed on it was a poem that I'd never seen before.

I read, "In Flanders Fields" by John McCrae.

In Flanders fields the poppies blow
Between the crosses, row on row,
That mark our place; and in the sky
The larks, still bravely singing, fly
Scarce heard amid the guns below.

We are the Dead. Short days ago
We lived, felt dawn, saw sunset glow,
Loved and were loved, and now we lie,
In Flanders fields.

Take up our quarrel with the foe:
To you from failing hands we throw
The torch; be yours to hold it high.
If ye break faith with us who die
We shall not sleep, though poppies grow
In Flanders fields.

As I was returning to my place, I heard Ron's voice over the microphone, The wreath-laying part of the service will now take place.

I saw Carrie step forward, carrying the wreath she'd made, and lay it at the base of the flagpole. She stepped back and waited. Two other people, a man and a woman, stepped forward and did the same; then two school children, a girl from Chandler Public School and Darryl Williams from my school stepped out from among the school children, were given wreaths by adults and laid them with the others. All the wreath-layers stepped back from the flagpole, bowed their heads, waited a moment and returned to their places.

Alex spoke, Our Anzac Day marshal, Mr Ron Diamond, will now read "The Ode" by Laurence Binyon, taken from "For the Fallen".

Ron stepped up to the microphone and read slowly:

> They shall not grow old, as we
> That are left grow old.
> Age shall not weary them, nor
> The years condemn.
> At the going down of the sun
> And in the morning
> We will remember them.

To which the assembly responded,

> We will remember them.

A soldier stepped forward, turned to face the flagpole, raised his bugle to the sky and played "The Last Post".

A minute's silence followed. Only birdsongs could be heard. The bugler then played "Reveille". A man from Wollomombi raised the flag to full mast, stepped back and saluted it. At the end of "Reveille" Ron Diamond read over the microphone, Lest we forget.

The people replied, Lest we forget.

Alex spoke, Ladies and gentlemen, to conclude our ceremony, we will now sing "God Save the Queen". Please stand.

From inside the church the organ began. As one, the assembly sang the National Anthem, in strong voices that proclaimed their loyalty to Queen Elizabeth II. The Anzac Day service at Wollomombi finished on the most strident of notes, a fitting tribute to all, living and dead.

*

The community hall was packed. Trestles had been set up at the front and ladies from Wollomombi and Jeogla were putting out refreshments. Cakes, biscuits, sandwiches. An urn, tea and coffee making facilities were arranged on a separate table. Outside, further back behind the hall, several of the younger men, station-hands mostly, had grouped around cars and utes, opening beer bottles and lighting up, laughing, joking, with much back-slapping and camaraderie. The serious part of Anzac Day was over, now the drinking and two-up would begin. A few others called out they were going to Ebor, on to Hillgrove or into Armidale. Most were staying here, Where the grog's as good as anywhere, and there was plenty of that in the ice buckets of the utes. There'll be more blokes arriving, others called out. Day's just startin'.

The service had taken three-quarters of an hour, and now, with people standing around and talking, milling around the church and slowly making their way into the hall, it had taken close to another half an hour.

Ron and Alex came up to me. Ron shook my hand, Alex slapped me on the back. You read the poem just right, mate. Alex said.

Both lit up a cigarette.

You might have told me, I said.

Nah, Ron said. You're a natural. New England might make a poet of you yet. Got to go, mates. Talk to some people from Armidale. By the way, Don't you think John Challis did a great job? Nothing like the talk of war and sacrifice to make us appreciate what we have in Australia. With a drag on his cigarette he was gone, merging into a crowd that parted at his arrival and then closed in behind him. You could see people looking at him, trying not to stare but obviously proud of him. After all, this was Ron, one of their very best.

Jill came out of the church to join us and said she could do with some refreshment.

Beer's out the back, darling, Alex laughed. Or there's tea and coffee in the hall.

We better try some of Carrie's cakes, I said, otherwise she'll be upset.

Inside the hall, I was surrounded by children from Jeogla; they formed a circle around me.

What's up? I asked.

Nothing, sir, Roslyn Turner said. We're happy you could make it. It's nice to have our teacher here – isn't it? She asked the others.

All of whom said, Yes.

Ian Moult added, Makes me proud.

Why? I asked.

Just does, he said. Our dad's over there. By the way, sir, my spelling's getting better.

See, clever boy, I said

I saw him wipe a tear. He quickly turned and ran away. I thought that was a strange comment for him to make about his father, especially as all the Moult boys were so non-committal about themselves or their parents. I had never met either of the Moult boys' parents and started to walk over to meet him, but he became lost in the crowd and when I next saw him, the three boys and he were getting into somebody's truck and were being driven away, presumably back to Jeogla.

Within half an hour of food being put out the hall was packed and people were eating heartily. Plates of sandwiches first, cakes and scones next. Conversations flowed in all directions. The elderly were sitting around the hall on chairs. Many were being waited on. Out the back, the young men were tossing coins into the air. A two-up game had started. Gerald had gone out to join them. I'd heard Carrie say, as he left the hall, Mind yerself now – and don't go being a fool. He reddened, turned and left the hall in a hurry, escaping his mother's stern look. Now, one leg up on the tailgate of a ute he seemed at home among the boys, whoever they were or wherever they'd come from. I don't think I'd seen him looking happier, more relaxed, joking and laughing, while drinking a beer.

There was a tap on my shoulder and I turned around to see Lex McCrae, a beer in one hand, his pipe in the other, smiling, as he asked, Yer haven't forgotten what's on Saturdee?

No, Mr McCrae, I haven't. The referendum for the New England New State.

We'll finally have it, young feller, a state that's all ours.

I really didn't know how to answer him, and I didn't want to offend by saying the wrong thing.

Good, I said. I hope it turns out just the way you want it.

Yer not jest sayin' that, are yer?

No, I'm saying what I think is right. You country people want your own state, and I suppose it's right to ask, Why not?

Knew yer'd come aroun' to our way o' thinkin'. He swallowed a mouthful of beer, wiped his lips and was gone.

Carrie had been watching me. Let 'im go. Someone' ll bring 'im home.

What about Gerald?

I'll have a look-see before I go back.

Want me to bring him home?

Sure, if yer hopin' be to be home after midnight.

Midnight?

That's what they'll do. Drink 'emselves silly an' then go somewhere else. Or they'll sleep it off right 'ere. Yer can try and bring 'im home but he'll say no....Jimmy Browning most likely will do the honours. Always does. Jim doesn't drink much, yer see. Keeps a clear 'ead. Better leave 'im be...I'll check before I leave, okay?

Okay.

Now I'd better go and see if people 'ave eaten me cakes. They always go quick.

I found Jill in the hall. Alex was mixing with different groups of parishioners; he was balancing a cup of tea in one hand and a cigarette in the other.

He's in demand, I said to Jill.

Busy, busy, busy.

Your organ playing sounded beautiful.

Thank you. Those hymns inspire me, make me try harder every time. Strong community spirit, here, don't you think? Everybody knows everybody.

And I suppose everybody knows everybody's business? She smiled but was careful with her reply, So I've been told, she said.

I know what you're referring to when you speak of community spirit, I replied, after that visit to Kilcoy. Live here and die here.

This is a big event for you, isn't it? she asked.

Yes, and another on Saturday for the New England New State referendum.

Oh yes, she smiled wryly. Won't there be a big fallout if it doesn't get through?

Will it?

I don't know. The locals think it will, but I wonder. The vote's being taken to include Newcastle....That'll be interesting to watch the outcome. They've been waiting for decades, lobbying politicians and so on. We'll just have to wait and see.

I'm manning the school with Lex McCrae.

I've heard him referred to as Father Time. Always gets what he wants in the end.

A bit like Death, eh?

Did you like the surprise Ron and Alex sprung on you?

Loved it, I said. Glad it was a poem I had to read and not a hymn I had to sing. I can't tell a B from a bull's foot and couldn't carry a note if my life depended on it, I said bluntly; but I love poetry and enjoyed reading that poem. Soldiers die, but the birds keep singing in the fields.

I was enjoying talking to the lady from Sydney, the woman who scorned the weather on the day I arrived but now had a sparkle in her eye that matched the sun. Beautiful weather for a day of remembrance and celebration, I said.

You just wait until it's winter, she said. Frosts every morning. Teaching in your small school will be like teaching inside a freezer. You'll be wearing two or three jumpers at the one time and they won't keep out the cold. Make sure you put anti-freeze into your radiator. You teeth will chatter from the moment you open your eyes until the moment you close them and try to sleep. Make sure there's a good supply of firewood in the school – and make sure someone shows you the correct way to light the heater in the school. The kids will know anyhow...If the rains set in you'll think the Great Flood from the Bible has started. Wollomombi Falls will roar like you've never heard a roar. You'll think the Creation of the World has started all over.

She said all this with a smile but I knew she was dead serious. She was giving me information but she was also giving me a warning. She changed the subject. Are you going home for the May holidays?

Oh yes.

Flying again?

No, this time I'll be driving. I want to go into the city and buy some books. Poetry and art. See what else...Bring them back. The Sloggetts put a bookcase into my room over Easter and I can have my own books there...Makes it feel a bit more like home.

Surround yourself with the familiar.

Books and music...What else?

Go into town. See the art collection at the Teachers' College. There's the Armidale Theatre Club and playhouse. Musical groups, too...Performances are held in town and up at the university.

I saw "Othello" last year at the Roundhouse and loved it; so seeing a play might be good, I said. Thanks for that information. I'll follow it up after the May holidays.

Other people joined us, people I knew and those whom I didn't, many were from Wollomombi and Jill introduced me to them. Some from far away as Yooroonah. We talked, drank tea, ate biscuits. I wandered out of the hall and back in, finally deciding to return to Jeogla. The assembled people were leaving, although the crowd was still fairly large.

Then I saw him, Professor John Challis, the dignitary who had delivered the Anzac Day address.

Why hadn't our paths crossed before now? I wondered.

Ah, the new teacher, he said, coming towards me and holding out his hand. I thought you read the poem most sensitively, with a lot of feeling.

Glad you liked it, I answered. It was sprung on me. No one had told me beforehand. Still, it was an honour to be asked.

Up close, Professor Challis was taller than from a distance. A solidly built man, he looked more like a boxer or brick-layer, his black hair almost all turned to silver, his handshake was strong and firm, and my hand disappeared into his when he shook it. *Ouch*, I thought, but stopped myself from crying out.

Do you have plans to advance yourself academically, after you leave Jeogla?

I want to return to university studies, I replied. I have an English pass from a course I did at Sydney university, but where I failed everything except English.

Good, good. Excellent! Studying is a bit like warfare, I think. You don't left one lost battle discourage you from winning the war.

That made sense, I thought, but I said, I liked your references to Ancient History.

Anything in particular? he asked.

Hannibal, I said. He's always been my favourite.

Brilliant tactician, he replied. We will never know what might have happened if he'd made that march on Rome; but he'd been on the move a long time, his men were tired, his elephants and supplies worn out. Home seemed the best option. You've read about him?

A little. I thought the use of trumpets by Scipio Africanus at the Battle of Zama to frighten the elephants was a stroke of genius…I also like to read about the Roman occupation of Britain, and how they kept out the enemy from the north by building Hadrian's Wall.

My, aren't you an interesting young man? Are your parents professional people?

No. My father works for the Water Board as a "pick-and-shovel man". My mother cleans people's houses in Strathfield.

And you've ended up here in Jeogla to learn some of life's lessons?

I think I've just ended up in Jeogla.

I hope we meet again sometime, Peter, but in the meantime I have to start making tracks back to town. I have a wife and two daughters and they're expecting me back for lunch. I'm running late as it is.

Again, we shook hands and said our goodbyes. I watched him getting into his car and drive off, waving as he passed me.

I knew it was time for me to leave also. Within ten minutes I'd said my round of goodbyes and returned to Jeogla, deciding to go up to the school and preparing the next day's work. The weather remained warm, and as I drove along the dirt road from the Chandler turn-off, it occurred to me that this had been my first attendance at an Anzac Day service. Real-life, not just watching it on TV. I was pleased with myself for attending and for reading the poem.

The dogs barked happily in greeting when I returned, the geese honked as if there was a fire and the white cat ran across the front garden playfully, waving in and out among the dahlias, as if playing a cat-and-mouse game with me. Peek-a-boo, it seemed to be saying. Here I am. Catch me if you can.

I took a thermos of cold tea from the kitchen and drove up to the school. I put on The Beatles "Please Please Me" album and when the first song, "I Saw Her Standing There" came on I sang along with the Fab Four, feeling so elated, so high, it was a joy. Whatever records I played up at the school – because of the positioning of the record player near a veranda window – the songs blared across Ron Diamond's paddocks with the cattle and sheep listening.

I remembered the conversation with Professor Challis and the references to Ancient History that we'd made. This was Anzac Day but it was also an acknowledgment of sacrifices that are made in all wars. I thought hard of my mother's brother, the one after whom I'd been named. What were the actual circumstances of his death in fighting for the Russians? Whenever I'd ask my mother, she would say she didn't know. She'd left the Ukraine and travelled to Germany when the war broke out. She was in Germany when she learnt that he'd died. When the Beatles sang "Do

You Want to Know a Secret?", I said, No. It's too late for the secret of Uncle Peter's death to be revealed now. What difference would it make? And when they sang "There's a Place" I knew they were singing of the here and now, not only for themselves, but also for me. Not the place where he died in Europe but the place where I was standing, remembering him, in Australia on Anzac Day, 25th April, 1967.

New England New State Referendum

Saturday, 29 th April 1967

During the week a truck arrived from the Electoral Commission delivering materials to the school for the New England New State referendum; these included electoral rolls, voting papers and a ballot box. There was also a book of rules and directions for the Returning Officer and Polling Clerk, as well as a list of voting procedures, all of which I had to sign for. The arrival of all the materials felt intimidating and I was told that when the voting was finished I had to take all the materials to Chandler Public School. Mr Bill Higgins would take delivery and return them to the electoral office in Armidale.

The children had been watching my unease during the delivery, and how unsettled I must have looked. When the truck left, Wayne Moult, who once told me he wanted to be a journalist, said, Don't worry about all that stuff, Mr Skrzynecki, I've seen other teachers doing it, and it's real easy. I'll come up and help you if you like.

I thanked him and said it wasn't necessary. I'll follow the directions and do a check-list before I go home. That's all that has to be done and tomorrow morning I'll be ready to start by eight o'clock. Mr McCrae will be here to help me.

*

Next morning I awoke and thought I was sleeping inside the freezer that Jill spoke about, and knew there was a frost outside. I'd experienced frosts before, but they were "light" as Carrie put it; but this was something else. Afterwards in the kitchen she said it was a sign of things to come. The frosts were a bit slow, coming like they did in April, usually it was in March, at the start of autumn. She explained it meant they'll be late but they'll be stronger and there'll most likely be "black frosts". She said it was when the temperature dropped so low it burnt the roots of the grass and left it dead. After a while, the ground looks like a "fire's been through it".

Yer haven't forgotten what day it is?

Of course, not, I said. Voting day up at the school. I have to leave early.

I'll go up ahead of you. I know exactly what to do and where ter put things out. Have yer breakfast and come up then. Votin' don't start till eight o'clock, yer know that, don't yer?

I must have overlooked it in the paperwork, I replied guiltily. I thought it was nine o'clock.

I'll put on the urn and take up some milk an' biscuits. His Nibs will probably be there before us both.

The Sloggets weren't going into town today. Afterwards, Carrie would return to the house and she and Elmo would bring Granma. Gerald was too young to vote, Carrie told me as she left the house.

Sounds like a perfect arrangement, I said.

First school an' now in charge of votin'. My, my, yer comin' up in the world, Mr Peter, she chuckled, as she went to her car, carrying her basket.

When I arrived at the school both Carrie and Lex McCrae were already there, having turned the school into a voting booth, with portable desks joined at the front to form a table for Lex and myself. Here we would check the electoral roll and issue voting slips. People would vote on separate desks on one side of the room. The ballot box was placed at the door. Refreshments were available on the veranda where people could also stand around and talk; it all seemed very co-ordinated and civilised. All we needed was for voters to arrive.

By nine o'clock there were no voters. Each of us drank a cup of tea. Lex and Carrie kept telling me not to be discouraged. Even if no one arrived, at least they'd have voted and the day would not have been a failure. We just had to be patient; this was Saturday and people slept in, or they travelled into town and left voting to the end of the day.

Lex told me to go for a walk into the bush, and that might calm me down. I explained that I hadn't been prepared for a job like this. Again, he suggested I go for a walk. Why you might even get lost! He laughed. Carrie told him not to be disrespectful or she'd tell a few tales out of school, and that would shut him up "real quick". He looked at her, surprised. Try me, she said, staring him into the eyes. He puffed harder on his pipe, and I wondered what he was thinking about.

By late morning the voters began to arrive. The day had warmed up. Birds sang around the school, noisy soldiers-birds and parrots alike. The school yard had come to life. Lex's horse grazed at the back of the school yard; he'd left a bucket of water for it near the shelter shed.

First it was the Diamonds, then the Frizells, George Gray, the family from the post office, Noel Williams and the Cundys, all the parents of the children from the Oakey River Hydro-dam. Wayne Williams's parents, Marie and Dave. George Gray returned with the parents of the Moult boys, giving them a lift in his truck. Mrs Moult was a large woman and seemed to have trouble walking. Mr Moult looked older than her and I learnt he was a returned soldier. He made a point of telling me that if anything happened to him "Legacy will look after the boys". I wondered why he said that to a teacher he'd never met before. They were a strange couple, different from the other locals and left with George Gray almost as soon as they voted. Before leaving, they invited me to dinner at their home. They asked, Maybe next term? I accepted.

Everyone knew everyone else, and spent time talking on the veranda or out in the yard. Carrie was acting as a hostess, telling me at the same time just to concentrate on the paperwork. Whenever Lex said he'd look after things, she told him to sit there like a "good boy" and reminded him it was the teacher who was in charge.

Not long afterwards, she left and said she'd return with Granma and Elmo. She'd also bring up some lunch for me. How would I like ham and tomato sandwiches?

She gave Lex another censoring look and left.

It felt awkward being alone with him. I asked, You still don't like me, do you?

Never said I didn't, he replied gruffly, getting up and going outside. You an' me are just different, that's all.

While he was outside the Stace family arrived, Jennifer and Andrew behind them. Lex appeared and followed them in, adding, Remember we've been waitin' for sixty years to get this vote. You know which box to cross. He stood up and followed them over to the desk, at the back, where people voted.

Hey, Mister McCrae, I called out, You can't do that.

Says who, sonny?

That's the law. You have stay with me, up here at the desk. Voters vote alone.

He was embarrassed. He pulled himself up his full height, adjusted his belt and walked outside again. I reckoned because the Staces were newcomers to the district they didn't know about him or his overbearing tactics; but they were registered New England voters, and must have an informed opinion that didn't require interference from anybody.

After they dropped their votes into the ballot box, I said, Sorry about that. They said they understood and asked about their children's progress. They moved around the district, the father explained. He went wherever there was work, and sometimes that meant the children didn't stay too long in one school. They're coping, I answered, and they're still fitting in with the rest of the school. That seemed to satisfy them.

Straight afterwards, an elderly couple arrived towing a caravan down the Kempsey Road. From what I'd heard of the road down to Kempsey it didn't seem to be a safe thing to be doing. They wanted to get the voting over and done with, quickly, soon as possible. Can't waste time on a beautiful day like this, can we? the woman asked.

When I remarked how dangerous I heard the road was, the man said, That's what makes it so exciting. The thrill of doing what we've never tried before.

I agreed, and off they went, hauling a caravan with a car that looked like nothing more than an oversized Matchbox toy.

Shortly, Carrie arrived with Granma and Elmo, and my sandwiches. The whole family voted, with Carrie helping Granma to the voting desk and leaving her while she made her cross and folded the ballot. Elmo stood outside with Lex, the former smoking a cigarette, the latter lighting up his pipe. They enjoyed a cup of tea while Granma sat in a chair specially brought out for her and looked over Ron's paddocks, smiling and nodding her head. Whether or not she heard what was being said, it didn't matter. As I read her face, I think she must have been remembering something, or someone, or some place, similar to this or another voting day and another.

I asked Carrie, Do you ever think about what she's thinking when she's like this?

She'll be remembering Billy, her husband, me father. They'd sit like this fer hours down by the Styx at the old house, watchin' us kiddies playin' aroun'....Yer know what, Peter? No one ever got hurt. We had our parents and we had our pets, an' we kiddies were the happiest on earth. By golly, it was beautiful down there; it was like growin' up in the Garden of Paradise.

I was speechless, and before I could reply I heard Elmo's voice. Time ter head back, Mum. I didn't know if he was referring to Carrie or Granma; but it was Granma who stood up, reached for her walking stick and headed towards the veranda steps, her black velvet broad-brimmed hat concealing her face, as she bent her head and Carrie helped her towards the car. I'll be back directly, an' stay with yer until closin' time. I'll help yer pack up everythin' and you can take it over to Wollomombi…Dear oh dear, I wonder if we'll get the vote?

While she was gone, I was surprised to see two cars and a van pull up outside the school gate; they'd come from the east, driving very fast, leaving clouds of dust in their wake. As I watched, people whom I'd never seen in the district spilled from the motor vehicles and headed towards the door. Good, the more the merrier, I thought. That should take the voter count up to about thirty. A decent number for a small school out in the forest, but I couldn't help noticing their clothes, ragged and worn. Most of these people were barefooted and looked like they hadn't shaved or washed in years. Where did they live? What did they do for a living?

Ah, Lex's eyes lit up like the tobacco in his pipe. All the "bushies", them's that we never see except when they have ter appear. They must have got my message to come out of their hidin' places and make their vote count. He was virtually running towards the door.

Welcome, welcome! He cried out. Line up here, will yers all, please. Teacher will just cross yer names off the roll and then I'll show yers where ter put yer crosses.

I crossed off the names of these new arrivals while Lex continued telling them how they should be voting.

We've been waitin' sixty years or more fer this day. Make yer vote count. Youse all know me. Would I lie?

I protested against this breach of correctness, and each time I stood up he told me to sit down. To mind my own business.

A young man, although it was difficult to say how young or old he was, wouldn't leave his mother's side. He clung to her, almost desperately with a pleading look in his eyes. I thought he might start to cry. The mother spoke up. He can't read, mister. He don't know what ter do.

Lex took the young man's hand, put it into his, and said, Here, son. Put a cross into this little square. That's how yer want ter vote, isn't it? The young man nodded.

I walked over, almost shouting. That's enough. You can't do that. Let go of his hand. He votes, but you don't vote for him. The young man began to shake, tearing himself away, back to his mother.

She thrust the ballot paper into the box and called out, Alright, all of yers. When you've voted, git back inter the cars. Let's git outer 'ere.

I stood in the middle of the room, trembling, speechless, as they departed, one by one, half-running, wide-eyed, determined to avoid at what might become a physical confrontation between the teacher and their friend Lex McCrae. When they'd driven off, he said to me, Happy now, are yer? They didn't even stay fer a cuppa tea? That's yer hospitality, is it?

Don't try and change the subject, sir, I replied. You know what you were doing!

Think whatever yer like sonny, he said, and calmly returned to the desk, lighting up his pipe as he did, sitting down, stretching out his legs, and looking up to the ceiling as though he was observing a fly walking across it.

As the dust of this confrontation settled, Ron Diamond entered the school with two very elderly people. These are my parents, Peter, he said. They've come to vote. G'day, Lex. You been up to your old tricks again? I hope not.

Lex leaped to his feet, No, no, Ron. Me an' the teacher are sweet. Aren't we, sir?

I said nothing.

Ron took a deep breath, and said, Right, then, let's do some voting. He drew deeply on the cigarette dangling from his lips. He gave me a wink.

A small dog's barking filled the room. Suzie had entered

the school. Come in, Suzie, Ron said. You can vote too.

After Ron and his parents voted we all sat on the veranda, enjoying the afternoon warmth, each of us having a cup of tea. Lex walked round the yard, talking to his horse and smoking his pipe. There won't be many more after that lot, Ron said, unless we get a few stragglers running late because they won't make the coast on time. Absentees voters,

That's all. The locals've all been and voted.

Who were those people? I asked him. I've never seen them before – and no one's spoken about them either.

That's a good question. They live right down on the Styx – past the old saw mill, and whatever huts still exist that once belonged to the mill. Some live in caravans, some in old buses, some…well, someone live wherever they've put up a cabin or shed and make do with what they can. They come into town infrequently, stock up on basics and head back to their life; they are registered voters, but they mind their own business and don't cause problems. Leave them alone and they'll leave you alone…Isn't that right, Carrie?

I hadn't noticed Carrie returning, as she walked round the corner of the building and spoke to Ron's parents, G'day, Tom…Whatever you say's right, Ron…Whatever…

Not long afterwards, Ron left with his parents and there were no more voters. Six o'clock arrived and it was time to close the booth.

Lex said he'd be off, seeing I had Carrie to help me put things away. I watched as he tipped his horse's bucket of water onto the garden, put the bucket into the shelter shed and hoisted himself into saddle. Puffing on his pipe, he said, We'll win, Mr Teacher, wait an' see. The yellow gate was open and off he went, clip-clopping along the footpath until he reached the road and the sound of his horse's hooves were lost in the grass and dust. There was an air of solitariness about him that was both mythic and lonely. He belonged to a past I had no experience of, and he seemed to regards me as a threat. Was it my name, my European background, the fact that he thought I didn't fully appreciate what this vote today meant?

It didn't take long to pack up the electioneering material into my car. Carrie had locked away the urn and put the leftover food into her basket. We rearranged the desks and tables to their original places. Off yer go, Carrie said. I'll close the school.

*

I doubt if they'll get it, were Bill's first words when I asked him about the outcome of today's referendum.

Why?

Just think about the land they want? One of the juiciest carve-ups in the state's history….An educational centre, a harbour, coal mines, a steelworks, all the milk and dairy products of the Hunter Valley, cattle, sheep, timber industries, sugar cane They weren't being stupid when they drew up the boundaries, were they?

No, I guess they weren't…Who are they?

Country Party, mate. Country Party.

I listened to Bill talk about the workers of the state, of the country. He railed about the fairness of the pay packet and social justice with a conviction that bordered on the obsessional. He challenged me to think for myself, and not be driven to conclusions that steered me away from the roots of my heritage. He reminded me of my parents and the obligations I still had to them. He lit up his pipe and, like Lex McCrae, drew on it more rapidly the more emotional his speech became. Never forget why your parents came here…

I interrupted by saying, They came because they wanted a better life.

That's right, to escape a war caused by totalitarian oppression. Where do you think you'd be if Adolf Hitler hadn't come to power?

I have no idea. It was out of my hands. My parents came to Australia; they have no regrets about that and neither do I. They've always said what a great country Australia is…

It occurred to me that if I wasn't arguing with Alex about religion I was starting to get into deep water with Bill over politics.

I told him what had happened with Lex McCrae interfering and trying to sway the voters.

See, that's exactly my point. Blokes like him think they've got a God-given right to interfere with a democratic process… Exactly, my point! By the way, you know there's a state election early next year, don't you?

No.

Well, you'll be running that one also.

Good, I replied. Lex and I should be mates by then.

So we talked. I'd had thirty-something voters at Jeogla. Bill had more than a hundred at Chandler. He said, Wollomombi is a bigger village, of course, and we get the travellers going straight through to Grafton.

I'd promised Carrie I'd be home for dinner. Signing off on the delivered materials, I waved goodbye from the car. It was starting to get dark. The air was chilly. I forgot it was late autumn. Cold weather or not, the experience of running the school as a voting booth had exhilarated me. At first the responsibility had seemed daunting, but in retrospect it was not too difficult. Common sense prevailed, even in the dealings with an old farmer on a horse.

On the drive back, I remembered how Wayne Moult had offered to come up and help me run the polling booth.

*

It was several days before the final count came in for the result of the referendum; the push for a New England new state had been defeated. It was close, but most strategists predicted a final count of 54% against.

Hard to say definitely what the feeling was in the Sloggett home. Elmo was away at work, that only left Carrie and Granma and Gerald to discuss it. The latter said he didn't care one way or the other, Carrie said it was a pity but didn't elaborate. Granma smiled and nodded her head when I asked her what she thought of the result. She continued eating off the tray on her lap, watching TV and slowly going off to bed, her walking stick leading the way to her bedroom. I'd observed this ritual so many times I knew that I was starting to take it for granted.

Lex McCrae was nowhere to be seen, not around his horses or on the ridge of his property that overlooked the Sloggett home. Ron didn't appear around the school, and those parents that dropped in for a quick chat before school were not to be seen. A heavy silence had settled over Jeogla – it was like the whole district was in mourning, a sadness that not even the songs of rosellas could brighten.

The atmosphere in Wollomombi was the same, a pall hung over the village; people were obviously wanting talk about the result but were too sad to even try and start a conversation. All those years of planning were now lost. Even if the movement got off the ground again, it would take decades to rebuild and launch. The old graziers were too old, and who knew what plans their successors would make?

Frank Robson rubbed his hands on his apron, and shrugged his shoulders. Oh well, that's the way it goes.

The only two people I was able to talk about it were Alex and Bill.

Alex said he'd predicted the result, although he thought the margin would be a lot greater. Bill said the referendum would be defeated. Labor had put up a sterling effort in campaigning against it, but the Country Party's mistake had been to include Newcastle and the Lower Hunter in the boundaries. The Novocastrians are essentially urban people, he explained, and tied to the steel works – and Sydney – for their future. And being tied to Sydney means belonging to New South Wales.

You'll be on holidays soon, anyway, Alex advised. Time to put all this behind us. Everyone needs a break from political parties and all that talk.

Bill was taking his family for a holiday to the coast.

Alex had work in the parish and couldn't leave. A minister's work is never done, mates, school holidays or no school holidays. Babies get born all the time and must bechristened, people die all the time and funeral arrangements must be made, others get married. There are sick people to visit in hospital, sermons to write and church council meetings to attend. The books have to stay balanced. All for the love of God, he winked and laughed, drawing on another cigarette and sipping a whiskey. We were all in the manse, sitting in the lounge room.

When he put it like that, I hadn't really thought of all the work his ministry entailed.

I was counting the days until school ended on Friday 12th May. My plan was to leave as early as possible next day, and hoped to be Sydney after lunch time. My parents had advised against driving at night. Of course I argued that I'd had plenty of experience driving in the country at night by now, and I would be safe. Yes, they agreed, but they also said it would still be safer if I drove during the day. So do it for us, was their final request, and I agreed.

For some reason, the memory of writing "Wyatts Creek" flashed into my mind. Why should I remember it now, after the talk of politics and planning to drive to Sydney? The night when I argued with myself and ended up by writing poem I might never have expected. That poem was somehow a turning point in my life, and not since then, had I felt as I did, even though I had written other poems; but they all lacked a vehemence and depth of feeling, an intensity of self-expression that was unconquerable, except in the writing of the poem. Something stirred in me now that hadn't stirred for a long time, and I began an argument with myself, between the two warring halves of what my life was becoming, the teacher and the poet.

The prospect of the long drive home was exciting. Not since arriving in the rain had I gone on a long drive, a distance that would challenge and educate. Travelling down the Moonbi Hills, seeing the countryside in reverse, the imagined sea on my left, the western slopes on my right.

When I returned in the second term I was hoping to start a story with the children, even though we were still reading and discussing poetry.

I'd made a selection by cutting poems out of the "School Magazine" and creating a personal anthology. I even designed a cover for the book in green, blue and red colours. The Sea, Water and Rain were popular topics. We read poems by Henry Longfellow, James Reeves (The children thought the first line of "The Sea" – *The sea is a hungry dog* – was an amazing metaphor). We read Kenneth Slessor and Hugh McCrae. One poem the children liked was written by Anon:

The rain it raineth every day,
Upon the just and unjust fellow,
But more upon the just, because
The unjust hath the just's umbrella.

I explained what Anon stood for and they laughed and started calling each other "Anon" instead by their real names, and for the rest of that day there were fourteen "Anons" in the school, each claiming they were a famous poet.

Last Day of Term

The last day of term, in a sense, was an anticlimax. I'd completed the term returns of enrolment and attendance, forwarding the Original to Head Office, and because my school was classed as a fourth class school, the First through the school inspector to the north-west directorate. I retained the Second copy in the school.

I also submitted the required form, to the school inspector, of those organisations that had used the school during the term, in this case it being only one, the Jeogla District Dingo Destruction Association. I'd arrived at school an hour earlier than my usual time, and this paperwork was done before classes started. The mail was addressed and prepared for Gerald to pick up around noon.

First term ended today, Friday 12th May.

Second term would begin and all schools reopen, Tuesday, 23rd May.

Allowing two days for driving at either end of the holidays, I'd have nine days at home.

I couldn't wait!

And even though Carrie would be up after school to clean up we spent part of the day in a general clean-up, not just the schoolroom but the yard also, including some weeding of the garden, around the roses and dahlias. Cones had fallen off the pines at the far end of the yard, so we gathered these up, put them into wooden boxes and stored them in the shelter shed. When they dried out, we'd have them for firewood, and with winter coming we'd need plenty. I'd already watched as they burnt, the resin hissing out of them, crackling and popping at the heat made them explode, then finally burning and giving the most intense heat from each cone. I took a small branch with several cones attached, put it into the boot of my car and said I was taking them back to Sydney, as a souvenir, to show my parents. I explained this to the children and I could see how they stared at each other wonderingly, as if to ask, Why?

In the afternoon we talked about what we'd be doing in the holidays. Most of them weren't going anywhere; some said they might go to the coast to visit friends or family if mum or dad had the time to drive them over – and then have to come and get them later. Whatever, they all seemed content with their lot of staying at Jeogla or at the Oaky River dam. That's where their fathers worked, and that's where they'd play. Or they'd go into town during the week with their mothers; that was something always to look forward to.

I told them I was hoping to catch up with friends and I wanted to go into the city to buy books – lots of books, poetry and art books, as well as go to a big record shop in George Street and buy some new LPs.

After dismissing them and wishing everyone a happy holiday, I returned inside the schoolroom, made sure all cupboards and windows were locked. Carrie would be up here in less than an hour, and I knew she'd double-check; then I closed the school, wired the yellow gate closed with its own piece of fencing wire and drove down the yellow-dust road, pleased it would be the last time for almost two weeks. The Anzac Day service and the New England New State referendum suddenly became events of the past, whose images that were blown away and disappeared in the swirls of dust that rose behind my car.

After Carrie drove up to the school I began to pack. Books would stay behind, the small portable record player and a handful of record albums would come with me. Clothes were kept to a minimum. I planned to leave at sunrise, even without having breakfast, travel into Armidale, fill up with petrol and maybe stop once more after leaving the upper Hunter Valley, then through Singleton and along the Putty Road to Windsor, onto Parramatta and Regents Park.

But Carrie would have none of that "without breakfast" talk.

Ribbon of Highway

Next morning Carrie woke me at six o'clock. Come an' have a light breakfast, an' then yer can be off.

I'd said goodbye to Granma and Gerald last night at dinnertime and, now, after breakfast, I was on the road.

Giving Carrie a hug I told her I'd be back the day before school started. Drive carefully, now, yer hear? The same caution, the same tone of voice that I'd heard her use with Gerald many times.

With the sun rising behind me I started on the winding road home, away from the Slogget house, past Jeogla Station and where I knew Ron's parents lived. Driving over the Oaky River, I slowed down. Waterbirds were all over it, coming to life as the day came to life. I wound down my window and listened to songs that were soft and loud, that whispered and screeched, and then were gone.

When I reached the Grafton Road and turned south, a phrase from Woody Guthrie's folk song "This Land Is Your Land" sprung to mind ...*a ribbon of highway...*

There'd been no traffic until that point, but now the occasional truck or car passed me with its headlights still turned on. After I filled the car's tank in Armidale and drove away I felt as if I were ten feet tall. For a while I kept the window down. My head swam with exhilaration. The countryside around me was all light. There were green paddocks and yellow-brown paddocks, mauve in the distance, grey and brown, dotted with livestock, farmhouses, towns and charming small villages with their war memorials, their pubs and milk bars, their grocery stores and newsagencies.

The day was clear but windy, full of sunlight that sheared off solid formations or sunk deeply into the earth, changing its collective colours, enriching them, setting a fire to them,

The granite rocks and boulders that had looked monstrous and threatening on my drive up in the rain in

January, were filled with a solid but luminous presence. The leaves on trees, in the last grip of autumn, swayed and were filled with transparent red and brown colours, oranges and yellows.

I drove over creeks and rivers lined with weeping willows, many of whose waters exposed rocks that formed flat stepping stones from one side to the other; and all the time, without fail, there were birds in the sky…Magpies, galahs, cockatoos, hawks, parrots, crows, cranes, small birds and large birds, birds whose names I knew and those I didn't.

When I reached the Moonbi Hills I knew the ocean was far to my left by now, in the direction of Kempsey and Port Macquarie, over forests and ranges, bluish-green in the distance, rivers and more creeks flowing to the east, to the tributaries and outlets where beaches fronted the Pacific Ocean, turquoise waves and breaking foam, the salt-sea air with its invigorating power. Below lay the city of Tamworth, and the slopes and plains of New South Wales beyond, far, far ahead in a haze of light. I could only imagine the patchwork greens and browns, the ploughed and unploughed paddocks.

Coming down from the Liverpool ranges and passing through Murrurundi, I was in coal-mining country. Coal trucks stood by railway sidings, some trucks were full, others waiting to be filled, ready to be hauled by diesel locomotives. These were the hills of the Upper Hunter with their rich lodes of coal. Scone, Aberdeen and Muswellbrook lay ahead, and then Singleton, where I planned to stop and have lunch.

Black swans on Lake Liddell were a watercolour image painted by an artist on a hazy distance. Out on the water and among the reeds, their heads bobbing, they belonged to a different world from the power station, almost directly opposite, on the other side of the New England Highway, where thick clouds of steam rose like signals from the giant concrete chimney stacks.

I bought a sandwich and milkshake in Singleton and had these in a park, topped up the car with petrol and turned right for the Putty Road. This was the longest haul, perhaps, through forests and negotiating hairpin bends; there was little or no room for overtaking. I calculated it was about 100 – 120 miles before I reached the outer zone of the Sydney area. My ribbon of highway brought me into a green shaded part of the map, and that meant forests and mountains range, with little or no signs of human habitation.

The further I travelled from Singleton, the taller and deeper the forests became, trees that grew on both side of the road and permitted only the barest of sunlight to penetrate. Shadows were green. Reflections were green. I heard whipbirds in several places when I slowed and wound down the window. At one spot, negotiating a difficult hairpin bend, I'd almost stopped. By the side of the road was a dead kangaroo, and tearing into it was a wedge-tailed eagle which ignored me until I sounded the car horn. I'd wound the window up and then stared right into its eyes, as it spun its head around and looked up, unafraid. If it were a human I'd say it glared at me, in a warning, its wings slightly spread.

Once out of the forested area, properties appeared. Unlike the farmhouses elsewhere that I'd passed along the highway these were mostly acreage holdings and might have been what city people called "hobby farms". At Colo Heights, I pulled over and stopped to look at a one-teacher school that reminded me of Jeogla. Within throwing distance of the road, I could see there was no electricity connected to the school. One school building, a shelter shed and two toilets, in the middle of a clearing, surrounded by sandstone formations and more forests.

After the Colo River with its rattling wooden bridge, where a marble plaque was fixed to a wall of green rock and water was streaming and looked down at what appeared to be a grave – there were more hairpin bends and steep climbs, probably the steepest since leaving Jeogla. Semi-trailers held up traffic which didn't thin out until the Wilberforce and Windsor districts. In my blood I could sense Parramatta wasn't far off, and that only made me more impatient to get to Regents Park.

By the time I'd reached the Bankstown area, coming in from Woodville Road, I knew I was home even though I wasn't there yet.

My ribbon of highway had run out, with less than ten minutes of driving left.

First Things First

As I expected, my father wasn't at home, but then neither was my mother; that surprised me because it was my parents who insisted I not drive at night. My father would be at work, but my mother, where could she have gone?

Bobby the dog ran around me in circles, barking and madly wagging his tail. He ran up and down the garden,through the potatoes and cabbages, turning up plants and breaking off leaves. Finally, exhausted, he lay at my feet, as if to say, I'm happy to see you!

I had a key to the back door and let myself in, went to my room and plopped on to the bed; tiredness hit me and I felt myself falling asleep, travelling in a strange motor vehicle out of daylight, along a highway that ran alongside a forest and then into it, accelerating until my head was thrown back, my mouth unable to close and I couldn't breathe; but the sleep was deep, restful, and there were no dreams, unless it was the highway, the force of acceleration and the forest.

My left shoulder had snagged on something. I shook and tried to break free – but was held fast. Back and forth it was shaken. Then I heard, Alright, stay sleeping. My mother's voice came from above me.

Hello, Mum, I said, blinking. I'm home.

She apologised for not being home – because she had to "run up to the shops" and get some fresh meat for dinner. I'm glad you did the right thing and let yourself in – and got some rest.

*

We were seated in the kitchen. She said, First things first. It's too early to have dinner, but I've made you a sandwich, and you can eat that while you tell me about your trip home.

When I said there wasn't much to tell, she said, Nonsense. You've driven nearly eight hours. There must be a million things to tell me. Or you can wait until your father comes home, then you can tell us both.

I agreed. In the meantime I'd unload the car and even give it a wash. My mother thought it was a good idea to wash the car, and said that since tomorrow was Sunday I'd be driving my parents to Mass.

She asked me, When was the last time you washed it? It looks filthy.

Not since before I left in January, I replied.

How do you keep it clean?

I don't. The rain washes it.

Very well, if you hurry up you can have it washed before it gets dark. There's no need to polish it; but you can do that before you return to Jeogla.

The car belonged to my parents, but as neither of them drove I was allowed to take it with me to Jeogla. A godsend, from my parents. Why would I want to disobey either of them when it came to matters relating to the car. Yes, Mum.

*

My father came home, just as I was finishing. Ah, Peter, Peter, he smiled. It's so good to see you. We hugged and I gave him a kiss on the cheek. He smelt of Velvet soap, that thick, yellow soap I knew the men washed with when they finished for the day on the Waterboard sites. My mind slipped back in time. I remembered when I was younger I'd travelled with my father to some of these sites in the school holidays, and watched how they stripped off to the waist and washed themselves using just a basin of water.

We talked during dinner and I told my parents of my plans for the holidays. I'd rung P and we were going into the city on Monday, having a meal and going to a movie. Later in the week we thought we'd go to the museum or the art gallery – or go to both. We'd just play it by ear.

My mother asked, What's it got to do with music?

I said, Nothing. It has nothing to do with music. It's just an English expression meaning we'll just do whatever comes along, not making any specific plans.

Then you should say exactly what you mean. Older people like myself, especially the ones from Europe, have enough trouble coping with words. Remember, Say exactly what you mean.

Yes, Mum. You're right. I thought that maybe P and I would go for a drive one day – maybe down to Kiama, and have a picnic; but I also want to go into the city and buy books – lots of books.

Why, Peter? My father asked. Don't you have enough books?

No, no, no, I replied rapidly. Not nearly enough...Dad, Mum, you can never have enough books. Don't you know that? I don't just learn from books and enjoy them. They become my friends. Books keep me company...So does music.

As I spoke I could sense tension in the room, an argument brewing, especially if my mother bought into the conversation, so I changed tack and said, There won't be many books, just a few – besides, I'll take them back with me to Jeogla. You won't even know they exist. Now, can I tell you about everything that's happened at Jeogla since I returned after the Easter holidays.

Of course, my father said warmly, take your time.

My mother washed the dishes and my father wiped up; when I offered to help they refused and said I had enough to do. Just talk, my mother said, We're both listening.

I told them about the Anzac Day service and about the people I'd met, people like Professor John Challis from the university in Armidale. I told them about the small schools conference I attended and what it was like to work on a polling booth for the New England New State referendum.

We saw the results of that on TV, my mother said....And

we thought of you. Imagine, you worked on a polling booth. Did you feel important? Was it interesting? she asked.

No, I didn't feel important. At first I thought I couldn't handle the job – until one of the boys offered to help me; but it was more interesting than I can describe. You see a side of people you never expected to see, especially when they are so passionate about local politics.

Just then the phone rang. It was P. My mother took the call, and then called me to the phone. After a few minutes I returned and told my parents that I'd been invited by P's parents for dinner tomorrow night at their home.

Have a good time, my father said.

Remember Mass is tomorrow – at noon, my mother added. We're going to St Felix's at Bankstown. Good thing you washed the car.

V

The Future

I hadn't eaten at P's home since before Christmas last year. I was overjoyed to see her and couldn't stop looking at her and smiling during the meal. I even winked across the table, hoping neither of her parents had seen me. Her father was the second-in charge of a large multinational company, he worked in the city and was often overseas; her mother had been a teacher but now, with her three daughters grown up and moved out of home, confined herself to working as a volunteer charity worker.

So, what's Jeogla like? Mr R asked.

It's probably boring to people like you, I said (but I was surprised that he pronounced it correctly)...Cattle, sheep, cold weather, lots of rain. Armidale is 33 miles away and I go in there once a week, on Saturdays.

How many children do you teach? Mrs R asked.

Fourteen.

I had thirty in my little school. Did I tell you I taught in a small school? That was in the wheat belt of W.A.

Yes, you mentioned it once, I replied.

All this time P kept her eyes down on her meal, as if not wanting to intrude on her parents conversation with me.

Mr R was a tall man, partly bald, bespectacled, with a wide, friendly smile. He leant back in his chair from time

time, adjusted his glasses and ate his food with gusto.

Again, I thanked them for inviting me over.

We ate in a long space that was a dining room at one end and a lounge room at the other. Book shelves ran along one entire wall. I kept looking at the books, and thought of the book case in my room at Jeogla.

Mrs R saw me looking at the books. Would you like to borrow one? she asked.

No, thanks, I said.

They're mostly history books, P said. Mum loves history, especially English history. She could easily teach it at university level – that's how good she is. Dad, on the other hand, loves reading novels.

Not business books? I asked.

Goodness me, no, he laughed. They're boring, boring, boring.

So how you keep up with business? I asked, trying to impress.

Oh, P interjected, that all comes from experience. Dad keeps all that business information in his head. He's got a marvellous memory. Retains everything. Plus there's all that boardroom stuff we mere mortals can only guess at.

Experience, Mr R, said. Best teacher in the business world.

Pity some of the kings and queens of England weren't more business-like in their lives, instead of getting themselves tied up in having affairs and wars that never made sense, said Mrs R. All about victories and glory, it was. Never mind the people they taxed to death and trod on. What about the Potato Famine, dear, are you interested in that? I have a marvellous book on that...Little wonder the Irish dislike the English so much...All that waste of life. How those poor people suffered. What a tragedy that Potato Famine turned out to be...

Told you so, P said and laughed. Don't get her started.

She obviously cares about people, I said sympathetically.

After dinner we retired to the lounge room where coffee, tea and biscuits were served.

What are your plans beyond Jeogla? For the future? Mr R asked me.

I'm not sure what "beyond Jeogla" means? I said. I intend enrolling at the University of New England next year, as an external student, to complete my B.A. After my three years of country service are completed, I'll apply for a city appointment. That's all. Nothing beyond the next three years.

Well, P is hoping to go overseas. Mrs R said. Although, mind you, we'd rather not lose another daughter overseas. One is enough… But if she does go, at least we'll have our eldest in Sydney.

Yes, I know that, I replied, feeling uneasy about the direction the conversation had taken.

P said nothing, neither did Mr R. It was like both were observing a situation they were aware of intimately, but chose to say nothing.

How are your parents? Mr R asked.

Thanks for asking, I said, feeling nervous. Both have their health. Both are working. They're saving money to have the house brick-veneered.

What's the house made of? Mr R asked.

Fibro, I said. That's all they could afford when they bought it. They paid it off in four years – and soon they'll have a brick house, something they've always wanted.

I've always admired your parents – and people like them – said Mrs R. People who came to Australia with nothing, asked nothing from the government, worked hard, saved their money and rebuilt their lives from scratch. The so-called True-blue Aussies can learn a lot about that work ethic.

Apart from this somewhat scattered conversation there was little response from P towards me, except once for a brief, sweet smile. When it came time to leave, I said goodnight to Mr and Mrs R, and thanked them for having me to dinner.The former shook hands with me, the latter said, Goodnight, dear. P will see you out.

We sat on the steps of the veranda and talked for a while longer, about what I'd been doing at Jeogla and she told me about her studies – as well as her plans for moving out of home before the end of the year, maybe even in the next few weeks, as soon as suitable accommodation could be found close to Sydney University. Mrs R's coughing, several times in the hallway behind us, was a hint for P to come inside.

Will I still see you tomorrow? I asked.

Yes, as we've arranged. Why not?

I thought tonight's dinner might be replacing our meeting?

Why should it?

Just a thought.

We kissed goodnight and I drove off, pleased with the evening, still smelling the scent of flowers from the garden.

Nothing in the World

We met on the steps of the Town Hall and went for a cappuccino with raisin toast to a coffee shop in Rowe Street, our plan being to take in a movie and then have lunch down at Circular Quay.

A pale autumn light was falling onto the city when I emerged out of the semi-darkness of the railway tunnel at Town Hall, and stepped out into George Street. P was already there, waiting for me, smiling her irresistible smile; we walked into the heart of the city, holding hands, swinging them, without a worry in the world. I was so happy to be alive. She pointed to one of the top floors of a building in Market Street. That's Dad's office up there. Can you imagine what it must be like cooped up inside?

No, I can't, I said.

It was exciting to stand in Rowe Street, more a laneway than a street, with its art galleries, bohemian clothes and jewellery shops, restaurants and cafes, with Rowe Street Records where one could order records from overseas. We must go there, I said, if not today maybe some other time. There's not a record shop like it anywhere else in Sydney.

I know, P said.

Down a small flight of stairs, and into a coffee shop, we ordered the raisin toast and cappuccino, and sat at a small dark-timbered round table. Parisians scenes and faces hung in frames around the walls. Many of the men in these photos wore berets and smoked cigarettes, while the women were thin and had long blonde hair, looked wistfully over their shoulders or stood in groups on corners. The Eiffel Tower, the Bridges of Paris and the Seine stared at us while we stared back and thought we were knowledgeable.

Wouldn't you like to go there sometimes? P asked.

Yes, I said, but I wonder if I will?

I intend to, said P emphatically.

When? I asked.

Maybe next year – or as soon as I get away from Australia. She waited, before she said, That's what I want to talk about.

About Paris?

About my going away – and us.

I paused, mid-breath, to hear the next words.

At the moment, she said, I can't see a future for us – not like this anyway. You've got this year and two more years of country service to complete in the bush, and I can't wait to get out of Australia.

So?

So, I think we shouldn't see each other anymore – at least not for the present.

And…?

And we can still stay friends. Or you can wait until I return from overseas…

You want me to wait until you get the travel bug out of your system – go and see Paris and Dublin and London and the rest of Europe – and then we pick up where we left off. Is that it?

Well, yes.

She looked me straight in the eyes and I knew exactly what she was doing.

So, we're breaking up?

I'm sorry, Peter, but the uncertainty of this relationship has been weighing on my mind for a long time. I need to say it now. Sooner than later.

So last night was The Last Supper?

Last night was last night. This is now. Last night was very special. My parents have no idea I'm doing this today.

My raisin toast tasted like dry bread and my cappuccino like dishwater. I pushed them away and stared at a picture of the Seine in its frame, tranquilly flowing nowhere, trapped in its time-frame.

I don't know what to say, I almost stuttered. I'm shocked.

I'm so sorry.

Me too.

A customer had walked in, sat down and lit up a cigarette. From the far corner its menthol aroma drifted across to us and made my eyes water.

Please, she said, taking my hand…Please try to understand.

How does one understand saying goodbye to someone you've known for three years, and had a relationship with – tell me that? It's not about understanding, don't you see? It's about handling the emotions – and at the moment they're swirling inside me like planets that have collided!

Peter…

Fine, I said, withdrawing my hand from hers. Goodbye.... The day was too good to be true. They should be playing "Autumn Leaves" for us, don't you think?

She said nothing.

I wanted to sit there and plead with her, make her reconsider what she'd said, but she'd said so much in so few words I knew it was useless. This wasn't a spur-of-the moment decision, this was a speech prepared in advance.

The silence was brief but painful, intense. The planets continued to collide. I had no idea what to do next.

We stood up simultaneously, looked into each other's eyes, hugged and kissed, and she was gone – up the stairs, turned left, and left again, into the city.

I followed, but instead of turning left I turned right, towards Circular Quay.

*

At first, the salt air burnt my eyes. I knew I must be crying because everything was watery, out of focus. I sat on the steps of a building and dried my eyes many times until the tears stopped.

I kept seeing images of the scene in the coffee shop. The

wind off the water was strong and blew whatever words I could remember around in my head and out of my head, some bounced back, others disappeared.

Seagulls swooped overhead with noisy cries, searching for food.

Ferries traversed the harbour, ploughing through water, leaving white furrows of foam in their wake, their green and yellow coloured bodies resembling giant shell fish. The harbour bridge looked like it had been drawn on the sky with a crayon.

People fished off the quay's piers and walls, some with fishing rods, others with cork handlines, baiting hooks with prawns and bread.

I walked around Bennelong Point and into the Botanic Gardens, then returned to the heart of the city, going into the Angus & Robertson bookstore in Castlereagh Street where I bought poetry and art books. In Nicholsons record shop in George Street I bought *Big Hits (High Tide and Green Grass)* by the Rolling Stones and the *Help!* album by the Beatles, as well an album by the Mamas and the Papas; but best of all was finding *Dylan Thomas Reading His Complete Recorded Poetry* in the Spoken Word section of the shop. A double album for only $12.40.

*

Goodness me, my mother said, when I walked in the door. What's happened to you? And what're all those bags you're carrying?

They're mostly books, Mum – and I look how I look because P and I have broken up.

Oh, Peter, I'm so sorry. She put her arms around me and hugged me, books and all. I'm so sorry, she kept repeating.

In my room I sorted out the books and records I'd bought and thought they made a solid pile. I read through the titles of songs on the albums but didn't have the heart or inclination to play any of them. I decided to leave the books until later.

I rang Kevin and told him about my breakup with P and he commiserated. He was going to Swansea Heads with his family to visit two aunts, Mary and Peg, who lived there but told me he'd call when the family returned.

My father said, It's all for the best, Peter. In the long run, it's all for the best. You'll see.

I stood in the back garden and found solace among the vegetables and fruit trees. My parents always grew stone fruits and the garden was coming to life with these winter crops. The garden shone with a subdued light, grey, but warm. The cabbages were gigantic, their leaves resembling metallic steel-blue plates. The chooks clucked in the yard and the dog wagged its tail. What more could I have wanted? Nothing. But nothing in the world could have prepared me for the shock of separation from P in the morning. My parents would object vehemently to what I was considering, and I would have to choose my moment to tell them.

A Hard Choice, but

Over dinner, after I'd praised my mother's cooking, I said, Mum and Dad, I'm going back early to Jeogla

You're what?

Going back early to Jeogla. Maybe even tomorrow or the day after. I want to get out of Sydney. Forget yesterday. I don't want to mope around the house doing nothing.

But, but… my mother began to interrupt but the look she got from my father made her stop. She said nothing more.

My father said, We don't want you to go early, Peter, but if that's what you want, of course we'll support you. We understand what's happened and if you feel that getting out of Sydney is best for you, so be it.

This isn't easy, I said. It's a hard choice, but, that's how I feel. Staying here with you or just disappearing north. I don't want to keep thinking about things as they were. Ok? I'll wash the car again, polish it, chrome and all. Who knows what the weather will be like up there when I return? The car's got to look good, yes? And when Kevin calls after I've gone, tell him I'm back at Jeogla. He'll understand.

My decision went down better than I thought it would. There were no objections.

*

I left on the morning of the second day after my breakup with P.

At 6a.m. I drove my father to the railway station for him to catch his train to work at Warwick Farm, and two hours later I drove my mother so that she could catch her train to work at Strathfield. The goodbye scenes were not as emotional as I thought they'd be. I promised both parents I'd stay in touch and would drive safely. I'd ring as soon as I got to Armidale. I hadn't informed Carrie, but my plan was to ring her from Armidale.

My father had said, This will all work out one day, Peter. The change has started.

As she got out of the car, my mother's last comment was, You've changed overnight. Do you know that?

Scone

When I drove over Silverwater Bridge in Sydney I saw a pelican flying north, along the Parramatta River and over the suburbs, in the direction that I was heading. From Hornsby I followed the Pacific Highway, through the towns of the Central Coast and into Newcastle.

There wasn't much traffic on the road, and as I left each city, the landscape changed to semi-rural and rural. Farmhouses, cows in paddocks, hens in a yard, saw mills, orchards, abattoirs, mining villages, main streets and side streets, shops and pubs, signs to wineries, petrol stations, small schools, bridges over creeks and rivers. Sydney and Newcastle disappeared further into the rear vision mirror. Maitland, Singleton, Muswellbrook, Aberdeen, Scone. The New England Highway and its townships was beginning to look familiar.

I sat in a park in Scone and ate fish and chips. A railway line ran across the main street and off into the green distance.

You okay, son?

An old man on a bicycle stopped behind me. He looked like he hadn't washed or combed his hair for weeks. His bicycle had a hessian bag tied to a frame over the back wheel.

Just hungry, I replied.

Goin' far?

Armidale.

He kept looking at my food.

Have a chip, I said.

Thanks, son.

I tipped several into his hand and broke off a piece of fish.

He sat down next to me. What'cha do? he asked.

School teacher.

Oh?

Are you going far?

Oh, just ridin'… I got friends in Goonoo Goonoo. Might stay with 'em…Fred's me name, he said. Used ter be a newspaper man. Fell on hard times an' now I jest travel from place ter place...Do the odd job, make a bit of money....an' move on. Sleep under the stars. What's yer name?

Peter.

Pleased ter meet yer.

We shook hands. I gave him some more chips and another piece of fish. Now all the food was gone.

What makes you ride into the distance like that on a push bike?

Well, I don't have a car. Me bike's strong. I don't ride fast. I just decided I wanted to leave...Spur of the moment thing, if yer know what I mean... Well, Peter, I gotter push on. Thanks for the fish 'n' chips.

Goodbye, Fred.

The bike wobbled as he left, across the railway line and downhill, riding by the side of the road, joining a line of strung-out cars and semi-trailers. I thought he might look back and wave, but he didn't.

His words about "the spur of the moment thing" struck a chord in my head. I decided immediately not to travel any further. I would stay overnight in Scone, in this beautiful small town surrounded by green paddocks. To my left, and further behind was a motel, one that looked like it had been newly built. Perfect.

Back in Sydney I'd bought *The Life of Dylan Thomas* by Constantine Fitzgibbon and couldn't wait to start reading it. Together with the poetry recording and the *Collected Poems 1934-1952* that I already owned it seemed I had everything needed to keep my passion for Dylan Thomas's poetry alive. I was disappointed to find that *The force that through the green fuse drives the flower* was not included on the recording. The biography was a grand book, an impressive tome, with its Augustus John portrait of Dylan Thomas in full colour on the cover.

After I checked into the motel I bought a milkshake and

walked round town, using a street map that the receptionist at the motel had given me, taking in the sights and mingling with the locals in the main street which was still the New England Highway although it was called Kelly Street. Library, police station, fire station, RSL. Further back from Kelly Street, I found a church, St Luke's Anglican, that I thought was a very impressive building. I wanted to go in, but it was locked, so I asked a man where the Catholic Church was. He told me, St Mary's Queen of Peace, in Short Street, not that far a walk, mate.

Built of bluestone it was just as impressive with its square belltower, looking more like a medieval castle than a church, surrounded by pines; it was open and I walked in, sat in one of the pews and let my mind wander over the altar, the crucifix, unlit candles, the sanctuary lamp. The pews smelt of wax. I started to think of my altar-boy days and remembered the smell of burning incense, the way I'd sneeze when resin was sprinkled over the burning charcoal during Benediction.

A Mamas and Papas song came to mind, "California Dreamin'" – about a person in New York going into a church and pretending to pray. Why would anyone pretend to pray? You either wanted to or you didn't. You can't fool God. New York was cold and grey. So leave, I always thought to myself. Deep down, that singer wanted to stay a dreamer.

Nothing happened out of the ordinary. I sat there and found myself saying a Hail Mary, over and over. I blessed myself, stood up, genuflected and left.

There was plenty of daylight left so I checked my map and found there was no scenic lookout in Scone, as there was in Armidale, but there were lots of hills. I returned to the motel, got into my car and drove out on to the Gundy Road. Again, it was a shot in the dark, following an arrow that pointed to Lake Glenbawn, Moonan Flat, Belltrees and other places. Lake. Bell. Trees. A poetical combination of words!

Gundy itself was a small rural village with a general stone and a pub; but further along, I stopped and stood on a hill that resembled a ridge. I looked down on the township of Scone on one side and the Glenbawn Dam on the other. The water was deep, ultramarine, shining with silver reflections. The hazy distances were more blue than green, yet the whole countryside was green, dotted with trees and small patches of forest. Signs had pointed to various horse studs in the district and you could these spread over the countryside, with their white fences and gates. Horses grazed in these paddocks.

When I stopped and looked back in the direction I'd come from, songs of birds filled the air, the scent of eucalypts blew strongly in the wind and I began to feel heady, perhaps from standing too long in the sun. I thought of Wyatts Creek and the loving way Ron talked about it.

In Moonan Flat I slowed down to have a look at the Catholic weatherboard church, Immaculate Heart of Mary. I thought it resembled a small school; it had a small belltower on top, like something out of a colonial history book, old but quaint.

From a distance the "Belltrees" homestead looked magnificent. Resembling a residential castle, it stood at the end of a long driveway and I stopped and got out of the car, at an open gate, to admire it. Painted white, of an Italianate design with all-enclosing verandas on both levels and decorated with wrought-iron, it stood out against a green backdrop of undulating hills. Cattle grazed in the foreground and pink-flowering trees grew along the perimeters of paddocks.

These sights were bewildering, but they were starting to confuse me, and I knew it was time to return. The drive was giving me a headache. All this stopping and starting. I'd had enough of it. I needed to freshen up, clear my head, have dinner and read the Constantine Fitzgibbon book. For whatever reason, the drive back seemed longer than the drive out.

I rang my parents from the motel and told them what I'd done. They repeated their advice about driving safely and asked me to let them know when I arrived at Jeogla.

Are you sure everything is fine? both parents asked.

Never been better, I said. Despite the headache, I meant what I said. I hoped they were proud of me for making the decision to leave Sydney early.

⁂

Two hours later I was back in the motel, having taken a shower and gone out for a mixed grill in one of the cafes in town.

The room I had was at the back of the building, the "quietest here" I'd been assured. So it seemed: no sound from rumbling semis or cars on the highway. My room overlooked open space, flat grass paddocks and a forest in the far distance. Magpies could be seen stalking the ground, galahs wheeled overhead.

The books I'd bought in Sydney included *Poems* by Kenneth Slessor, *Five Senses* by Judith Wright and *Selected Poems of Louis Macneice*, edited by W.H. Auden, as well as a book of children's poetry, *A Child's Garden of Verses* by Robert Louis Stevenson; this was illustrated with the most brilliant pictures by Brian Wildsmith. I'd never heard of Brian Wildsmith, but he was a genius, I thought, for the images and colours he used. A small stack of art books included pictorial biographies of van Gogh, Chagall, Toulouse-Lautrec, Rodin, Post-Impressionist artists and El Greco.

The portrait of Dylan Thomas stared out from all these books and others that I'd brought in from my car, as if the book was saying, *Read me.* I had never read the biography of a poet before. *Start*, it continued speaking.

Getting into bed, turning on a lamp, I started to read,

but first stared at the photograph of Dylan standing in the graveyard at Laugharne, waist-high in flowers, leaning against a railing, surrounded by headstones and trees, the caption underneath the photograph read, "Time has ticked a heaven round the stars." I knew it from *The force that through the green fuse drives the flower.*

The sound of a train woke me. I'd fallen asleep and the book had slipped off my chest. What was the time? Two or three in the morning. A train was tunnelling through the night, not far away. Turning off the bedside lamp I stumbled to the back window and peered into the darkness. The whole landscape was washed in silver light – as if an invisible beacon was shining overhead, something stronger than the moon, closer, more immediate, illuminating the scene I'd looked at earlier. Instead of returning to bed, I stood at the window, absorbing the spectral landscape, being drawn deeper into it, listening to the noise from the train as it receded, until I felt exhausted, my eyes burning, and I could keep them open no longer. I went back to bed.

Breakfast! A voice called.

There was a knock on the door and I took the tray left outside on the step. The air was crisp, sharp. The grass in the grounds of the motel was a sheet of frost, glittering in the light. Magpies stood around in the sun, throwing back their heads and singing. How good is this? I thought. Songs going up to Heaven before breakfast!

Good morning. Sleep well? It was the man from reception, delivering breakfast to another room.

I did, thank you. Isn't this something?

Can't beat the rising sun, he replied, and was gone, back to the office.

An hour later I was on the road, heading north towards Murrurundi, Tamworth, Armidale and Jeogla – at a point along the road remembering Fred on his bicycle, and wondering how he fell from grace as a newspaper man.

Well, Look Who's 'ere

The drive from Scone had gone without incident; when I arrived in Armidale I stopped in Beardy Street at the IXL café and ordered a pot of tea.

What would I say to the Sloggets about returning early? Or to the Clarks?

As I drove, the last few days kept running through my head, especially the break-up with P. My parents' reaction and their understanding of my decision to leave home early.

The meeting with Fred led to my stopover in Scone and the commencement of my reading of the Dylan Thomas biography. I wondered if the trip around the district had been for nothing; but getting up at night, looking out onto the silver landscape, precipitated a series of conversations with myself. They bordered on the angry and quarrelsome. It was like I'd been looking at myself, and something that I couldn't articulate sank into me. The reaction was similar to the conversation I had with myself before I wrote "Wyatts Creek".

Here was the story of a poet I could identify with. Aspects of his life related to mine and, without apology, I felt empowered. I started to realise I should never apologise for being myself. No matter how difficult things became or what people thought of me.

I read that Dylan Thomas was at the bottom of the class in every subject except English. So was I. In primary school, words came easily, the ability to construct sentences, to understand subject, verb, object, predicate, clauses and phrases, prepositions. Later, in high school, it was metaphor, imagery, symbolism, hyperbole, personification. I would hear a word or lines from a poem and remember them. I made up rhymes. I loved listening to the lyrics of a song because I heard it as a poem, set to music, thereby creating a melody.

No one in my family read Shakespeare to me, as Dylan Thomas's father had read to him, but my mother told me stories from the Ukraine, poems and songs she sang. I heard about a great Ukrainian poet named Taras Shevchenko. He was to the Ukraine what Shakespeare was to England. He wrote of the country's landscapes, mountains, rivers, the lives of people in the history of the Ukraine. Most of all, he wrote about liberty.

The biography helped to deepen the affinity that I felt when I first read Dylan Thomas's poetry.

*

Before going on to Jeogla I stopped at Wollomombi when I saw Alec and Jill's car parked outside the manse.

Cassie came bounding from the paddock behind the manse, barking at me and almost knocking me over.

Alex came outside. Hey, mate. You're back early. What's up?

My girlfriend and I broke up.

Oh, he said, cupping his hand to his mouth. Is that all? He asked. Coming over, he put an arm around my shoulder. Gee, I'm sorry. I didn't mean to laugh.

That alright, I replied. Better than crying.

Jill came out of the manse. Alex beat me to an explanation. He's broken up with his girlfriend.

Oh, you poor thing, Jill said. Come inside and have a cuppa.

I just had one.

Well, have another. It won't hurt to have another.

Here, let me get you a whiskey, Alex said. I'll have one with you. Let's relax.

And what?

Contemplate our navels, mate.

It felt good sitting inside the manse again – where it was cooler than in my car; but I passed up on the whiskey and had a soft drink instead.

The mountain air smelt differently than in the city or in the Upper Hunter, sharper, it went straight into your lungs, you could feel it when you breathed in. I felt comfortable being here, and was glad to be back.

By the way, Alex said. The Robsons have invited us to dinner on Saturday night and I think they'd like to have you over as well. I'll check, but I can't see it being a problem. Frank's talked about it for a while now, and it would be good to go with you. We've been there, done that before, and Frank's always trying to be the big shot out here, you know, Mr Entrepreneur and that kind of thing.

He runs a general store in a country village, I replied. It's hardly David Jones in Sydney.

Ah, mate, you're letting your prejudices show. They're country people.

Just like we are, added Jill. At least while we're living here.

So, what happened with the girlfriend? Or would you rather not talk about it?

Our lives were going in different directions. She wants to travel – and I'm doing country service for the next three years.

You'll find it's for the best, Jill said.

I know, mate, Alex said, from experience, that nothing teaches you more about life than a broken heart.

Is that right? asked Jill.

I said nothing and quickly the talk turned to other matters. I still had to face Carrie with the reason for my early return, but I said I felt good about explaining the situation to her, just as I did to the Clarks.

You'll be just fine, Jill kept saying.

Alex became more philosophical. In the sum total of all things happening on the face of the planet, it's no great deal, Peter. The sun continues to rise and set. The earth turns and we humans continue to stumble.

Well, I'd better go, I said. I'm glad I'm back early.

They saw me to the door, even Cassie – barking like a firing cannon.

*

Well, look who's 'ere, Carrie said, shading her eyes as she watched me getting out of my car. What brings yer back early? Don' tell me yer got homesick fer Jeogla?

No, I said, looking her in the eyes. Nothing like that… Can we sit down for a minute, please?

We sat on the bench under my window, facing the west, between the wall of the house and tree where Willy-wagtails sang by moonlight.

I told her my story and why I felt I had to leave Sydney.

Oh, yer a poor little feller, she sighed. Broken heart, so far from home…

That's the point, Carrie. I wanted to come back. My parents understood me wanting to come back early – and I hope you don't mind that I did? I'll pay the extra rent.

Why don't yer jest unpack yer things and get some rest, hey? Yer must be tired. My, yer car's lookin' a bit flash. Got a wash 'n' polish, did it?

Yes. Thanks for noticing.

Like some tea?

No, thanks. I stopped at the Clarks and had something to drink.

I unloaded my belongings, and it felt good being back in my little weatherboard room. There was a warmth to it that I'd forgotten while I was away. I kicked off my shoes and curled up to have a sleep before dinner.

Cold Days

The start of the new term was a cold day and indicative of what kind of weather would follow.

Wait till the pipes freeze over and there's no water from the taps, Carrie said over breakfast. Yer'll git used to it, all the teachers do.

I made a trip out to Wollomombi Falls and Hillgrove Gorge, out to Scots' Corner and drove down to the Styx River. I was tempted to get out of my car and explore the river, but something stopped me, something that was no more than a strange feeling that said, *This isn't the right time.*

I submitted three poems to the *Poetry Magazine* published by the Poetry Society of Australia in the hope of getting an acceptance. Frank Davidson, my former lecturer at teachers' college, had taken out a year's subscription for me and I had been receiving the magazine

Ron and Dof stopped into the school to say hello, surprised to see me back early. I began to explain about the break-up with P, speaking in staccato sentences as I did, but before I could finish they said there wasn't any need to say anything more; their daughter Joan was just returning to Newcastle after a few days at Jeogla but was first visiting their other daughters, Wendy and their twin girls, Jill and Sue, all of whom lived in town.

Ah, Peter, Peter, Ron said in sympathy. All part of the process called growing up. Pity you can't get yourself a little dog while you're up here –it'd be good company to have instead of spending nights by yourself preparing lessons. Besides, it might turn out to be a friend for Suzie.

The days passed, some slowly, some quickly. In June the weather grew very cold and I took to wearing warmer clothes – although at times the winds were so sharp they went straight through them. The night winds sounded like they were blowing in from Siberia. When the temperature dropped below zero in the mornings all the jumpers and warm shirts I wore made no difference.

Letters from Sydney trailed off but I didn't seem to mind that and, except for writing to my parents, I wrote none back. One piece of exciting news was that I had two poems accepted for *Poetry Magazine*. They would appear sometime in the next three months and I would receive payment of $2 per poem. I immediately thought of P and wished we were still in communication. She had encouraged me to write from the beginning of our relationship at Sydney University and I felt that she should be told; but I stopped myself from writing or ringing her. I did drop Frank Davidson a note and told him to look out for the poem in the magazine in the next few months. I had dedicated one of the poems to him, *The Snake* and, as well as P, I wanted him to share the good news.

As I drove to work, I noticed there was a quietness in the trees, even when a wind blew, as if they were bunkering down for the coming season. This was the metaphorical season of death in nature, when the earth was going to sleep. The trees brooded over the roadway leading up to the school, and those around the building seemed to drip moisture from the night. The ground beneath the pines was always wet, covered with cones that had fallen off. Carrie had added to the store of cones in the shelter shed, and we continued adding to these. As they dried out they could be used for fuel in the school's heater.

On the first morning of lighting the heater, after I filled it with newspapers, twigs. woodchips and cones, I couldn't find any kerosene to start the fire, but I found some methylated spirits in one of the handicraft cupboards. The children cautioned me against using it.

She'll be right, I said proudly. I know what I'm doing.

I crouched down, poured in the methylated spirits and children around me stepped back.

I lit a match, threw it in and flame shot out through the door of the heater with a roar, followed by an explosion that sounded like a bomb. *BOOM!* I was thrown off my feet, and landed on my backside, feeling as if my face was on fire. I thought I was blinded.

The fire died down and so did the commotion. Smoke cleared to the side of the blackboard where the heater was situated. I heard the crackling of firewood, closed the door of the heater, and stood up, my hands still up to my face. There, I said, now we have a fire, trying not to feel embarrassed.

The children watched me uneasily.

Sir, can you see? Michael Burleigh asked.

You should wash your face, sir, Christine Frizell said, Get all that smoke off your face and wash your eyes out properly.

I felt like a child who was being reprimanded, and did as I was told. I half-expected someone to say, *See we told you so*, but nothing more was said about the incident.

After that near disaster, I made sure there was a supply of kerosene in the school.

*

The pattern of routines that had been established between myself and the locals continued.

During the district athletics carnival involving all the small schools at which Jeogla Public School came second, I met more locals from the Wollomombi and Jeogla districts; some of these were farmers from around the Kilcoy area, others were from properties at Yaroona and down the Big Hill, towards Kempsey, and many of these rarely came to visit the school; if they did it might have been in Ron's company or George Gray's or Wally Frizell's. They'd nod, say a few words as a courtesy, and return to discussing farming matters. I did note that Lex McRae never stopped in with anyone to say hello. Occasionally, I'd see one or two of these people at the general store and always told them what a happy time I was having, living and teaching at Jeogla. I doubt if they believed me, but most of the time I meant what I said.

In mid-winter I accepted an invitation to have dinner at the Moults, in a house they rented and way down on the Styx Road, past the disused sawmill. When I arrived the table had been set and the three boys, their parents and I sat down to eat in a room where the walls had been covered with newspapers. A single light hung over the table and it swayed slightly every time a wind blew. Then I noticed the house seemed to be moving, or at least the walls swayed, first from one side, then the other. A chicken ran through the room, followed by another and another. They were bantams, clucking as if escaping from a calamity. Did they sense something bad was about to happen?

Ignore them, Mrs Moult, said, they'll settle down. She instructed the boys to chase them out and make sure every door was closed. Mr Moult talked about his war experiences. Legacy was looking after them now, and would continue to do so in to the future. Whatever the future held, as I'd heard said before among the locals. The boys would be looked after.

As I was leaving, Mrs Moult said they'd be happy to sell me some bantams that I could take home to my parents.

We could get some cages fixed for the backseat of your car, she said. They'll survive the trip.

I said I'd think about it.

*

When I returned from Sydney I drew up a program of Creative Writing centred around themes: Childhood, Birds and Animals, Scenery and Environment, Feelings.

Sections of the walls were set aside for examples of Handicraft, Art and Poetry, this last part consisting of the children's creative writing accompanied by their own illustrations, either drawings or paintings.

The back wall was mostly examples of what could be done with paper – this included free tearing, crumpling, rolling, snipping, fringing, tooth, pinpricking. The more colourful, the more attractive the presentation looked.

*

I'd found an old Esso calendar in one of the cupboards with a painting by a different Australian artist for each month. I cut out the prints, glued them onto thick cardboard and made a small gallery of Australian art. My favourites were "Solveig's Song" by Pixie O'Harris and "Old Windsor" by Franklin Bennett. If nothing else, the inspector would find walls covered with paintings, colours and words.

The little school was like a home to me now, and I found joy in seeing what I was doing with it – mostly with the creative side, but also the "mechanical", the teaching of Basic Skills.

The school's startin' to look real pretty, Carrie said one evening after returning from cleaning it. I haven't seen it look like that ever, I don't think. Like it's Christmas. Yes, real pretty. I might being Granma up ter have a look. Do yer mind?

No, bring her up, Elmo and Gerald too.

*

One Sunday in July, Ron turned up at the Sloggets and asked if I'd like to come out for a drive to Wyatts Creek with him.

We'd had a lot of rain but the day was sunny, the air shone with a light that was dazzling and frosty. I jumped at the chance of going back to the piglets and sows. As before, Suzie sat between us in the cabin of the truck. Her growling at me had stopped, she wagged her tail and even listened to when I was speaking to Ron.

When I commented on this, Ron replied, See, I told you. She listens all the time to you now – as if it was me who was speaking to her. Suzie woofed in agreement, madly wagging her little tail.

We arrived and looked down on the property. I wasn't prepared to what I saw: a sweep of golden colour from the farmhouse, on both sides of the land, to the horizon, the same distance where we'd walked before.

You didn't bring me here just to feed pigs, did you? I asked, but meant it more as a statement.

Ron said nothing; he kept smoking his cigarette.

Under a pale blue sky, in a cold yellow light, they glowed like fire. The wattles! The golden trees.

We got out, fed the sows that were without piglets, and strolled through the golden display.

Finally, he spoke. Let's walk a bit.

Magpies sang. Rosellas flew around us.

He told me how proud he was of Joan, his daughter going out teaching, and asked me how I was feeling about the break-up with my girlfriend.

I shrugged my shoulders. Getting better, I replied, but not sure if I meant it.

When everything else fails, he said. Learn from nature.

I quoted him a Polish saying of my mother's that had a religious overtone. The One who sends the rain will send the sun.

Couldn't've put it better myself, he said. Hang in there, Peter.

We didn't walk as far as last time. Nor did we stop to drink from the creek.

Seen enough? Ron asked.

I nodded.

We walked back to the truck without speaking.

Styx River

The visit with Ron to Wyatts Creek set off something disruptive inside me, a feeling of dislocation that I couldn't equate with preparing the school for the inspector's visit and where the future might lead me as a result of the inspection? For the rest of the week this notion kept nagging me.

The following weekend the weather was drizzly. On Saturday, when the Sloggetts were going into town, I decided not to go, instead, would go beyond Wyatts Creek, and visit the Styx River. I'd gone down before with Carrie and Elmo to visit her brother Jim and his family, but there were time constraints and limitations to how many times I could ask the Sloggets to stop the car, because I wanted a better look at the river or forest. I needed independence, and I needed to be alone.

After the family left for Armidale, the rain began to clear and by mid-morning I set off, driving several miles past the school to where a sign indicated the Styx River. The road sloped down over a wooden bridge and I pulled over from the road, parking under a tree. That way, I wouldn't impede other motor vehicles, especially those hauling caravans.

The air smelt differently, more earthy, mossy; it was colder than at Jeogla. I hadn't even thought of bringing an umbrella but it didn't seem important now, although water dripped from overhead branches. I pulled my jacket tightly around me and my beanie over my ears, and walked across the bridge. From reading and talking about the Styx I knew it rose below Point Lookout in the Snowy Range, a part of the eastern escarpment of the New England Tablelands, it flowed in a south-westerly direction, was joined by two minor tributaries before joining up with the Chandler and flowing into a deep gorge and then into the Macleay. I knew there was a waterfall further back, but from where I boarded and where I was able to park, there was no access to it

Turning left I edged closer to the river, off the roadway

as far as I could, stepping over rocks and climbing over boulders wet with spray.

What were those birds? Whipbirds?

I heard black cockatoos, their cries long and doleful.

Black waterhen appeared, peeping out from foliage, and disappeared.

Smaller birds whistled in the undergrowth, scattered and regrouped. They sounded like wrens.

Something stirred and rushed away from me in the bracken. Maybe it was a wallaby?

The further down I walked the more I became surrounded by a forest, trees taller than cathedrals, ferns with leaves as broad as plates, a density of growth I had never noticed from the roadway. There were types of heath and shrubs that must flower in summer.

As I stumbled over rocks and granite boulders, I knew many of these trees to be Stringy-barks, others were Beeches and Coach-woods, Blackbutts, Tallow-woods and Blue Gums. I'd heard Elmo and Carrie talk of these giant trees that grew in the Styx Forest, which ones were better for firewood and which should be avoided. Their buttresses were covered in lichens, growths of mosses thick as a carpet. Bird nest ferns, stag horns and orchids grew out of them. Vines grew down from their branches. Frogs croaked.

The icy water that rushed over rocks, boulders and stone ledges created a music that was bewildering as it was delightful; it was like the kind of music one might associate with spirits of a forest. Together with the bird songs, the atmosphere was magical, mysterious.

By now I'd lost sight of the road, disappearing further under a canopy of treetops where sunlight barely broke through. Despite my warm clothes, I was getting colder. After an hour my clothes were soaked through. In many places I had to push through heavy undergrowth. My hands were cut and bleeding. My face was scratched.

In some places the river was broad, in other places it was narrow, struggling to find a way through a constriction of rocks. Once it was free, it would rush ahead, creating a mini-flood from the overflow.

I sat down on a boulder and took stock of my situation. The scent of eucalypts was strong; the damp vegetative smell that I picked up as soon as I'd stepped from my car had increased, but I didn't find it objectionable. What kind of world was I walking into?

A pool lay ahead, very calm, at a spot where the river broadened, maybe the widest spot I'd come to at that stage of my walk. Leaves floated on it. Then I saw a ripple, then another and another. Looking closer I saw the water was shallow. A movement below the surface was followed by another wriggly movement. I stepped into the water and saw fish, rainbow trout that I'd been told lived in the Styx. These were bred and released from the trout hatchery on the Point Lookout Road further upstream. The Sloggets, Ron and most of the locals talked about it. They said that a visit to the hatchery was worth the effort. These fish made no effort to escape; they swan around my feet. Their backs and sides were spotted, although they were dark in colour, like stones; their sides were also spotted. Their gills were pink with the line of pink running the length of their bodies. When they turned, light was reflected off them, silver and golden. A glorious sight.

As I walked I thought of the associations in Greek mythology with the river; it was one of five rivers that separated the world of the living from the world of the dead. This was the "river of hate". Anyone wishing to cross it safely and not spend eternity in Hades, had to pay for their passage; and this was done by the family of the deceased. A coin was placed with the body, sometimes under the tongue. Charon, the old ferryman, transported the body to the other side where its soul waited to be reborn.

A short distance further on I came to an intersection

where I saw a sign to the Barwick, the Little Styx and Wattle Flat which sounded like it might be a campsite. I knew I'd had enough for one day, even though Wattle Flat sounded enticing. Signs might mean meeting people and I still wanted to be alone. Besides, the return journey was uphill, and would take longer. I'd forgotten to bring my watch and had no idea what the time was; but down here by the river knowing the time didn't seem essential. I felt thirsty. Kneeling down, I drank from the river, stood up and turned to walk back.

*

From the position of the sun I knew it was late afternoon when I returned to my car; it was setting and the spot where my car was parked was in shadows. Rustling noises came from the undergrowth around me, short, scurrying sounds as if animals were rushing to hide. Birdsongs sounded low and mournful, detached from the sky and falling to earth. It occurred to me that in all the time I was alone, I hadn't encountered another human being; but now I was shivering and needed to dry off.

I turned the car around and drove straight to the school. The Sloggetts hadn't been told where I was going, but I figured I'd be home in time for dinner. First I needed to dry off and get warm.

Inside the school I lit the heater and the fire quickly came to life. I took off my wet jacket, beanie, shoes, socks and shirt and lay them across the backs of chairs, arranging them around the heater. I made a cup of tea and sat as close to the heater as I could, sipping it. One hour. That was all I needed, to at least get my clothes warm enough to put back on. My underwear and trousers were only damp, but I could cope with that discomfort.

As soon as I sat down I began to feel uneasy about my future – the very thought that drove me from the house down to the river –and remembered my home in Sydney.

Occasionally, since returning from the May holidays, I'd ask myself, *Do I really want to leave New England?* There was never a definite answer to that question. My mind would go off in one direction or another, and the conundrum would remain. Was it to do with my break-up with P? Or was it something else, something deeper?

After an hour the schoolroom was warm, I'd drunk my tea and was preparing to leave when images of the river came back in a burst of fragments – water, rocks, trees, ferns, birds, images of the New England ranges that'd accumulated in my mind. There was a harshness in this cold landscape but there was a sweetness, also, that I sensed but couldn't comprehend.

I heard a voice in my head – the same that argued with me when I'd written the Wyatts Creek poem, and the one I'd been waiting to hear for a long time. I can't even be sure what it was saying but it was urging me to put my feelings into words, these contradictory sensations about where I should be and where I am. And why?

Taking sheets of paper from my desk, I wrote:

Styx River

If time and frost have spared these hills
why should a man curb the stream?
Deeper than sound in a bone's hollow
has the river cut into this flesh of earth.
The waterfall, crashing out of forgotten centuries,
throws up an arc from inside the sun.

In pools of thorn, deep as an eye's lens,
rainbow trout and water-hen glide
through ripples of leaves that, once seen,
wash into the mind's sleep, reshaping a dream,

unearthing the destinies of voices and stars.
Families live scattered along banks
of yellow clay, biding sleet and winds of summer
with words the colour of sunflower seeds.

I shall never walk the bottom
To disprove its name and origins – confirming
myths of Hades or the stories
brought back by men from the city.
Let myths and tales remain
in the colour and shape of trees,
in the sound of hail breaking against granite –
sunlight piercing the eyes of trout:
winds threading their needles
around Tablelands chimneys and doors.

Let myths remain, with their gullies and secret ferns,
and begin journeys along rivers as this
only when conscience and self
look to lands beyond the earth of hard flesh:
beyond the bridge spanning day and night
where Charon himself is a passenger
and the mouths of the dead are empty.
And you, all journeys ended, knowing time has come
for waterfalls to be silent, fall
on your knees to drink from the river.
As time and frost slowly enter your blood
no draught of hemlock could have tasted sweeter.

Again, it was a poem written without any rewriting. Straight through, a clean sweep. On two pieces of paper.

When I finished the fire had died down and my clothes were almost dry. I dressed, got up to leave. There was a knock on the door.

It was Carrie. Are yer ok? We got worried. Wally Frizell said he saw yer drivin' down to the Styx and we thought yer might've got lost – or fell in.

Fell in? Is that what you think of me?

It's past dinner time, now, an' yer not home. Not tellin' us where you were. Worried, that's all we were…

Carrie, that's very kind of you to come up and check. I got a bit wet, that's all, and decided to stop in and dry off. Thanks for coming up. Thanks for your concern.

Well, come back now. I'll git yer dinner. She spoke, almost like she was apologising for the intrusion.

*

Later that night it started to rain. After I went to bed I read through that part of the Dylan Thomas biography where he gives his response to a young man about his poetry, and which was then reprinted in the *Texas Quarterly* under the title of "Dylan Thomas's Poetic Manifesto."

There were five questions the young man had asked, and I'd marked the answers in the margin. The answers ran for seven or eight pages, their simplicity amazed me; There was a depth to them that was natural, innocent, pure. I felt he was speaking to me directly, and I absorbed every word. The young man had asked, why and how he began to write poetry, his influences, was there a deliberate use of devices, was he attempting to create something "new" in the style of the Surrealists, what was his definition of poetry? In his answers he spoke of his love of words, and that part of the explanation, I understood above all else, "*I wanted to write poetry because I had fallen in love with words….Words were as the notes of bells, the noises of musical instruments, the noises of wind, sea, and rain…*"

Winners and Oedipus Rex

Friday, 14/7/67

Dear Mum & Dad,
Just a few words during my lunch hour.

Today is a nice warm day; but the nights are very, very cold. The frosts are bigger than before, and yesterday morning it was icy. In the mornings the ground looks like it's covered with snow. The water in the puddles around the tanks is frozen over.

But at night the stars are very clear and it is so beautiful. Quiet and lonely, but beautiful.

Mum, do you want some bantams, chooks and a rooster? I can buy some very cheaply here and I could bring them home with me during the next holidays. They are very little and lay eggs that are small as pigeon eggs.

Tomorrow I will be going into Armidale. There was a book competition at the library last week for all the schools in the district and Jeogla won a first prize, got an equal second and one entry was highly commended. This is good for the school, and puts us on a level with the Demonstration School in Armidale. Miss Enid Isaacs will make the presentations. She is the librarian and comes out to the school to bring new books.

Recently I went into town to see a performance of a play called "Oedipus Rex". It's a strange play and one day I must tell you about it. The main role was played by a man called John Challis, a professor from the university whom I met during the Anzac Day service in Wollomombi.

I also went up to the teachers' college and had a look at their art collection. It took my breath away.

Your loving son,
Peter

School Inspection

The dreaded day arrived. Thursday, 3rd August. An overcast day at the end of winter, with a prediction of fine weather towards noon and no rain.

I got up early, had breakfast and was up at the school. Carrie reminded me to invite Mr Harris to come back and have afternoon tea with us. Jest don't git nervous. Remember what Ron's told yer. He's a fair man. Yer gotta trust Ron.

The children had been asked not to be late on the day. When I arrived, one hour before school assembly, the Moult boys were waiting. The others arrived by half-past eight. The inspector arrived as the Frizell children were being dropped off by Wally. I heard him fussing over them. Now, children, please be very good today. Extra well-behaved. Tell sir I said hello. I won't be popping in today.

They are well-behaved, Wally, I thought, standing from where I was at the window. Stop pleading with them.

After greeting Mr Harris, shaking hands, and extending a welcome to the school, he and I came out on the veranda where I rang the school bell, and the children lined up for assembly.

Mr Harris, drew himself up to his full height, put his hands behind his back, stood alongside me and said, Just carry on as if I wasn't here.

I introduced Mr Harris, told the children why he was here, and asked them to welcome him.

Welcome Mr Harris, they replied unenthusiastically.

Thank you, children, I'm looking forward to spending the day with you.

I briefly revised rules of good behaviour towards each other in the playground, and stressed the importance of observing loyalty to the community and towards the flag. Patriotism was an essential factor in the country, and many of these children's relatives had their names on honour boards in churches and civic centres as members of the Australian Defence Forces. I told them that duty begins at the grassroots level, in the family and in the school.

As a tree is planted, so shall it grow. I quoted a saying of my mother's from over the years. From the corner of my eye, I thought I saw Mr Harris nodding in agreement. Let us enjoy this beautiful day, I said, and be happy to be here. I thought maybe I'd gone over the top, and I left it on that point.

We said the Lord's Prayer and saluted the flag that I'd brought out and stood against the wall on the veranda.

I brought the school to attention. We turned and filed in. So far so good.

I wished it was bell-time, and the day over.

*

Thursday's lesson program in the morning began with Number, Spelling and Reading for the Juniors, and Spelling, Reading and Arithmetic for the Seniors.

Basically, while I did oral work with one group, the other group worked from set work on the blackboard or from pages in a text book. Then, the process would be reversed; while I did Spelling with the Seniors, for example, the Juniors did their set sums and tables exercises.

And while I taught, Mr Harris walked around observing, listening, stopping to look through a child's exercise book – or he would stop and ask a question. He also took notes into a small note book that he took from his inside coat pocket. That was the most nerve-wracking experience of the whole day, whatever the subject. *What are you writing?* I thought. Every time a child answered correctly, you could feel a collective sigh of relief from the rest of the children and myself; if the child answered incorrectly, there would be an embarrassed silence until Mr Harris would say, Carry on, Mr Skrzynecki.

By recess, the tension had got to me and I felt like running away, thinking, Goodbye, Education Department. Hello, Whatever, Wherever. I thought of Fred at Scone, on his bicycle, riding towards an invisible horizon, and wished it were me.

Mr Harris and I poured cups of tea from our thermoses and walked round the school while the children played. Did I mind if we skipped "little lunch" and stretched our legs, he asked?

No, I replied enthusiastically. Whatever you prefer. I felt like asking, Well, what do you think so far?

As we walked he asked me about my feelings of being sent so far from Sydney. Did I feel the appointment would benefit me in the long term? How did I feel about being isolated?

Isolated?

Yes, alone up here – away from your parents and friends in Sydney? Surely you must miss them?

Of course I do.

So, how do you feel about this isolation?

Sometimes I like it – I don't mind it – but mostly I don't like it. Is that saying the wrong thing?

No, you must speak the truth.

So, physically, I feel isolated but in my head – in my mind – I know I'm not alone. I have books, music, art. I go for walks. I see things in nature – in a way that I never have before. I speak to the locals. I go into town.

Are you writing poetry?

Yes.... I've had two poems accepted for a national poetry magazine. I said this with some pride in my voice and regretted immediately that I'd told him. *You must speak the truth.* Those were his words, and there was a Biblical ring to them. According to St John, telling the truth will set me free.

He watched my face and saw that I was deliberating. He waited for my answer.

Bureaucracy, he said, Mr Skrzynecki. What about

bureaucracy? Do you ever think about paperwork, the Department's need for copies of requests and reports to be filed in duplicate and triplicate?

I hate it, I snapped back.

So you are a captive to rules and regulations too. As I am. As the Area Director is. As the Director-General of Education is.

This man is strange, I started to think. He walks around the playground with me, instead of sitting at a desk and eating cake and drinking tea. I almost blurted out, Are you happy, Mr Harris, doing this job?

Just then a group of children ran past us, and he said, Let's go in shall we, or we'll forget the real reason why I'm here today.

Between recess and lunch there was Physical Education and Oral Expression with Juniors and Seniors, Social Studies with the Juniors, Language Study with the Seniors and Singing with both Seniors and Juniors. This last lesson I was dreading the most. At teachers' college I never completely grasped the skills of teaching Singing. Recorders, tuning forks, singing in parts. So when it came time for Singing I turned on the ABC's *"Let's Have Music"* programme. At the appropriate time, when a song had to be sung, I alternated between having the children singing with the presenter and sing without the radio. I doubt whether Mr Harris thought this the most appropriate method, but I did see him nod three or four times when the children sang with gusto. We got through "Flash Jack from Gundagai" with much joy. The children applauded themselves. They were beaming. I don't think Mr Harris knew what to make of it all. He continued taking notes.

For Physical Education we did exercises using medicine balls and hoola-hoops; then finished off the session with a Tunnel Ball competition, using a mix of Juniors and Seniors to make up two teams called the Kookaburras and the Rosellas.

For Oral Expression there were short- part play-readings from Shakepeare and poems, mostly from the Romantics for the Seniors and poems from "A Child's Garden of Verses" by Robert Louis Stevenson for the Juniors. This proved so popular that we ran overtime and I asked Mr Harris if it could be included as part of Language Study that was planned for the afternoon. I thought he would disagree, instead, he smiled and said, Whatever you like, Mr Skrzynecki. You're the boss.

During lunch the children ate in the shelter shed. Mr Harris and I sat inside the school, eating sandwiches and drinking tea.

Are you from Sydney originally? I asked him.

Oh yes, he replied happily. We hope to return there in my retirement. A beautiful city. There's no other harbour like it in the world. Which part of Sydney are you from?

Regents Park, I told him, and gave a general account of our coming to Australia in 1949, my father working for the Water Board while my mother and I lived in the migrant camp in Parkes. After two years, we moved to Sydney, where my father had put a deposit on a house. I spoke quickly and probably – what must have seemed emotionally – to Mr Harris, and for whatever reason I can't say. Nerves had the better of me – and perhaps I'd been unprepared to go down this road of conversation with someone I barely knew.

Again, he suggested we go outside and walk around. We finished eating and strolled around the perimeter of the schoolyard. He asked questions about who lived where. When I pointed out Ron Diamond's house he nodded knowingly, but said nothing. He asked if I went to church while I was living here.

Sometimes I go to the Mass at Wollomombi, I replied. I said I liked to pray in the cathedral in town when I went in. I liked the "aloneness" of being inside a big church.

But we're never alone, are we? he asked.

Not in the sense I think you mean.

Do you think God ever abandons us? he asked.

No, but it feels like that sometimes. People despair, lose hope. I wasn't at all certain where this was leading.

God felt abandoned, didn't he? On the Cross. He cried, Father, Father, why have you abandoned me?

I've never felt like that since I came to Jeogla, I said. Standing on the Oaky Bridge or going down to the Styx, I said, I feel like I'm inside a church. Creation of the World all over again – and I'm smack bang in the middle of it.

He laughed, what an interesting turn of words!

The sheep from the school's yard on the other side of the fence came up to us and bleated pitifully. I broke off two flowers from a dahlia and fed one to each of them. They continued bleating, wanting more.

There were three sessions of classes after lunch. While the Seniors did their set Social Studies exercises, I took the Juniors through Writing and Reading. To my surprise, for the latter, Mr Harris joined us on the small infants chairs and read with the children, sounding out words and helping with creating sentences. He didn't hurry any of them, taking as much time as was necessary – as if the whole afternoon could be spent, reading that one page. Afterwards, Natural Science was a combination of Juniors and Seniors and we looked the life cycle of the cicada.

More notes into that small notebook.

Finally, the children were given Library, where they could take whatever book they'd borrowed from the box that Miss Isaacs brought. For those who wanted to listen to poetry, I read from "A Child's Garden of Verses" that I'd bought in Sydney. Their favourite poems to date had been "My Shadow", "Bed in Summer" and "From a Railway Carriage". We acted out the parts, and Mr Harris joined in that activity as well.

Time go home, Mr Harris, said, looking at his watch and

getting up from a mat on the veranda. It's been an illuminating day, Mr Skrzynecki. Thank you – and you, also, children.

Mrs Sloggett's invited you back for afternoon tea, I said. Do you have time?

I'd love to, he said. Let me see you dismiss the children, and we'll pack up.

Everyone packed their bags, stood to attention next to their desks, and waited.

Say good afternoon to Mr Harris, I said.

Good afternoon, Mr Harris, the children chimed in chorus. They filed out exactly the same way the filed in in the morning, except the process was reversed. They could be heard, chattering and laughing, as soon as they were outside.

Another successful day, Mr Skrzynecki, Mr Harris said.

I hope so, Mr Harris, I thought under my breath. Instead, I said, Tomorrow's Friday, I hope they keep their energy up.

*

We sat around the kitchen table, sunlight from the western window shining into our eyes, Mr Harris's and mine; Carrie sat with her back to the window and watched us, never taking her eyes off the school inspector – who seemed unnerved by this inscrutable attention.

Lovely scones, Mrs Sloggett, he said.

Thank you, sir, she replied, and I thought she might curtsy, even from a sitting position.

Have you boarded the school teachers for a long time? he asked.

Long as I can remember, she said. Before the war and after. We was always the place they wanted ter stay.

Must be your cooking, he laughed.

Hope so. An' the room we always provided. Warm. Comforts of home. Three meals a day. Yer only need ter ask Peter, 'ere. Isn't that so?

Oh yes, I replied keenly. Just like home.

There's a very "comfy" feeling in the house, I must say, Mr Harris added. One can feel it upon entering. You make people feel welcome, Mrs Sloggett.

I try ter. Thank yer fer the compliment. Would yer like ter see the yard.

Of course.

For the next ten minutes we followed Carrie around while she showed off her flowers, her chickens, her geese and showed what pride she took in her home. Elmo's too, of course, she added, giggling.

I must be off, Mr Harris said finally, as we returned to the house. Thank you so much for the refreshments. Your hospitality is second to none, I assure you.

Why, that's so kind, Carrie said.

I saw Mr Harris out to his car. Oh, by the way, Mr Skrzynecki. I almost forgot. A small gift. You might find it useful – or at least interesting.

He handed me a book with a lemon coloured cover; its title was "Lectures on Poetry", published by the Inservice Training Branch of the Department of Education. Thank you, I said.

If you find no value in it, feel free to pass it on.

Thank you, I said.

I've had an enjoyable day, and I wish you all the best in your career as a teacher and poet. You should have your report in two weeks. Goodbye.

We shook hands.

I watched as he drove off and waved as his car turned left, followed by a cloud of yellow dust, into the bush of khaki colours, just as the sun's light was beginning to set fire to them.

Golly, Carrie said, when I returned to the house. Didn't he jest say some nice things. Wait 'till I tell Elmo. Bet she'll be yeller when she finds out the school inspector called in 'ere.

And she named a woman who lived in the district.

School Report

Exactly two weeks plus one day after the inspection, I received my report. It consisted of two parts, the first an overall assessment of the school under the headings POLICY, ORGANISATION and GOVERNMENT and INSTRUCTION.

The second was the REPORT OF INSPECTOR UPON TEACHER. It was this that I read first:

Overcoming some initial misgivings Mr Skrzynecki has thrown himself wholeheartedly into the work of his school. His vitality and gifts have fired the imagination of the children and his sincerity has compelled their liking and cooperation.

His complicated, self-critical and mercurial temperament is both servant and scourge in the teaching situation but he is winning through to self-discipline and balance. In this he is aided by a strong commitment to the welfare of the children, intellectual honesty and the ability to find friends.

It is RECOMMENDED that his efficiency be determined as satisfying requirements for his position and status.

(signed) H. Harris / Inspector

The first part of the report was favourable in all respects except the teaching of music: faults of pitch and tune had to be eliminated before Singing could be regarded as adequate. Everything else – all aspect of the teaching of the curriculum were favourable, especially work on the cultural side: poetry, verse-writing, art and craft.

The report praised promoting the reading of library books and the helpful relationship that had been achieved with the Municipal library and staff.

In conclusion, this formal side of the report stated, *This school has come to life under the infectious enthusiasm of the teacher. Much remains to be done but the lines for progress have been soundly drawn.*

There was also a second letter in the mail that was related to Mr Harry Harris; it was from the Area Director, in Tamworth, informing all schools in the Armidale inspectorate that Mr Harris was going on leave at the end of the term and would not be returning to Armidale. From then, until further notification, all school correspondence should be sent to Mr G. W. Falkenmire, Inspector of Schools at Tamworth.

I was overjoyed at the positive report that I received from Mr Harris, at the same time I felt sad because he was leaving the district. I wasn't sure exactly why I felt like this but it had nothing to do with him inspecting Jeogla Public School or the report he'd written; it was something deeper, distant, something that I might never discover. I sensed but did not understand how he'd made an indelible impact on my life. Maybe it had to do walking around the school while children played and rosellas whistled in the pines – or the way he watched me when I fed flowers to the sheep and responded to their bleating? Or was it the time we talked about God and abandonment? That was so strange! In all my years, I could not remember speaking to my parents about that subject.

Or was it the book of poetry lectures that he gave me? The book that I knew I would never give away.

School Numbers

Sunday, 6/8/67

Dear Mum & Dad,

The weather is warmer now although the nights can still be very cold. In the morning the ground is all white.

And how are you both? Don't think that I have forgotten you, and think of you all the time. I hope you are both well and happy and that everything is fine.

We have three sheep belonging to the school now. Recently one of the sheep had twins – 2 lambs – a girl and a boy. They are such sweet little things with their long legs and long tails. They jump about in the sun as if they were on strings. I wanted to get a photo of them, but whenever I come near the mother runs off with them.

When I come home I must go to the dentist. A little piece of tooth has fallen out of one of my right back teeth.

The school is losing a child on Friday and this brings us down to only 12. We need a daily average attendance of 9 to stay open. Otherwise, the school is coming along nicely and quietly. I should do some gardening. The roses need pruning and there are some rockery plants to put in. But there's other work too – programming for the kids and working out lessons every day.

Holidays soon. It will be good to be home again. I suppose Sydney is as crowded and noisy as it was? Nothing like quiet country life.

See you soon, your loving son.
Peter

Three Chooks and a Rooster

Monday, 21-8-67

Dear Mum & Dad,

This will my last letter before I come home. It was good to hear your voices when I last rang. I am pleased to say that I received a favourable report from the inspector. When I come home I will bring it and show you.

I'm bringing home 3 chooks and one rooster. They are bantams, but not the very small kind; these are the large sort. Mr Moult has made me a special cage to put on the back seat of the car. When I get home you will have to cut their wings. They are not used to being in cages or behind wire. They are used to just running around the yard. If you breed this lot you will get chickens with lovely colours.

Yesterday I found one of the lambs dead. The crows had picked out its eyes.

Well, that's all for now. See you on the weekend. I have presents for you both. God bless.

Your loving son,
Peter.

VI

Point Lookout

Not long after the start of school in September, I went on a picnic to Point Lookout in the New England National Park with the Burleigh family: father Maurice, mother Jean, sisters Christine and Sharon, and Michael.

After travelling along the Armidale-Grafton Road, we entered the park and travelled further along a gravel road to the main lookout area.

We were on top of an escarpment that seemed to be vertical. I felt giddy looking straight down. I had no idea that such a place existed in Australia!

The panorama below us was breathtaking. The Dorrigo Plateau, the Bellinger and Macleay Rivers, their valleys. A sweep of green vegetation, rugged and mountainous, ridges and gullies.

The sky was clear, not a cloud in sight. Maurice handed me a pair of binoculars, There's the Pacific Ocean, he said, some eighty or ninety miles away.

Signs informed us that this was the highest point on the east coast of Australia, and was 5280 ft above sea-level; they pointed to various track systems, and it was decided we would have lunch and then go for a walk.

We ate at a picnic table. The children finished first and played around us, as well on a nearby stone monument.

Photos were taken of Michael and Christine climbing it. Also of the three of them, Sharon, her arms around the younger two.

It was the change of temperature that I noticed first, how much colder it became after only walking a short distance, down the track, surrounded by greenery and giant ferns and trees on which mosses grew. Maurice explained that many of these trees were Antarctic beeches and snow fell here in winter. Stag horns grew at every point we passed. Strangler vines hung from tree to tree. Broken rocks, also covered in mosses, ran down parts of the track. As we walked down, mist was rising from further down in the trackless valley, enveloping us, leaving tiny specks of water on clothes and skin.

The birdlife reminded me of the walk along the Styx River: whipbirds, screeching cockatoos, small birds and large birds, birds that seemed to run up tree trunks. Large birds passed among the giant trees, flapping like bats.

I commented on the variety of birdlife.

Oh, you'll see everything down here, Maurice replied, if you return and take a longer walk. There are lyrebirds, king parrots, crimson rosellas, honeyeaters, riflebirds, bowerbirds, robins, varieties of scrub-birds. This is part of a sub-tropical forest. Kangaroos live down here, too, wallabies and glider possums.

Frogs were croaking.

Are we nearly there? Michael asked.

About an hour's walk, all round, Maurice replied.

No longer cool, it had become cold. Most of us said we wished we'd brought warmer jumpers and jackets.

Light broke through the canopies of trees in bright yellow shafts, illuminating those parts of the greenery it could reach, leaving the rest in shadows.

Here we are, Maurice said, Weeping Rock. The rock we've come to see.

We were standing at the foot of a huge wet, green cliff-face that Maurice told us was basalt. Water streamed across it nonstop, silvery in parts.

Where's it coming from? The children asked.

Hidden springs, Maurice replied. The man seemed to know everything about everything.

Maurice is very knowledgeable, Jean said. He should be writing books.

I became even more aware of the coldness, a chill that penetrated my clothes, skin, and passed through me as if I didn't exist.

Under the rock's face, at the edge of a forest that could have been its heart, I shivered, noticed how each of us reached out to touch it – the stone, the water, the moss, as if to acknowledge our kinship with it.

Okay, said Maurice, let's start back. Mind your step, now, it's pretty slippery down here.

As we walked, I kept looking back at the rock – tall, green, majestic – sunlight streaming on to it – through the trees, and thought how much it resembled a headstone.

The New Inspector

A letter arrived from Area Office informing all schools in the Armidale inspectorate that the new inspector, replacing Mr Harry Harris, was Mr N. Baker, B.A., B.Litt., formerly of the Casino inspectorate.

I wondered what he was like. If, with those academic qualifications, he had any interest in literature or poetry?

Bill Higgins told me the new inspector was planning to visit all the small schools in the inspectorate, getting to know the teachers and, as secondary reason, assessing school enrolment numbers for the future.

The future? I asked.

Immediate, he said.

How immediate is "immediate"? I asked.

Hard to say, he said. You know all this is political.

Political? How come?

Politics and economics. The bean-counters in Head Office assess the viability of keeping small schools open. Say in your case, the numbers are low. One teacher is teaching a handful of kids. It's called "luxury teaching". That teacher could be teaching twice that number or more elsewhere. So they'll move you on.

Will they?

Hard to say, as I said. They do projections into the future. What the numbers are now and what they'll be over the next the two, three or four years. If the projections are good, the school stays open; if there's no prospect of the numbers picking they close the school down – or, rather, they officially "withdraw the teacher" and the minister, then, closes the school. That's the protocol.

I'd never heard this explanation before; it made sense but it also left a sense of disquiet in my mind.

Anyway, Bill said, it doesn't happen overnight. A lot of thought has to be put into closing a school. They're the centre of the community, in lots of cases, and the inspectors have to be careful not to alienate the community; then it might have political repercussions.

What Bill said made sense, and you couldn't help but see it through the eyes of the Department of Education or the government who, after all, was my employer; but Bill also made me think of the politics involved. Alone, I would never have considered that line of reasoning.

Don't let it get you down, Bill said. You won't be out of a job. You'll get moved on, probably to another small school. North or south, east or west. What's it matter? There'll always be a job for teachers...And while you're single, you're easy to be moved.

Again, he sounded wise, especially when he puffed on his pipe and looked to the sky, beyond the row of trees at the end of the Grafton Road, outside Chandler Public School, where we were standing.

Like a Tourist

After the visit to Point Lookout with the Burleighs, I began to make trips around the district by myself, as people suggested I should do more often – like a tourist – go beyond the regular visits to places like Wollomombi Falls, Styx River and Kilcoy.

Boulders rose out of the water at Blue Hole, a popular picnic area off the Grafton Road. I had seen the sign to it every time I drove into town and returned to Jeogla. Surrounded by gum trees and casuarinas, it was an idyllic setting. A tree hung over the water at one spot with a rope and tyre hanging from it – a likely jumping-off point for children splashing into the water. For some reason it reminded me of a gallows, with that grim sight of a black tyre silhouetted like a noose.

As at the Oaky, waterbirds were everywhere, an abundance of water hens, ducks and swans that swam and splashed and ignored me. Swallows dived and rose from the water, swimming joyously through the air like porpoises. Reeds and bulrushes grew on the fringes of the hole; although there was nothing "blue" about the water, which was more grey or a seaweed brown, under a blue sky.

The boulders seemed to have eyes in them, staring and glaring at me, as I tried to ignore them.

*

I'd visited Gostwyck Chapel near Uralla before, in autumn, on the prompting of Jeogla locals who said I should see the vine-covered chapel and the avenue of elms leading up to it – as beautiful as Elm Avenue at the university.

When I first saw it, the chapel was covered in deep orange, red and purple colours, vines and leaves that seemed to have sprung from the stones of the chapel itself, drawing their blood from the fire in the stones.

On this visit, the chapel's winter shades hadn't disappeared. More browns and greys, still with ice and frost evident, awaiting spring, before its colours came to life; but the chapel still retained its medieval appearance, like something out of an Arthurian legend, in a story book, set permanently into the stones of the earth, awaiting a knight or saviour to release it from the spell of a magician.

The elms also, bare, stripped of their green and gold, much of it lying on the roadway, scattered or piled up by winds, turning into brown dust, out of which more green and gold would grow.

*

One Sunday I drove up to Glen Innes, to visit Balancing Rock.

Again, it was the Jeogla locals who suggested I go.

Between Armidale and Wollomombi, on the western side of the road, I'd noticed egg-shaped granite boulders, sitting or balanced on each other. They were not very large, and some were more rounded than others. After a storm or windy weather, I half-expected to see them fallen over, lying in the paddocks, but they remained upright.

None compares to Balancing Rock, people would say. Go and see it. South of Glen Innes.

I made enquiries at the Armidale tourist bureau, got myself a map and some pamphlets, and left early on Saturday, right after breakfast.

It didn't take long to arrive at the rock after leaving Guyra, and I followed the sign on the New England Highway to the Stonehenge reserve. A short distance from the turn-off was the sign to the rock, on a private property.

A rock among other rocks, balanced on its edge, on top of another rock. Neither egg-shaped nor round, it reminded me of an inverted pear, held up by invisible wire. Of course there was no wire. Just this phenomenon.

I got out of my car and walked over, closer to it. Crows descended out of nowhere, perching on fencing-wire and dead trees, cawing, watching me suspiciously, as if I had intruded into their domain. Getting over the fence, I stood face to face with the rock, running my hands over it, reading patterns of moss and lichens that could have been hieroglyphics from another age, Ice or Stone.

Despite the season, the ground was covered in weeds and thistles.

The sky was streaked with fleecy clouds, but it was cold, and the dismal cawing of crows only added to my feeling of isolation.

Driving home I remembered Weeping Rock, the boulders in the water at Blue Hole and the stones of the chapel at Gostwyck; these locations were all connected in my mind through rocks and stones – and now Balancing Rock, sitting like Buddha, pointing to the earth, to the here and now.

Spring

19/10/67

Dear Mum & Dad,
Today we had a very heavy cloudburst and the hail fell as big as birds' eggs. We were out gardening so everything had to be left as it was. The grapes that I brought back with me in May and planted here are starting to grow – there are little green shoots coming out from the stems. Our school strawberries are also coming out; and I am building a small fence for some climbing roses that are here. I don't want to do too much here in the way of gardening because the next teacher may not want to keep any of it and might want to take it all down. In a small school gardening should be done and, besides, it is fun, and the children love it.

Now it is spring and there are baby-everythings: baby sheep, baby horses, baby cows and baby birds. I think the nicest thing I saw yesterday was a lamb only a few hours old. Its mother had left it, and when I went to pat it, it began to suck my fingers. Oh yes, Mrs Slogggett's cat has kittens again.

There is no news really since I wrote to you last time. This is the seventh week coming up.

The new inspector, Mr Baker, paid a visit and we discussed the school numbers. It's serious but it's not. By the looks of things the school will not be closing, so I'll probably be here next year. But I don't mind now. I've put so much work into this place, I will feel sorry when the time does come to leave. This is the seventh week coming up.

My health is back to normal, but I miss those bacon and eggs meals of yours.

I'm reading too much, I think, because my eyes get sore very quickly; but besides writing poetry, it's something I enjoy and something extra to do to fill in the time. I wish I had people my own age to talk with. Out here there is only Gerald. Sometimes I feel like screaming and coming home; but that would prove nothing. You don't solve problems by screaming..

The weather is much warmer now, and I have to take off blankets because it gets too hot. But it's spring.

It's nearly 11 o'clock and I am up here at the school, and I better get home to bed. God bless.

Peter.

First Published Poems

I received a copy of "Poetry Magazine" that had my two poems, "Rosella" and "The Snake", in it.

A photograph of A.D. Hope was on the cover, and the magazine was 1967, Number 5: October.

I turned the pages excitedly and my hands shook as I flicked through it until I found the page they were on.

After returning to Carrie's, and while she and I had tea, I showed the poems to her.

Look, two poems written at Jeogla! I've been here nine months – not counting January – and I've had two poems published in a national poetry magazine.

She looked at the poems seriously, reading them slowly. Hmmm, she finally responded. Yer poor little bugger, I didn't think you'd last nine days.

She must have seen the look of disappointment on my face, because she said, Only jokin', only jokin' – and she burst out laughing. That's it, she said. School's waitin' ter be cleaned.

I changed my clothes and lay on my bed reading "Poetry Magazine".

Poems by A.D. Hope, Christopher Pollnitz, Norman Talbot, Jill Hellyer, Eric C. Rolls; the best in my opinion was "The Floating Head" by Eric Irwin, a poem about Orpheus after he'd been torn apart by the maenads in a Bacchic frenzy.

I was fascinated by all these poems, riveted to the different voices I could hear in them.

In the list of office bearers of the Poetry Society of Australia published at the back of the magazine, I read that Roland Robinson was its President. I hoped that one day I would meet him.

Rumours

By the end of October the rumours about the school's closure were a topic of conversation, at Jeogla and at Wollomombi. Whenever I'd stop at the general store, I'd be asked, What's the latest on the future of the school? Or, Any news since the inspector's visit?

Bill Higgins said he'd heard rumours that more small schools in the Armidale district had been earmarked for possible closure.

You learn a lot in pubs on a Friday afternoon. Schoolies talk, he said, drawing on his pipe and looking pensive.

The Clarks were curious, too, but more sympathetic to the children's needs and my future.

The children will have that extra travel every day. A school bus will have to bring them from Jeogla to Chandler and then back.

What about those living down the Styx? The Frizells and the Moults? I asked.

No one knows, Alex said. They'll work out something if it comes to that... Anyway, you'll be moved on. You won't be out of a job.

Ron Diamond's response to the rumours seemed to be ambivalent. We've got to fight to keep the school open of course – without a doubt – but there's a change in the wind, you can sense it; change is coming and we have to keep up with the change...Like farming, bringing in new fertilizers, modern breeding programmes. Education is changing too.

If I didn't know better, I would've said he knew something the rest of us didn't.

A letter was received from Area Office in Tamworth saying that if the school numbers didn't go up, the school might have to be closed.

As a result of this, a public meeting was organised; attended by parents, George Gray, Ron Diamond and

Norman Baker. Alex came from Wollomombi to lend moral support to the community.

The enrolment numbers for the next five years were "projected", scrunched to make them as viable and optimistic as possible. The upshot being – with no possible solution for the raising of enrolment numbers and getting a daily average attendance of nine – the school would have to be closed; but the P & C would write to the Department of Education requesting that the school be given "grace" for twelve months. Farm workers were often itinerant, they came and left a district, many of them travelled with families. Numbers had fluctuated in the past, this could happen again.

Despite the gloomy prospect of the school possibly closing next year, it was a pleasant evening, with tea, coffee and biscuits provided by the P & C afterwards.

*

Meanwhile, life in the school continued: examinations for those in Sixth class going on to high school; setting and marking papers, filling in transfer cards and other administrative business.

On the 27th of October I wrote a letter to my parents, in it I said: *only 35 more school days left.*

November and December

November and December proved to be busy and exciting months.

The University of New England gave me credit for English I from Sydney University and I enrolled as an external student for 1968, however, I could not do another English course straight off so I chose to study Reformation History. This sounded like an exciting new area of study. I couldn't wait to get started.

By now I thought I'd began to understand Jeogla's weather – cold, hot or in-between. By November, it was very hot by day and warm to cold at night.

The flies had become terrible and we were lucky that screens had been installed in the school the previous year. How did children and teachers survive all those years without them?

I wrote to my parents, "*These days the flies are terrible; they don't leave you alone for a moment and they are everywhere. There are flies called March-flies, and they are as big as Christmas beetles. If they land on a person they can sting badly.*"

With the hot weather settling in, I began to see black snakes in the district. The first and second times they went sliding across the road as I was driving towards them; each time I watched them escaping into the grass.

Another time was in the school yard, behind the boys' toilet. Pressed against the wall of the toilet it looked like the snake's escape was cut off. One of the children saw it and called me over.

Forgetting what Alex had told me months ago about leaving them alone, I ran forward.

Stand back, stand back, I'll get it! I called out. Grabbing a piece of wire hanging on the back fence I came running over, the wire raised above my head, ready to remove the threat. As the children stepped back to make way for me, the snake saw its chance to escape and rushed forward, twisting as it did. I brought the wire down, missing it. Again, I brought the wire down – and again I missed it. By this stage the snake slid away and disappeared under the school.

The children commiserated with me. Never mind, sir, they called out. Better luck next time!

By the first week of December the weather had become intolerably hot; it would be 85 or 90 degrees Fahrenheit in the schoolroom in the afternoons and in the playground it would reach 100 degrees or more.

The bakery in Wollomombi burnt down and that became a serious setback for the village. Debate continued as to the cause of it, and whether or not it would be rebuilt. In the meantime, fresh bread was brought to Robsons' general store from Armidale.

I didn't know the family who owned the bakery, but believe I'd met them during the Anzac Day service.

By the end of the first week in December we'd begun rehearsing for the Christmas Tree Party that would be held in the local hall.

Children volunteered to play the parts of the Nativity scene. A doll was used for the baby Jesus. Costumes were made of rudimentary clothing and we recited poetry, a couple of Christmas carols sung to recorded music.

In a letter to my parents, I wrote…

"*these Infants are a delight to watch; but sometimes you feel like screaming out of exasperation.*"

The Christmas Tree Party went off without hitch. A pine tree was used as a Christmas tree and decorated with tinsel, glass baubles, candles, stars and cotton wool for snow.

No one knew who Santa Claus was although people believed it was George Gray; at least he sounded like George – even though he didn't speak, just gave his hearty

Ho-Ho-Ho.

The occasion was for the whole community and everyone in the district attended, even Lex McCrae whom I'd hardly seen in recent times.

Presents were exchanged, promises made by those going on to high school to stay in touch with the rest of the school. Wally Frizell played the piano – for children and adults. After presents were opened and carols sung, sawdust was sprinkled on the floor. Adults danced under a watery light from bare light globes long into the night to whatever waltz Wally played. He seemed merrier than I'd ever seen him, his face glowing happily – as if a camera was trained on him, filming every movement he made. At times I thought he was asleep, dreaming, playing from memory.

*

On Monday,11th December, 1967 I wrote my last letter home for the year.

Dear Mum & Dad,
Last Saturday at 2 o'clock in the morning, Mr Sloggett had another heart attack and the ambulance had to rush out from Armidale and then rush back and take him to hospital. I didn't know he'd had an attack once before. So it will not be happy Christmas for the family here.

This will my last letter before I come home for Christmas. I expect to be back here next year, so that I will not be bringing all my books back with me.

Everyone here feels a bit nervous, what with Mr Sloggett's health being as it is. It's easy to say don't get upset but that is easier said than done.

Keep smiling. I won't leave right after school on the Friday but will wait until Saturday morning
I thought a bit seriously about our lives and think we

are very lucky to have each other.
See you soon.

Your loving son
Peter

P.S. I have had another poem accepted for publication next year.

VII

Like a Falling Star

When I was a little boy and lived with my mother in the migrant camp in Parkes while my father worked in Sydney, she would take me for walks at night around the camp's perimeter.

Sometimes, we'd see a falling star. She always said that was the soul of someone who'd died and the soul was on a journey to Heaven.

But I noticed that the closer the star got to the horizon, the faster it travelled. Then It disappeared. Or burnt out.

Looking back to 1968, my second year at Jeogla, the days seemed to pick up a momentum of their own – a force I had no control over – heading towards a horizon that was invisible, but waiting, day and night.

When I returned, I drove up to the school and was surprised by what I saw. Carrie had told me, Go up, have a look.

Carrie accompanied me.

The school had a fresh look about it, parts of it were brand new. There was a new water tank, new ablution block, new guttering, new railings and floorboards on the veranda, a new door, the weather shed also had many of its old and rotting timbers replaced.

How come? I asked. I didn't request this.

I think the previous inspector might've had a hand in

this…Always told yer he was a fair man, didn't I?

When was this done? I asked.

Over Christmas an' the New Year. Two blokes from Public Works in Tamworth were 'ere fer a month, slept on site. Nice men, too, I sometimes brought 'em a cup of tea an' some of me scones.

Does this mean the school will stay open an extra year?

Dunno, she said. No use askin' me…But I wouldn't complain, not if I was you.

I won't.

*

There were also two new enrolments, a girl in Kindergarten and a boy in First Class, children of farmworkers. As we'd lost three pupils going to high school at the end of last year, our enrolment numbers seemed healthy, but deep down inside myself I didn't feel so optimistic.

The weather changed to cold and it began to rain, the same as it did last year but not as heavily and it didn't last as long.

I started going into town on Fridays as well as Saturdays, having meals in cafes or restaurants, doing shopping for myself, returning to Jeogla and preparing lessons the rest of the weekend. I was also having a 2-hour sleep in the afternoon so that I could stay up longer at night, reading or writing.

By the middle of February two children left the school, regulars from last year and that sounded a warning I couldn't ignore.

Speaking to Bill, Alex, Ron and Carrie I found they all sympathised with the situation, but said they'd heard nothing new since the meeting last year with the inspector. They understood when I said that I didn't want to see all the work that I'd put into it go for nothing; but the school wasn't really my property and there was nothing anybody could do to change the situation. I was happy to have an enrolment of 13 or 14 but we were down to 11, and there was no way we could average a daily attendance of 9 for the rest of the year – let alone make a prediction for the next five years. Another girl left the school and the enrolment was now 10.

My parents wrote to say that Bobby, the dog we'd had ever since I could remember, had to be put down. His back legs "were gone" and he was beyond being saved. I felt sad for many days, thinking of how he'd played with me all those years when I was growing up, under the fruit trees and before we had lawns – when there were rows of vegetables and he'd run among the potatoes and cabbages, his tongue hanging out, barking, happy to chase or be chased.

While I fretted about the school's future, Mr Baker came out on a surprise visit to see how I was getting on. He was pleased with the school's academic progress and said to carry on as usual and not to be worried.

On Saturday 24th February, the State elections were held and voting was again in the school. The same people, almost to the exact number turned up as they did for the New State New England Referendum. I was Returning Officer again and Lex McCrae was the Polling Clerk. This time there was a cordial relationship between us that bordered on the suspicious. He made no attempt to influence people's voting and kept his distance when Ron came in to vote. Politeness was the order of the day.

The election was won by the Liberal/Country Party coalition led by Robert Askin that defeated the Labour Party led by Jack Renshaw.

In early March the Burleighs invited me to their home for dinner one Saturday night; it was exciting to see them again and talk about our visit to Point Lookout. I left their home that night feeling on a high, elated that I friends there, like I did with the Clarks at Wollomombi and Ron Diamond at Jeogla.

The inspector rang again to say that, in the event of the school having to close, he would try and retain me in the

North-West Region of New South Wales, perhaps near Inverell. I neither agreed nor disagreed: the region was vast, and perhaps I'd get an appointment closer to home.

Another telephone call from the inspector a few days later.

Pure officialdom at work. No other word could describe it.

Like a naptha flash, I remembered what Harry Harris had asked me about bureaucracy.

Inspector Baker informed me that the school was officially closing on Friday 15th March. He requested that I bring in all official school documents, such as pupil record cards, daily attendance role, enrolment books, punishment book, etc to his residence. Any time after school would do. According to the law, all equipment and books belonging to Jeogla Public School must be transferred to Chandler Public School and would I please make arrangements for the P & C to complete this.

I rang home and told my parents, again stressing to them not to worry about my welfare.

I did my rounds of good-byes to parents and friends in Jeogla and Wollomombi. I explained that the next few days would be busy and I may not get a chance to do it after Friday – as I'd have to start in a new school, somewhere in the North-West on Monday 18th March.

I wrote a very short letter to my parents, unsure when they'd receive it:

Dear Mum & Dad,

The inspector rang me this morning and my new small school is called Crooble, and it is not near Inverell but near Moree. I will be leaving Jeogla on Saturday. Don't write until you get my address. But I will ring when I arrive at my new school.

Everything is ok. Don't worry.
Peter

On Thursday after school I drove into Armidale and informed the Commonwealth Bank about the children's School Savings accounts. Would the bank enquire as to whether these should be transferred to Chandler Public School or elsewhere?

Yes, the bank would see to this matter.

I also transferred my own savings account from Armidale to Moree.

Then before 5 o'clock and closing time, I drove up to the External Studies building of the university and gave them my change of address from Jeogla Public School to Crooble Public School.

Lastly, back to Armidale and the library to say goodbye to Miss Enid Isaacs. I was almost in tears when I said goodbye to her. And so was she. We'd met many times since her first visit to the school and we always talked about poetry. She also spoke about her favourite English author, Jane Austen.

The Golden Bird

The atmosphere was gloomy that night at the Sloggets as we ate. Everyone was thinking the same thing but no one could say the words.

This was the end of an era at Jeogla. Once this school closed it would not re-open. There had been rumours that there was a move politically to try and build up Chandler Public School to become a central school; but no one could confirm or deny these rumours. They were Chinese whispers.

On Friday, I would have one more day left as Teacher-in-Charge at Jeogla Public School and decided there would be no formal classes. Those children who wanted to play could play, those who wanted to read or listen to music could do that, and those who wanted to paint or draw could do those activities. We would have recess and lunch at the usual times and in the afternoon we could clean up.

We did all those things, played music, read stories and poetry.

One last poem, I said, here's one last poem, I must read you, and read for them, from one of the magazines I'd found in the blue cupboard, "The Golden Bird" by Rex Ingamells, where the poet reminisces about being a boy and watching the moon fly into the sky like a golden bird. The bush is filled with the sound of kookaburras, frogs and crickets. With all these sounds, the rising moon – the new moon – the golden moon – becomes a laughing bird perched on high: when the poet was a boy and the bush was all around.

One day, you will all be like the boy in the poem. You will remember your lives in the bush and the new moon will rise just like it does in the poem – and it will remind you what your lives were like when you were young.

I could have sworn they were spellbound.

I told them not to worry about sweeping the floor or cleaning the desks too much. Mrs Slogget would still do it, that was her job; but they insisted. They took their own books home while I started packing the car with my own belongings.

We said our goodbyes and wished each other good luck.

I thanked them for teaching me about life in the country.

You were the better teachers, I said.

They listened.

Parents also came up to shake hands, thanked me and wished me all the best, wherever I ended up.

Waving hands and shouting, with motor vehicles heading towards the Styx River and the Oaky River Hydro Dam, the children left.

As I was leaving, Ron appeared from under the pines, followed by Suzie.

Like our very first meeting, he said.

Yes, I replied, when I tried to scare your bull.

Still got him. He's a good breeder.

Glad you came over, I said. Say goodbye to Dof for me… And thanks for everything. It's been a privilege knowing you.

That'll do. Let's not get sentimental, he said, drawing on his cigarette.

I mean it, I said.

He looked away, embarrassed, trying to sound unfazed by my compliment.

Where're they sending you?

Crooble.

Crooble, that's cotton country! Near Moree. Jeez, I know farmers from up there…Tell them you know me.

Okay, I will… I'll never forget you.

Okay, that's enough.

We shook hands.

C'mon, Suzie., he said. Let the teacher finish his work.

I finished packing and closed the door, hearing the empty echo in the room where I'd never return to teach.

I wired the yellow gate closed and drove away, without looking back, knowing that I had official documents to deliver to the inspector. My car was loaded down with cartons of books and records so I decided to unload them at Carrie's.

Have a cup of tea with us first, she said. Then I'll go up and do a proper clean. Gerald's here too, so is Granma. Come on, the inspector's not goin' anywhere an' you'll have plenty o' time ter get back before dinner.

Elmo had also come home by then.

Gerald helped me unload the cartons into the corridor that ran between our rooms. Not much was said between us.

Wonder where'll you'll be this time termorrer? Carrie asked.

Moree I hope. I'll go through Glen Innes, across to Warialda and then Moree. That's the plan. I'll stay overnight in a motel and get my bearings on Sunday. Make some enquiries and head for Crooble. Someone out there must board the teacher. The police station's always a good place to ask. According to the map it's a bit further north – off a side road.

You'll be right, Elmo said, pouring us all a cup of tea.

Carrie got out her tin of date scones.

Granma smiled at me and, stirring her tea, said softly, Goodbye.

*

I turned into the driveway of Chandler Public School, but Bill wasn't there, nor was his car in the driveway of the school residence.

When I arrived in Armidale I felt famished and, even though I'd had afternoon tea at Carrie's, I still felt hungry. Was it a state of nerves that was driving my desperation? Was my impending departure causing a state of anxiety that had to be compensated by eating?

Going into the Mun Hing Chinese restaurant, I ordered a prawn omelette; then I watched people walking by and ate, trying to memorise as much as I could of the scenery through the window: people, children in their different school uniforms, shoppers, cars, the buildings that fronted Beardy Street. Time had become a blur of nonstop movements.

It was starting to get dark when I arrived at the inspector's residence With the school records and official papers under my arm, I knocked on the door.

Mr Baker opened it, Ah, Peter, come in. He was wearing shorts, was in his socks and his shirt was hanging out. He was eating a chicken drumstick.

Good, good, I see you've brought the school records. Thank you. I handed them to him and he put them aside with the chicken drumstick. Good news, he said. Guess what? We're not sending you to Crooble. You're going to Kunghur. Right up on the Queensland border. That's right – Kunghur. On the Tweed. Outside Murwillumbah; but don't worry. We're giving you an extra day to get there. Go to this address and make contact with the inspector – a Mr Noel Howard. And his wife Norma. Lovely people. He'll fill you in on the details about where to board and so on.

My mind was reeling. *Kunghur. Tweed River. Murwillumbah. Queensland border.*

What happened to Crooble via Moree? I asked.

Change of plans, he said. You'll like it better up there. Beautiful country. Sunshine all year round. Teachers forsake promotions to stay on the Tweed. Believe me.

That was the extent of my conversation with Mr Baker. He saw me to the door and I stood there under the darkening sky, trying to collect my thoughts about what I should do next?

I stopped at the Clarks on the way home and explained what had happened.

No doubt about it, mate, the Education Department's giving you a bit of a run around, Alex said.

Would you like to stay for dinner? Jill asked.

I explained the food situation, that I'd eaten and still had to eat at Carrie's, but asked a favour from Alex: would he go to the Commonwealth Bank on Monday morning and ask that my savings account be transferred to Murwillumbah instead of Moree, and then go up to the university and request that the Department of External Studies send all my lecture notes to the address at Kunghur? Finally, tell Bill Higgins, that I'd stopped in to see him but he wasn't there.

It was difficult saying goodbye to Alex and Jill, somehow I never expected it to happen so soon. After all, I'd only know them some fifteen months and here we were, preparing to say goodbye. I thanked them repeatedly for letting me use their shower and for all the meals they'd invited me to. I felt an affinity with them, as I did with Ron –a special friendship – although different from what I felt towards Carrie and her family.

Jill summed it up, as I was leaving. We'll be seeing more of you, Peter Skrzynecki. This isn't the end of a friendship; it's the start of one that will last for years. Who knows, maybe Alex will get an appointment to Sydney in the future?

We hugged and said goodbye, then I drove off, seeing Alex standing with his arm around his wife who was coughing. I could hear Cassie's barking from the front garden.

When I arrived at Jeogla, I told Carrie I'd eaten a small meal in town but was still hungry, and then told her about the change of school from Crooble to Kunghur.

They're treatin' yer like a tennis ball, she said. Yer goin' all over the court.

I ate a little with them. Granma had gone to bed and I said I'd go to bed also. I'd planned to leave straight after breakfast. Most of my possessions were packed; the rest wouldn't take long.

I was glad I hadn't rung my parents. With all this changing of schools, I didn't want to upset them anymore. When I got to Kunghur, I would call them.

Try as I might to get to sleep, I couldn't, or if I did, it was only in fits and starts. I'd doze off, then find I was awake again.

At some point, that voice of argument that bothered me before, entered my head. I got up and wrote:

Jeogla

Rabbits scatter in fright behind tussocks
or into the hills of a blackberry hedge
as your wheels drum over the grid of a cattle ramp.
Lowries in flocks of pairs of rosellas
quickly settle back into a cluster of ironbarks.
Grass never strikes you as being too green,
except the clover, perhaps, with a scent
that somehow gets through the dust
and haze of sunlight that vision can't penetrate –
as if a shield was reflecting the stare
of an obstinate, silent god.

Autumn and winter were mornings of grey frost
on the stubble of granite – Herefords
grazing along the roadside and barbed-wire fences:
sentinels on the edge of timber ravines
or boundaries of creeks and ridges of eyesight.

Evening was a trail of smoke rising
in columns above the small Tablelands homestead;
stars hanging overhead, as if blossoming
from invisible branches, always just out of reach;
and always you thought of Tantalus
or the great Scandinavian ash:

found adequate words for conversation,
but none for the solitude of silence that spread
over your mind as night unfolded its blanket
and you reached out for a taste of native manna.

Perhaps the roads going east will someday
bring all the answers, join coast to mountains
and people to people – make it all more than just
names on a road mailbox or the discovery
of a village that isn't on some maps:
all the back-blocks where wooden floors
have witnessed lessons, childbirth and death:
where you find evidence of the seasons on the bark
of any tree – or in the eyes of a farmer
as he carries a backlog over to the hearth.

I didn't get back to sleep after that but lay there, listening to the night, hearing the start of birds singing and animal noises from nearby farms. Light broke through the curtains, and when I heard sounds in the house, of someone moving around, I knew that Carrie had returned from milking.

Turning Right

Breakfast was early as the Sloggets were all going into town, and I wanted to get away before they left. Not much was said but reference was made to the new school I'd be having, and they asked me to stay in touch.

I explained that I'd be passing through Armidale on my way home to Sydney for the holidays – unless I came down the coast road – and I'd stop in to see them, maybe even stay a night. There would also be residential schools at the university that I would have to attend.

Yer'll always be welcome 'ere, Carrie said. Jest let me know when an' I'll have yer room ready an' waitin'.

Promise I'll stay in touch. Promise to come out and visit you. Stay too, if it's not too much trouble.

Gerald helped me pack my belongings and by 8 o'clock I was ready to leave.

I thanked them all for having me as a boarder and said I would never forget any of them. They were like a family to me.

They all came out to see me, standing in the same place that they did when I first arrived. I shook hands with Elmo and Gerald, bent down to give Granma a kiss. She was smiling and gave my hand a squeeze.

Saying goodbye to Carrie was the hardest of all. There were tears in my eyes, and hers – although she stood tall as a soldier and held them back.

I kissed her on the cheek and gave her a hug. She did likewise.

Thank you, again and again, for looking after me. It will be impossible to forget you and impossible to say what Jeogla means to me. I didn't want to be here when I arrived – and now I don't want to leave. You were like a mother to me.

With that I turned around, got into my car and turned on the ignition. The car started and drew away, slightly uphill until I reached the road.

I paused, tooted the horn and waved, then it was time to be off, down the yellow-dirt road, still not fully dry from the recent rain.

*

I drove along the Jeogla road as I'd done dozens of times. Unlike yesterday, the day was sunny. I stopped on the Oaky River bridge and got out, surprised by the sudden cold touch of air on my face.

Waterbirds, as always, were feeding on the riverbanks and river, sending out ripples. Ducks flew overhead. Magpies sang in trees. Otherwise, the silence was deafening; it was like standing in a cavern where the rest of the world had been shut out.

I almost said something.

Getting back into the car, I drove away, uphill and around those winding bends, then straightening out. More rises and falls lay ahead in the road, before it levelled out, and I came to the Armidale-Grafton Road.

Instead of turning left, as I always did, I turned right, towards the coast and north to Kunghur, via Murwillumbah, to my new school on the Tweed River, at the foot of Mount Warning.

VIII

Letters and Last Poems

After I left Jeogla I continued with my studies as an external student at the University of New England until I graduated with a Bachelor of Arts degree in 1975. I completed a Master of Letters there in 1986, and between those years returned to Sydney University where I did a Master of Arts.

During 1968, whenever I travelled between my next small school at Kunghur and Sydney, I'd drive up the Pacific Highway from Sydney, but return on the inland route when travelling south; this way I got to see the coastal towns and rivers as well as the ranges and coastal plains.

On each of these southbound trips I'd leave after bell-time and drive to Casino, via Nimbin and Lismore. This "back road" as I called it, then brought me to the Bruxner Highway and on to Tenterfield, through to Guyra and on to Armidale: a long haul and I would only stop for petrol, knowing that after Armidale I'd go straight onto Jeogla and, whatever time I'd arrive, Carrie had a hot meal waiting for me and my old room.

On the trip south for the September holidays in 1968 I asked if I could stay for a couple of days: it would give me a chance to say hello to Ron and Dof, Alex and Jill, Bill Higgins, the Robsons and any other locals I might meet.

The school itself looked deserted. The keys had been taken

away by Public Works, including the key that Carrie had. All I could do was walk around it and peer through the windows.

The yard was overgrown with weeds. Sheep and cattle had eaten whatever flowers were left growing.

Six months since I left – and already the school was looking like a ghost.

But I felt a need to go back and retrace my steps to where I'd already been once before, and where I felt an affinity to – even though the place held a dread that I couldn't understand.

Point Lookout.

When I arrived the view was shrouded in mist, moving in from the coast like a form of amoebaean life, settling on everything it touched. Following the track that I walked with the Burleighs, I was soon standing at the foot of Weeping Rock, that huge wall of basalt that confronted me as it did before, the same green face – silver water tricking out of the earth above me, running over ferns and plant life, trees, stones, seeping down, into the earth.

The inner voice was there this time, urging me to hurry back to the car and write:

Weeping Rock

Only after reaching the bottom did we stop
and listen to the drifting echoes –
as long-dreaded farewells when words are lost to worlds
in the embrace of death: of flesh with unimagined earth.

From cracks and blotched furrows the water
trickled silver on to ferns, grass and flowers
where, bordered by moss in crevices,
icicles remained unchanged from winter frosts.

A cool spring it had been: and the same now,
miles and years and gorges away.

The rock's water seeped noiselessly into
the chasm from boulders and forests of gum –
streamed, as if the years in grief had come to claim
our presence: turn bone to rock and flesh to moss.

In 1968, while teaching at Kunghur, I boarded at Uki and in May was trapped in a house fire; I managed to escape, but had to come to Sydney on sick leave while my burns healed. At the end of the year, I requested a transfer closer to Sydney in case I needed specialist treatment. I was transferred to Colo Heights Public School on the Singleton Road, the school I stopped to look at on my trip south in 1967. This would be my third year of country service and, after that, I intended to apply for a city appointment.

I was still studying at the university and whenever I attended a residential school, I came out to visit the Sloggets.

They were happy visits except for when I went up to the school and saw it falling more and more into disrepair.

On one such visit I was shocked to find it gone. Only the shelter shed, water tanks, incinerator and toilets remained. The foundations where the school stood and the concreted area where assemblies took place were surrounded by weeds.

Carrie told me that Public Works removed the building, and it was transported to Armidale, to be used as a portable classroom at Ben Venue Public School. Tenders had been called for the sale of the water tanks.

The contact with Carrie and the Sloggets remained, however. She wrote letters and I replied, or I wrote letters and she replied. Photos were also exchanged.

The following are a handful of her letters that have survived, and I quote them in full, exactly as they were written. They are honest, realistic, full memories and domestic detail.

They are also the voice of a country woman, stoic in the face of tragedy.

Jeogla
16-9-69

Dear Peter

Hope you had a safe journey home, and found your mother & Father OK

My we have had some awful wind sleet and rain over the week end and was it cold

We went to coffs Harbour on Sunday was a lovely warm day down their had a most enjoyable day. Left granma down their for a fortnight to see if she can get rid of the flu.

I got word back about those tanks at this stage the tanks are not available for purchase the building is to be transferred to another centre, if the tanks become surplus, I will be given the opportunity to submit an offer for purchase

I have got that snap of Peggy & myself for you 12 years this month since I started to milk her; she had only one calf in the 12 years.

I think she is just about done for milking.

Its rather lonely since granma went away could always hear her moving around

Well Peter I must Hurry. Gerald is ready to go for the mail

Kindest Regards
Mrs Slogget, Elmo & Gerald

2-3-1972
Jeogla

Dear Peter

Only a few short line to let you know, that our darling son was Killed a fortnight today by a falling tree only lived, one hour

Must end cant write

Kind Regards
Mrs Sloggett & Elmo

Jeogla
26 – 5 -72

Dear Peter

Thanks so much for your letter & so pleased to hear you have a lovely little daughter & I love the name you have called her

Granma has been very sick, had about a fortnight in hospital but she is still not to good.

Has been misty rain on and off for a week no log carting the trucks cant get along the forest road, even in my garden was muddy today when I was trying to clean it up and plant some new flowers

I saw Ron the day I got your letter and told him the good new

Well Peter I must go I just cant set my mind to writing everything seems upside down here without our dear boy and Granma being sick

Kindest Regard Mrs Sloggett & Elmo

Jeogla

Dear Peter

A few lines to let you know that Granma passed away on 10 June, 1972. I just couldnt write before as the world seems so empty for me two closed rooms at my home I just don't know how I will get through, but I guess I must bear up but its hard.

Will tell you all when I see you again

Kind Regards to your wife and little baby.
Mrs Sloggett

Jeogla
3 – 3- 1975

Dear Peter

Thanks so much for the snaps of your children, they both look great, Judith is like you more than Andrew, only my Idea.

We have been having some lovely rain this last couple of weeks, 2 inches this month so far quite muddy around our back steps

Elmo was sick last night with that pain where he had been operated on, but was better this morning, so he said.

Hope you can all make it when your graduation comes off, will be great to see you again

I still look after that little mullen boy poor little fellow fell on a cordial bottle & cut his hand. They have had to take him to Sydney twice now for an operation cut a nerve between his finger

Well Peter must end or the mail will be in, once again thanks so much.

Kindest Regards to all
From Carrie & Elmo

Jeogla
Friday
16 – 5 – 1975

Dear Peter,

Thanks so much for the Photo of you, its real you, we were sorry we had missed you that day, but these things do happen

We are having a few cold frosts up here but lovely days after its quite hot today.

I have the flu have had it now for a month cough half the night, but Elmo is OK

Hope the family is Ok I guess two keeps you busy. How are your mother & father doing

We had church here last Sunday was quite a roll up didn't think the room would hold all but we managed, had a nice cup of tea afterwards, Our minister is from Sydney Roy Stephenson

I have just been up to see Ron's Mother & Father

They are such dear's one 91 the other 89 what a great age, Ron says he will never reach that far.

Well Peter I must close as the mail will soon be in, Thanks once again for the Photo

Kindest Regard to all
Carrie & Elmo Sloggett

21-6-1993
Jeogla

Dear Peter

I received your letter and the Photos which was very good thanks so much for them its really cold here this morning but no frost and still no rain, only that awful wind.

Olga & Dawn my two sisters are away on a bus for almost four weeks to Darwin, I felt very lonely yesterday as they always comes out Sundays so I worked out in the garden all day to make the day feel a bit shorter,

I am going in to the school at Wollomombi today having a special day for the blind and I have done quite a lot of cooking for there stall

If you manage to get up later on bring your children even if they are grown up I would like to see them again, your wife also.

well must go go or the mailman will soon be here

Kindest Regards
Mrs Sloggett

Jeogla
8-11-1993

Dear Peter

Thanks so much for your poetry Book it is really great. I enjoy reading of a night

It's a lovely day here, a few clouds coming up only wish it brings rain it is awful dry here, my poor garden is awful have a few tomatoes in but they don't seem to be growing

Sorry I never got this posted today, had Visitors, all day

Well Kind Regards to you all, hope to hear from you before Xmas. Thanks once again

Mrs Sloggett

30-4-1998
Jeogla

Dear Peter

Received the photos & thank you so much they are really great,

Its very cloudy here today hope it brings more rain its really needed

Thanks once again was nice seeing you.

Kind regards
Mrs Sloggett

This last letter was written after I visited Carrie in April, 1998 and subsequently sent her some photos; it was the last time I saw her.

I had accepted an invitation to attend the 60th anniversary of the college university establishment which was held during the graduation weekend.

I drove and arrived in Armidale on Friday 17th and left on Monday 20th.

After booking into the Westwood Motor Inn on Barney Street, I spent Friday night and all of Saturday rediscovering Armidale. I visited my friend, former lecturer and post-graduate supervisor Associate Professor John Ryan, and we attended the reception given in the Faulty of Arts building for the 60th anniversary celebration.

On Saturday morning I went for a walk around Armidale, similar to the one that I did on my first visit in 1967.

Later, in Uralla, at a second-hand bookshop called The Book Collector I bought a collection of Wordsworth's poetry and *Picked-up Pieces* by John Updike.

At Gostywck the walls of the chapel were covered in the red, orange and purple vines that I'd failed to see on my last visit; the elms were coming into their autumn fall, covering the ground with golden leaves, shining in the cold sunlight.

On Sunday morning I drove to Jeogla, detouring to see Wollomombi Falls; the camping area had been modernised and a viewing platform erected. As always, the view was spectacular, washed as it was in morning light, birds singing and not another human being in sight. The falling water turned into a whirlpool of mist as it hit the bottom, and the surrounding silence had that eerie, echoing sound of wind as it rushed into the chasm and rushed out.

At Jeogla I saw Carrie sitting in front of her house but drove past, waving as I did. It was just after lunch.

Getting out at the school yard, I discovered the water tanks were gone, only the shelter shed, toilets and incinerator remained. Animal tracks covered the ground. All the flowers and plants were gone, not a trace remaining of anything except blackberry bushes that had invaded the yard.

The wind in the pines sounded the same, creating its soft music, whispering, telling me a story that I now understood.

The car's wheels drummed over the cattle grid and I turned down to Carrie's house, to where she sat in the sun, in a thick cardigan, under a straw hat, a blanket over her knees.

I got out of the car and gave her a hug and kiss.

I just wanted to see the school – or what's left of it.

She smiled, and said, I knew it was yer car. I seen yer wavin'

She was larger than what I remembered, under her face a solemn mask of forbearance. She was knitting.

How's it been?

Pretty lonely on yer own, but I manage. I git visitors. People help out. But since I got the arthritis bad in me hips it's harder to move. Yer know Elmo died in 1980?

Yes, you told me in a letter.

I keep fergettin' a lot. How've you been?

Good, I said. I recounted my life: study, divorce, remarriage, birth of a daughter whom we named Anna. The change from primary teaching to tertiary. My parents were still alive and asked to be remembered. They're getting old, I said.

Yer still writin' them poems?

Yes...

Hmmm.

Carrie, I'd like to ask you about what happened to Gerald?

Thought yer would.

She let out a big sigh – slow, heavy, deep, as if she were mustering her strength, summoning a force out of the earth to help her say the words.

No one's ever told me the details, I said, but if you'd rather not.

No, Peter, I don't mind talkin' about it now... It's been sixteen years...Besides, yer gotter a right to know. He was workin' down in the Styx forest with Elmo. Him an' Alan Cundy were cuttin' down a real big tree. As it came down it sorter shifted as they sometimes do – an' one of the branches hit 'im. He lived an hour an' died in Elmo's arms. I was sittin' right here an' I heard the ambulance come screamin' through – and I knew it was Gerald. Jest knew. When they got me to the camp I saw 'im lyin' there, a thin line of blood comin' from his mouth. That's all I remember. Then I hit the ground...

As she talked her speech slowed down, as if she were telling the story to herself, and had become lost in the details.

After that, we sat and didn't speak, just let the sun warm our faces. Birds sang around us.

Will yer come to me funeral, Peter? Gerald an' Granma' are buried just behind Elmo – an' that's where I'll be. Next to Elmo.

Yes, I said. Promise. I've left my contact details with Olga. Do you need help with anything before I go back to town? Can I go to Wollomombi and get you something?

No, I got everything I need at the moment. Thanks, anyway.

She mentioned the name of someone I didn't know. She'll be aroun' termorrer. She'll bring what I need. By golly, it's slow getting' aroun'....I've been in hospital a few times now, but I manage to pull through. Don't wanter die in there. Jeogla's me home. Only feel happy 'ere.

It was mid-afternoon and a chill had crept into the air.

I gotter go in...Come an' stay a while longer. I know yer have ter go. Come on, jest a cup of tea.

I followed her into the house, past my old room. She left her blanket and knitting in the lounge room where a fire was burning. ' ere, she said, put a few logs in fer me, please – if yer don't mind – if yer still know how. And she laughed.

She made the tea and we drank, eating biscuits from a packet, not speaking.

When it came time to leave, I was lost for words to say goodbye.

Yer don't have ter say anythin'....Yer were okay. Thanks for stayin' in touch all these years. We liked gettin' yer letters an' snaps.

Thank you – for everything, I said. Everything.

At the front door I kissed her cheek and hugged her.

I got into my car and, as I did back in March 1968, drove to the top of her driveway, tooted the horn, waved and drove off, trying to commit to memory the image of her, alone in the garden, in front of an empty house.

*

On Wednesday night, 4th June 2003, I received a long distance telephone call from Olga, Carrie's sister in Armidale, to tell me that Carrie had died that day in Armidale Hospital. Did I still want to come up for the funeral? she asked.

Yes, I replied. When is it?

Tomorrow morning. Ten o'clock.

Tomorrow morning!

I was teaching at the University of Western Sydney and said, Olga, I can't. I have a lecture and three tutorials tomorrow. I can't cancel or reorganise my teaching schedule that quickly. Why the hurry?

It's the long weekend. The family doesn't want to wait till next week.

Did she suffer?

No, she went peaceful.

*

Not long after Carrie's death I made enquiries through the Armidale and Dumaresq Council to locate the burial details of Gerald, Elmo, Granma and Caroline. The Customer Service Officer, Debbie Gwynne, could not have been more helpful and supplied me with everything I needed to know. The Sloggetts were buried in the Presbyterian Section of Armidale Cemetery. Rows, lots, dates of death and ages at time of death were also provided.

*

In late 2010, I was invited back by the English staff at the University of New England to lecture on my poetry as part of an HSC seminar being held by the School of Arts, as I had done in 2007.

Arriving on an early flight the day before the lecture I'd booked myself into the Westwood Motor Inn and Gill Willis from the university picked me up and drove me into town; my room at the motel inn wasn't ready so we drove to the university; it had been raining in Sydney and it was raining in Armidale. When the rain eased, I asked if I could be taken to the cemetery. Dr Elizabeth Hale drove me.

That inner voice, the voice that I now associated with Jeogla, Wyatts Creek, the Styx River, Weeping Rock started to speak inside me softly, but insistently, as soon as we entered Memorial Avenue with its red trees blazing in the cold autumn light. Elizabeth returned to the university and I was left alone.

When I found the graves, they were exactly as Carrie said: she and Elmo side by side, Granma and Gerald behind them. The voice said, Write, write while you're here.

But the first line or lines didn't come, as excited as I felt for being here and guilty at the same time for not coming to her funeral.

I took many "snaps" of the red trees and the graves, and started my walk back to town. Halfway there it started to rain. I called a taxi and was driven up to the university.

My friend John Ryan was in his labyrinthine office, surrounded by his vast collection of books, and I met Professor Jennie Shaw, Pro Vice-Chancellor and Dean of the Faculty of Arts and Sciences. I made visits to the Alumni Office and visited the bookshop, library and stopped into the A1 Theatre where my lecture would be given tomorrow and where I attended lectures as an external student.

But still that voice, that insistent urging to return to the cemetery, was not giving up.

This time Professor John Scott, Acting Head of the School of Arts, drove me. I enjoyed his company immensely. At the cemetery I showed him where the graves were and he returned to the university.

I spoke to Elmo, Granma and Gerald, one by one, as I would have when I was living with them.

Finally, I stood at Carrie's grave and told her why I didn't come to her funeral. I apologised for letting her down and asked her to forgive me.

The only response was from the birds and the wind blowing through the red trees.

Rain started to fall, and a first line came into my head, a second and third. The poem had arrived with the rain.

Day. Night. Darkness. Light. The time could have been any of these.

A single impulse drove me.

Hurrying, I left the cemetery, half- running, half-walking over ground already wet with leaves and flowers, crimson rosellas flying ahead of me. Out of Memorial Avenue and over the railway bridge, down Faulkner Street, in the direction of Central Park and the Westwood Motor Inn, while the rain got heavier. The words kept coming, images also – as if my brain had taken the photos it needed to keep the momentum flowing.

The distance was a lot further than I anticipated, and

by the time I got to Room 4, I was breathless, wet, face and hands dripping water.

I sat down and wrote:

Red Trees

Impossible not to see them
once you cross the railway bridge
and enter Memorial Avenue –
the rows of red trees
along the cemetery's perimeter:

maples, claret ash, liquidambers –
cotoneasters where rosellas
hang upside down and feast
on berries like clots of blood.

The breath of next month's winter
hangs over them already
but they seem intent on proving
that winter is a lie –
that neither winds nor frosts
are permanent afflictions
and disappear as quickly as they arrive.

A family that I once boarded with
at Jeogla lies buried
beside the trees – mother, father,
son, grandmother:
all "born and bred" in New England
where I came to work
and left when the work was done –
where I once considered
settling down but didn't
for reasons I still can't explain.

The mother dead at ninety-three years of age,
the father at seventy,
grandmother at eighty-five
and the son at twenty-four.
On his headstone
it reads, "Accidentally killed
16th February 1972."
All of them buried
In Loving memory Of.
What can I do but pray?
Or be content to live on the memory of a single day
when we sat down and ate a meal together?

The wind pauses
and brings a moment's peace –
but still leaves my questions unanswered
hanging from the branches of red trees.

Leaving a ground strewn
with decaying leaves
I leave Memorial Avenue
and walk back towards the railway bridge.

The poem was written non-stop and finished in a matter of minutes. The voice that urged me to write was silent. All I heard was the sound of rain on the roof. Or maybe it was falling inside me? I found it hard to tell.

IX

Epilogue

In May 2007, I had flown to Armidale at the invitation of the English Department at the University of New England. I was going to speak to a group of HSC students from the region who were studying my poetry. I booked into the Westwood Motor Inn beforehand. Around noon, I rented a car from Realistic Car Rentals, intending to drive to Jeogla and to return by dinnertime.

The countryside was looking healthy. Names on signposts were a welcoming sight. A bypass had been built at Wollomombi so it wasn't necessary to drive through the village. The last time I was here was in 1998 when I said goodbye to Carrie.

The banks of the Oaky River were a film of lush green, almost bright, and I figured there must have been recent rain, although there was no sign of it on the day. Waterbirds dotted the scenery. Herefords and sheep grazed in the distance. Rosellas greeted me with bursts of flight.

Up the hill I drove...Three more bends and there would the Sloggett home. But where? Where was the Sloggett home when I rounded the last bend? Did I make a mistake? Did my memory betray me? Where a house once stood only an overgrown, fenced-off allotment confronted me.

Then I noticed an outhouse at the bottom of the land and

recognised the old toilet. This was the right place, but where was the house? The sheds?

Shock and sadness overcame me.

Driving up to the school, I discovered changes I could not have anticipated. Parts of the yard were recognisable. Others were not. All but one of the pine trees had been cut down. The shelter shed had been renovated and a caravan parked alongside it. Trellises were put up. New trees planted. The old incinerator was there. Someone had obviously bought the land.

The feeling of sadness that I felt when I discovered the missing house deepened. The Jeogla that I knew was gone. I would have no reason to ever return.

I took photos of the school yard and what remained of where the house once stood. The chill in the air was welcome because it obliterated how I felt inside. More photos of the Oaky River and I said goodbye to the beautiful waterbirds on the river.

Detouring to Wollomombi, I asked at the general store what happened to the Sloggett home. The few people in the store shook their heads and shrugged their shoulders. Said they'd never heard of them.

The drive back to Armidale was slow at first – then faster than it should have been: it was like I was trying to escape from something I didn't understand.

All the way back I noticed a daylight moon hanging overhead, just as it did when I drove out.

After returning the car next morning, I went back to the motel, silent, dumb with disbelief from what I'd been told.

I wrote:

Jeogla Return

1

Half a daylight moon
hung over New England
as I drove from Armidale to Jeogla –
just as I did forty years ago
for the first time
to take up an appointment
in a one-teacher school.

Names appeared on signposts
with a familiarity that surprised me –
Commissioners Waters, Gara River,
Hillgrove, Wollomombi –
until I reached the Kempsey turnoff
and Jeogla lay 9 km ahead.

2

The main building and water tank
of the school were gone.
The shelter shed had been converted
to a cabin and a caravan
was parked next to it.
Incinerator still there; also one toilet block.
The same footpath ran
from the squeaky yellow gate
now replaced by steel fencing posts.
The windbreak of pines cut down,
its burnt-out stumps standing.
Someone had planted saplings
and vines, built trellises and put up tool sheds.
The school yard had a new life.

3

Further back, towards Oaky River –
where was the house
that I once lived in ?
Where I boarded – slept, ate, wrote poetry
and listened to Willy-wagtails
singing in the pine tree outside my window
in the moonlight ?

An overgrown allotment greeted me –
its rusty fence and wire gate still standing.
A disused water tank lay
under the pine tree.
For a moment I saw my old car
parked beside a weatherboard wall
while water gurgled
into the tank from a downpour.
Only an outhouse
stood at the back of the yard
alongside a row of hawthorns –
before the empty chook-run
where bantams roosted in the trees at night.
On a slope, towards the dam,
two kelpies used to run at the end of a long chain.
No timber blocks or logs remained
from what had been a wood heap.
Once I found an axe on top of it
rusting in the rain.

Walking away through grass and dust –
stepping over blackberry canes,
taking photographs of the property
and surrounding paddocks,
I found a row of purple flowers

growing against the wire as if trying to escape.
Rosellas flying across the landscape
broke the silence but gave no joy or solace.

4

Next day in Armidale,
returning the hire car and talking
to the man behind the counter about the missing house,
he replied, "I knew that family –
me and my dad used to stay with them.
Well, blow me down – how about that !"
I asked what happened to the house.
He said, "the new owner bulldozed it."
"Why ?"
"Because he wanted more space on the land."

Walking back to the motor inn
across Central Park,
stunned by the coincidence
of what I'd just heard –
I barely understood my luck
in that brief conversation
or what the loss of the house meant.
I remembered the previous
afternoon, driving away, the half-moon
still hanging in the darkening sky like a broken host –
and thinking how, of all the cities in the ancient world,
Juno loved Carthage the most.

25/5/2007
Armidale

*